FOREIGN POLICY OF THE UNITED STATES
VOLUME I

FOREIGN POLICY OF THE UNITED STATES
VOLUME I

ERNEST SIMONE (EDITOR)

Nova Science Publishers, Inc.
Huntington, NY

Editorial Production: Susan Boriotti
Office Manager: Annette Hellinger
Graphics: Frank Grucci and Jennifer Lucas
Information Editor: Tatiana Shohov
Book Production: LaToya Clay, Patrick Davin, Cathy DeGregory,
            Donna Dennis and Lynette Van Helden
Circulation: Anna Cruz, Ron Hedges and Andre Tillman

Library of Congress Cataloging-in-Publication Data
Available Upon Request

ISBN 1-56072-850-7

Copyright © 2000 by Nova Science Publishers, Inc.
            227 Main Street, Suite 100
            Huntington, New York 11743
            Tele. 631-424-6682   Fax 631-424-4666
            E Mail Novascil@aol.com

Printed in the United States of America

CONTENTS

PREFACE

Foreign policy of the United States is a complex mechanism defined both by constitutional law as well as by various instruments of public and private pressure. Both the President and Congress play major roles in its development and implementation. Initiation can be by the President or by Congress.

This book examines first of all the foreign policy roles of the President and Congress. History has shown control of foreign policy has shifted between the Executive Branch and Congress depending on public opinion, perceived strengths of various presidents, congressional interest levels and willingness of power congressmen to oppose the president.

National interest as a foreign policy element is considered as well. Albeit a vague term that can and often is construed to mean whatever a particular president or congress is interested in the moment, there are several areas of general agreement; cheap oil for American consumers; halting nuclear proliferation; containment of Russia; following Israeli direction on Mid-East policy; trying to open Chinese markets for American companies; generally serving as an active agent of American business in global markets; maintaining and projecting American's military muscle throughout the world.

The book also examines the government organizations involved in foreign policy, the laws related to various countries, foreign election monitoring, economic sanctions as instruments of foreign policy, international terrorism and the War Powers Resolution.

Foreign Policy of the United States
Volume 1

FOREIGN POLICY ROLES OF THE PRESIDENT AND CONGRESS

Richard F. Grimmett

ABSTRACT

The United States Constitution divides foreign policy powers between the President and the Congress so that both share in the making of foreign policy. The executive and legislative branches each play important roles that are different but that often overlap. Both branches have continuing opportunities to initiate and change foreign policy, and the interaction between them continues indefinitely throughout the life of a policy. This report reviews and illustrates 12 basic ways that the United States can make foreign policy. The practices illustrated in this report indicate that making foreign policy is a complex process, and that the support of both branches is required for a strong and effective U.S. foreign policy. For a detailed discussion of how war-making powers are shared, see War Powers Resolution: Presidential Compliance. CRS Issue Brief 81050. This report will be updated only as events warrant.

Summary

The United States Constitution divides the foreign policy powers between the President and Congress so that both share in the making of foreign policy. The executive and legislative branches each play important roles that are different but that often overlap. Both branches have continuing opportunities to initiate and change foreign policy, and the interaction between them continues indefinitely throughout the life of a policy.

This report identifies and illustrates 12 basic ways to make U.S. foreign policy. The President or the executive branch can make foreign policy through:

1) — responses to foreign events
2) — proposals for legislation
3) — negotiation of international agreements
4) — policy statements
5) — policy implementation
6) — independent action.

In nearly all of these circumstances, Congress can either support the President's approach or seek to change it. In the case of independent Presidential action, it may be very difficult to change policy in the short term; in the case of a legislative proposal by the executive branch or treaties and international agreements submitted to the Senate or Congress for approval, Congress has a decisive voice. In most cases Congress supports the President, but it often makes significant modifications in his initiatives in the process of approving them.

Congress can make foreign policy through:

1) — resolutions and policy statements
2) — legislative directives
3) — legislative pressure
4) — legislative restrictions/funding denials
5) — informal advice
6) — congressional oversight.

In these circumstances, the executive branch can either support or seek to change congressional policies as it interprets and carries out legislative directives and restrictions, and decides when and whether to adopt proposals and advice.

The practices illustrated in this report indicate that making U.S. foreign policy is a complex process, and the support of both branches is required for a strong and effective U.S. foreign policy.

Contents

Introduction

The Constitution divides the foreign policy powers between the President and Congress but not in a definitive manner.[1] Edward S. Corwin wrote:

> What the Constitution does, *and all that it does*, is to confer on the President certain powers capable of affecting our foreign relations, and certain other powers of the same general kind on the Senate, and still other such powers on Congress; but which of these organs shall have the decisive and final voice in determining the course of the American nation is left for events to resolve.[2]

Events have confirmed that together the President and Congress make foreign policy, but they have not resolved the question of which branch originates or finally determines policy. The two branches share in the process and each plays an important but different role. The question of who makes foreign policy does not have a more precise answer for several reasons.

First, U.S. foreign policy is not created in a vacuum as some sort of indivisible whole with a single grand design. Rather, making foreign policy is a prolonged process involving many actors and comprising dozens of individual policies toward different countries, regions, and functional problems.

Second, the complex process of determining foreign policy makes it difficult to decide who should be credited with initiating or altering any particular foreign policy. The two branches constantly interact and influence each other. Under these circumstances, it is difficult to trace an idea back to its origin, determine when a proposal actually influences policy, and decide when a modification creates a new policy.[3]

Third, the roles and relative influence of the two branches in making foreign policy differ from time to time according to such factors as the personalities of the President and Members of Congress and the degree of consensus on policy. Throughout American history there have been ebbs and flows of Presidential and

---

[1]See appendix for excerpts from the U.S. Constitution relating to foreign policy powers.

[2]Corwin, Edward S. The President, Office and Powers, 1787-1957. New York, New York University Press, 1957. p. 171 (emphasis in original).

[3]Baldwin, David A. Congressional Initiative in Foreign Policy. The Journal of Politics, November 1966. p. 754-773.

congressional dominance in making foreign policy, variously defined by different scholars. One study classified the period 1789-1829 as one of Presidential initiative; 1829-1898 as one of congressional supremacy; and 1899 through the immediate post-World War II period as one of growing Presidential power.[4] Another study defined three periods of congressional dominance, 1837-1861, 1869-1897, and 1918-1936, with a fourth one beginning toward the end of the Vietnam War in 1973.[5] During the Reagan and Bush Administrations the pendulum swung back toward Presidential dominance, reaching its height in 1991 during Operation Desert Storm against Iraq.[6] In the post-Persian Gulf war era, both President and the Congress are confronted with issues in foreign policy that may well define which branch of government will play the dominant role during the first decade of the twenty-first century.

For many years a perception existed that the executive branch usually initiated foreign policy with the implication that this relegated Congress to an inconsequential role. Writing in 1950 Robert Dahl wrote, "Perhaps the single most important fact about Congress and its role in foreign policy, therefore, is that it rarely provides the initiative. Most often initiative springs from the executive-administrative branch."[7] In 1962 James A. Robinson studied 22 case studies of foreign policies over the previous 30 years and found three cases of congressional initiative: the 1943 repeal of the Chinese exclusion laws, the 1943 Fulbright resolution calling for postwar participation in an international organization, and the 1958 Monroney resolution proposing the International Development Association.[8] Francis O. Wilcox, who was Staff Director of the Senate Foreign Relations Committee from 1947-1955, and Assistant Secretary of State for International Organization Affairs from 1955-1961, has argued, however, that "some of the most imaginative and constructive foreign policies since World War II have originated in Congress."[9]

In the period after the Vietnam War, Congress reasserted its role in foreign policy. It on occasion initiated new policies and exerted decisive influence on policies initiated by the executive branch. One study on the subject concluded that "the fact remains that the President is still in charge of American foreign policy," but it noted also that "the American Congress has more power to influence foreign affairs than its counterpart in any other country."[10] Another study concluded: "For all the problems

---

[4]Cheever, Daniel S., and H. Field Haviland, Jr. American Foreign Policy and the Separation of Powers. Cambridge, Harvard University Press, 1952. 244 p.

[5]Franck, Thomas M., and Edward Weisband. Foreign Policy by Congress. New York, Oxford University Press, 1979. 357 p.

[6]U.S. Congress. House. Congress and Foreign Policy, 1991. Washington, G.P.O., 1992, p. 19.

[7]Dahl, Robert A. Congress and Foreign Policy. New York, Norton, 1950. p . 58.

[8]Robinson, James A. Congress and Foreign Policy-Making. Homewood, Ill., Dorsey Press, 1967. p. 66.

[9]Wilcox, Francis O. Congress, the Executive, and Foreign Policy. New York, Harper and Row, 1971, p.14.

[10]Crabb, Cecil V., Jr., and Pat M. Holt. Invitation to Struggle: Congress, the President and
(continued...)

caused by a resurgent Congress with unprecedented resources and a will to be involved more directly in foreign policy, the system is working much more the way the Founding Fathers devised it than we have seen in some time."[11]

This report identifies and illustrates 12 major ways to make U.S. foreign policy, six utilized by the President or the executive branch, and six utilized by the Congress. No attempt has been made to measure how often the various practices are used. However, the findings of the report are consistent with Corwin's classic statement that:

> ...actual *practice* under the Constitution has shown that, while the President is usually in a position to *propose*, the Senate and the Congress are often in a technical position at least to *dispose*. The verdict of history, in short, is that the power to determine the substantive content of American foreign policy is a *divided* power, with the lion's share falling usually, though by no means always, to the President.[12]

This report does not attempt to define how a policy is made within a branch, as this is a complex and varied process and would require a detailed study of each case. Several case studies of this type are indicated in footnotes, and illustrations mentioned in the report highlight some of the many individuals and groups within each branch who contribute to policy formation.[13] Similarly, the report does not examine the influence of groups outside the executive and legislative branches, but the illustrations show that such groups, including the judiciary, interest groups, the press, and the public at large, can sometimes play an important role.

---

[10](...continued)
Foreign Policy. Washington, Congressional Quarterly Press, 1980. p. 3.

[11]Ornstein, Norman. The Constitution and the Sharing of Foreign Policy Responsibility. In The President, the Congress, and Foreign Policy. New York, Association of Former Members of Congress and the Atlantic Council of the United States, 1985. p.64.

[12]Corwin, The President, Office and Powers, p. 171(emphasis in original).

[13]For a collection of case studies, see the Congress and Foreign Policy committee prints, prepared by the Congressional Research Service and published by the House Foreign Affairs Committee, annually, from 1974 to 1992. These committee prints are subsequently cited as Congress and Foreign Policy, together with their pertinent year of coverage.

The President as Initiator

Following are six basic ways the President or executive branch can originate or initially shape foreign policy. In these circumstances, Congress is put in the position of either responding positively to the President's initiative or seeking to adjust or reverse the impact of his position.

Response to Foreign Events

Current events in foreign countries or a sudden action by a foreign government often challenge U.S. interests. As spokesman and head of the foreign service, the armed forces, the intelligence services, and the bureaucracy, the President usually responds to such events and thus initiates U.S. policy. Congress ordinarily supports the President, but on occasion seeks a change in policy.

For example, Congress supported President Reagan in the Falkland Islands crisis between Argentina and the United Kingdom. After Argentina in April 1982 seized and occupied the Falkland Islands, which the United Kingdom claimed as a crown colony, the U.S. executive branch sought to mediate the dispute. When Argentina refused one of the U.S. peace overtures, Secretary of State Alexander Haig announced that the United States would prohibit arms sales to Argentina and provide material support for British operations. Both Houses of Congress passed resolutions supporting the U.S. action siding with the United Kingdom.[14] The crisis ended in June 1982, and in December 1983 the Department of State lifted the ban on arms sales to Argentina.

Congress helped bring about a change in Administration-initiated policy in response to events in Lebanon.[15] In September 1983, Congress reached a compromise with the Reagan Administration, and agreed to authorize participation in the Multinational Force in Lebanon for 18 months[16]. After a terrorist bombing attack in Beirut on October 23, 1983, that killed more than 200 Marines, President Reagan first took the position that the United States had vital national interests in Lebanon and would continue to participate in the Multinational Force. Prominent Members of Congress questioned the policy, and some proposed an amendment to cut off funds for participation. While the amendment was defeated, criticism of the policy continued. The Subcommittee on Investigations of the House Armed Services Committee and a Department of Defense Commission headed by retired Admiral Robert Long both filed reports in December 1983 that questioned the U.S. ability to achieve its objectives by the use of the Marines. Public opinion polls also indicated that a majority of Americans thought the Marines should be withdrawn. On February 7, 1984, President Reagan announced that the Marines would be redeployed to ships

---

[14]U.S. Congress. House. Congress and Foreign Policy, 1982. p. 10.

[15]For further discussions see Preece, Richard M. Congress and the Conflict in Lebanon. Congress and Foreign Policy, 1983, p. 11-28; and Laipson, Ellen. Congress and the Withdrawal of the Marines from Lebanon. Congress and Foreign Policy, 1984, p. 11-20.

[16]Multinational Force in Lebanon Resolution, P.L. 98-119, signed October 12, 1983.

off the coast of Lebanon, and in March he reported that U.S. participation in the Multinational Force had ended.

On August 2, 1990, President Bush responded to the Iraqi invasion of Kuwait the previous day by immediately applying full economic sanctions against Iraq, and, within a week, deploying U.S. Armed Forces to help defend Saudi Arabia against potential attack. In October Congress supported continued action through the United Nations, and enacted the economic sanctions into law. In January 1991, Congress authorized the use of the U.S. Armed Forces to implement U.N. Security Council resolutions.[17]

President Bill Clinton authorized U.S. actions in support of U.N. and NATO operations aimed at halting the fighting in the former territory of Yugoslavia, particularly in Bosnia. Under President Clinton, the United States participated in airlifts into Sarajevo, Bosnia, naval monitoring of sanctions, aerial enforcement of a "no-fly zone", and aerial enforcement of safe havens. In December 1995, President Clinton authorized the deployment of over 20,000 American combat troops to Bosnia as part of a NATO-led peacekeeping force to help enforce the Dayton peace accords aimed at resolving the Bosnian conflict. Subsequently, in December 1996, President Clinton agreed to provide up to 8,500 American ground troops to participate in a NATO-led follow-on force in Bosnia termed the Stabilization Force (SFOR). These actions were taken by the President in the absence of express congressional approval, and despite continuing disputes between the Congress and the President over the proper course of action for the U.S. in the Bosnian conflict.[18]

Following the seizure of Haiti's government by Haitian military leader Raul Cedras in July 1993 from its President Jean-Bertrand Aristide, the United Nations took a number of steps to support the restoration of Aristide to power, including an embargo, and in July 1994, authorizing a multinational force to facilitate the departure of the military leadership in Haiti. In mid September 1994, President Clinton sent a U.S. negotiating team to Haiti to urge the peaceful departure of the military junta, while ordering the U.S. military to prepare for an invasion of Haiti, if necessary, to restore President Aristide. The military junta agreed to leave Haiti peacefully in the face of an imminent U.S. invasion. Subsequently, the U.S. sent approximately 21,000 military forces to Haiti to disarm Haitian military and paramilitary forces, and to aid a U.N. peacekeeping operation in restoring civil government and order in Haiti. President Clinton undertook the Haiti operation without the prior approval of Congress and was criticized for this. Congress subsequently passed S.J. Res. 229 in October 1994 (signed as P.L. 103-423) which stated the sense of Congress that the

---

[17]See Mark, Clyde. Congress and Iraq, 1990, in Congress and Foreign Policy, 1990, p. 109-137, and Kenneth Katzman, War and Peace in the Middle East, Congress and Foreign Policy 1991, p. 21-53.

[18]See Grimmett, Richard F. War Powers Resolution: Presidential Compliance. CRS Issue Brief 81050. Woehrel, Steven and Julie Kim. Bosnia-Former Yugoslavia and U.S. Policy. CRS Archived Issue Brief 91089 and Bowman, Steven R. Bosnia: U.S. Military Operations. CRS Issue Brief 93056.

President should have sought congressional approval before deploying U.S. forces to Haiti and supported a prompt and orderly withdrawal as soon as possible.[19]

Administration Proposal for Legislation

On occasion, the executive branch wants to begin a foreign policy program that requires legislation or appropriations, and accordingly proposes legislation to Congress. Congressional approval in this situation is essential. Congress may play a more or less active role in the development of the legislation, modifying the Administration bill or developing entirely new legislation of its own.

The classic example of a policy proposed by the Administration but subsequently developed by both branches working together cooperatively is the Marshall plan.[20] On June 5, 1947, Secretary of State George Marshall proposed U.S. assistance for European recovery on condition that the European nations initiate and agree on plans for an aid program. The Western European governments responded with a proposal for a program based on 4 years of U.S. assistance. To allow sufficient time for consideration, President Truman requested an interim aid program that was passed by Congress in December 1947. He then submitted to Congress the proposal for the longer term European Recovery Program. Congress created a Select Committee on Foreign Aid that made an independent study of the needs in Europe. The Senate Foreign Relations and House Foreign Affairs Committees also held extensive hearings, and the legislation that emerged was widely considered to be the product of a bipartisan, joint effort of both branches.

Since then Presidents have annually proposed foreign assistance programs that Congress has authorized or appropriated after modifying as it saw fit, often using the legislation as a vehicle for initiatives of its own. In 1978, for example, Congress required a new emphasis in both bilateral and multilateral aid for programs designed to meet basic human needs, and also launched a Women in Development program to promote attention to women in the economic development process.[21] After democratic reforms occurred in Poland and Hungary during 1989, President Bush proposed an aid package and trade benefits for the two countries. As the year continued and all of Eastern Europe was transformed by the replacement of Communist governments with democratic reforms, Congress enlarged the package and urged more active U.S. support for the growing democratic movements.[22]

---

[19]See Taft-Morales, Maureen E. Haiti Under President Preval: Issues for Congress. CRS Issue Brief 96019.

[20]For further discussion see Hutchinson, Martha Crenshaw. The Marshall Plan Model: A Case Study of the Congressional Information Problem. In Executive-Legislative Consultation on Foreign Policy, Strengthening the Legislative Side. House Foreign Affairs Committee Print, April 1982. p. 77-85.

[21]See Sanford, Jonathan E. International Economic Assistance. In Congress and Foreign Policy, 1978. p. 73-100.

[22]See Miko, Francis. Congress and the Transformation of Eastern Europe in 1989, in Congress and Foreign Policy, 1989, p. 19-37.

President Clinton in April 1993 proposed a major increase in United States assistance to Russia following a summit at Vancouver, Canada, with Russian Prime Minister Boris Yeltsin. The $1.6 billion U.S. assistance package, using existing appropriated funds, included more concessional terms for agricultural loans and an increase in assistance targeted at privatization. Further, funding was targeted at resettling Russian officers and providing employment training to assist their return to civilian life, while facilitating their withdrawal from the Baltics. The President stated that 75% of the assistance would be used outside of Moscow to make it more highly visible to the average Russian citizen than earlier U.S. aid programs. All such assistance efforts were aimed at advancing democratization in Russia.[23]

Negotiation of International Agreements

The power of negotiation gives the executive branch a dominant role in making foreign policy through international agreements, but the President must take into account congressional opinion because often agreements must be approved by the Senate or Congress. Congress also influences agreements by placing in legislation instructions and views concerning international agreements, indicating through various means what kind of agreement would be acceptable, and attaching reservations or other conditions when approving an agreement.

A few international agreements might be called "sole executive agreements" because the President considers that he has the authority to conclude them under his own powers and does not submit them to the Senate as treaties nor to Congress for approval.[24] Examples are the Yalta Agreement of 1945, the Vietnam Peace Agreement of 1973, the Iranian Hostage Agreement of 1981, and the Afghanistan Settlement Agreement of April 14, 1988.

Most international agreements, however, have some form of congressional participation. The Senate must approve treaties by a two-thirds majority. The bulk of executive agreements are either authorized by Congress prior to their conclusion or approved after their conclusion, and might be called congressional-executive agreements. As an example of prior action, Congress has authorized the executive branch to conclude agreements on military and economic assistance, space and nuclear energy cooperation, and foreign trade, and has set forth goals, guidelines, and criteria in the authorizing legislation. As an example of action after conclusion, Congress approved the SALT I interim agreement of 1972 by a joint resolution, with the Jackson amendment which requested that the President seek a future treaty that would not limit the United States to levels of strategic forces inferior to Soviet levels.

---

[23]For further discussion see Tarnoff, Curt. U.S. Assistance to the Soviet Union and Its Successor States 1991-1996: A History of Administration and Congressional Action. CRS Report 98-43F. January 14, 1998. 31p.

[24]For further discussion of various types of international agreements, see Treaties and Other International Agreements: The Role of the United States Senate. A Study Prepared for the Committee on Foreign Relations by the Congressional Research Service. Washington, G.P.O., November 1993. S. Prt. 103-53. 384 p.

In the case of trade agreements such as the North American Free Trade Agreement (NAFTA) and agreements negotiated under the auspices of the General Agreement on Trade and Tariffs (GATT), Congress has authorized negotiations in advance but required that it approve the agreement prior to its implementation.[25] The implementing legislation for both the NAFTA and the GATT Uruguay Round agreements was considered under so-called "fast-track" procedures in 1993 and 1994 respectively. This process had been developed during the Nixon and Ford Administrations to protect a President's ability to negotiate trade agreements with some confidence that they would not be undermined later by Congress through the traditional rules applied to legislation. Under "fast-track" rules, Congress was given 90 days to take action on the implementing bill after its formal introduction. Congress could not amend the bill. Each congressional committee of jurisdiction was given 45 days to review the proposed legislation. The proposed bill was then only subject to a yes or no vote in the House and the Senate. Since Congress could not amend the final legislation, a practice developed over the years whereby informal committee markup sessions were held on the draft implementing bills to indicate to the President key areas of Congressional concern regarding the specific trade legislation. This process afforded the President the opportunity to address these concerns as he deemed appropriate prior to submitting a final bill to implement the trade agreement. The debates over the NAFTA and the GATT Uruguay Round agreements were very contentious. Following passage of the implementing vehicle for the latter in a lame duck session of Congress in late 1994, the President's authority to use "fast-track" procedures lapsed. A subsequent effort by the Clinton Administration to secure renewal of this authority was dropped in late 1997 due to insufficient bipartisan support for granting it. In the fall of 1998 a bill to restore "fast-track" authority failed to pass the House of Representatives[26]

Legislative-executive branch interchange has been especially complex in the treaties relating to strategic arms reductions. In preparation for the Strategic Arms Reduction Treaty (START), the Senate and House formed Observer Groups to monitor the negotiations. After the START Treaty was submitted to the Senate on November 25, 1991, the Soviet Union ceased to exist and Senators worked with the Administration in deciding how to handle the new situation. A new protocol amending the treaty was negotiated in Lisbon with the Soviet successor states. The Senate approved the START Treaty on October 1, 1992, with several conditions, including that Belarus, Kazakhstan, Russia, and Ukraine be legally bound to all the obligations of the Soviet Union in the treaty.

---

[25]Sek, Lenore. Congress and Trade Negotiating Authority. In Congress and Foreign Policy, 1991, p. 103-117.

[26]For additional background see: Grimmett, Jeanne J. Why Certain Trade Agreements Are Approved as Congressional-Executive Agreements Rather Than as Treaties. CRS Report for Congress 97-896A. September 29, 1997. 6p. Howe, Robert H. North American Free Trade Agreement (NAFTA) and Related Issues: A Checklist of CRS Products. CRS Report for Congress 97-907L. October 9, 1997. 4p. Wilson, Arlene. The GATT and the WTO: An Overview. CRS Report for Congress 95-424E. March 27, 1995. 6p. Pregelj, Vladimir N. Trade Agreements: Renewing the Negotiating and Fast-Track Implementing Authority. CRS Issue Brief 97016.

Policy Statements

The President also establishes U.S. foreign policy through unilateral statements or joint statements issued with other governments. Sometimes unilateral statements are broad descriptions of American goals and objectives. In an address to the United Nations on September 21, 1992, President Bush called for strengthening the peacekeeping capabilities of the United Nations. Other times, the President articulates policy on a specific issue. In the State of the Union Address of January 28, 1992, President Bush proposed that the United States and Russia eliminate all their land-based multiple warhead ballistic missiles. On April 5, 1991, President Bush announced the United States would join international efforts to airdrop relief supplies to Kurdish refugees along the Iraqi-Turkish border. In January 1994, the Clinton Administration proposed the expansion of the alliance at the NATO summit. With Congressional support over the next four years, a number of gradual steps were taken leading to the Senate giving its consent to the amendment of the North Atlantic Treaty on April 30, 1998, by a vote of 80-19, permitting the admission of Poland, the Czech Republic and Hungary to the alliance.[27]

Joint statements—policy statements made with other countries—are not legally binding international agreements, but they commit the President to a course of action. At the conclusion of the summit conference in Tokyo on May 5, 1986, for example, leaders of seven nations including the United States issued a joint statement pledging to fight terrorism through specified economic and diplomatic actions. At the conclusion of the economic summit of the Group of Seven on July 8, 1992, the leaders issued a communique embodying a wide range of policies including support for the strategy of cooperation between the Russian Government and the International Monetary Fund.

Congress may support the policy enunciated by the President, attempt to change it, or find a way to participate in the further development of the policy. After the Conference on Security and Cooperation in Europe in Helsinki, on August 1, 1975, President Ford and 34 other heads of state signed the Final Act of the Conference that provided for the freer flow of people and information between East and West Europe. Congress by legislation established a Commission on Security and Cooperation in Europe to monitor the implementation of the accords.[28] Since that time the Commission, 12 of whose 15 members are Members of Congress, has closely monitored the accords and played an active role in development of U.S. policy in this area.

The executive branch makes a policy statement when it casts the U.S. vote in international organizations. Most measures adopted by international organizations, such as United Nations General Assembly resolutions, are not legally binding, but they put the United States on record as for or against a proposed course of action. The executive branch also determines the U.S. position on resolutions of the United

---

[27]Katzman, Kenneth. War and Peace in the Middle East. Congress and Foreign Policy, 1991, p. 21-53. Gallis, Paul E. NATO: Congress Addresses Expansion of the Alliance. CRS Issue Brief 95076.

[28]P.L. 94-304, approved June 3, 1976.

Nations Security Council, which many authorities consider binding, such as Resolution 678 (1990) calling for nations to use "all necessary means" to uphold earlier resolutions aimed at getting Iraq to withdraw from Kuwait.

Congress sometimes influences the U.S. vote in international organizations. It has on several occasions directed U.S. representatives in international financial institutions to vote in a specified manner. For example, in 1992 Congress provided that the Secretary of the Treasury should direct the U.S. Executive Director of the Inter-American Development Bank to vote against funding for any project of the Multilateral Investment Fund if the project was likely to cause loss of jobs in the United States. Members of Congress also serve on inter-parliamentary groups such as the North Atlantic Assembly and the parliamentary assembly of the Organization on Security and Cooperation in Europe, where their views may affect the perspectives and votes of members from other participating nations.[29]

Whenever implementation of the measures promised by the executive in unilateral or joint statements requires legislation or appropriations, Congress has more power in deciding whether to support or modify U.S. policy. When the Administration pledges funds to the multilateral development banks, for example, the funds must be authorized and appropriated by Congress. The United States could not increase its quota in the International Monetary Fund for assistance to Russia in 1992 until Congress appropriated the necessary funds.[30]

Policy Implementation

Even when Congress establishes foreign policy through legislation, the Administration continues to shape policy as it interprets and applies the various provisions of law. This is illustrated in arms sales policy. Congress has established the objectives and criteria for arms sales to foreign countries in the Arms Export Control Act, and it has required advance notification of major arms sales and provided procedures for halting a sale it disapproves. But the executive branch makes the daily decisions on whether or not to sell arms to specific countries and what weapons systems to provide. As an example, on September 14, 1992, President Bush notified Congress of his intention to sell 72 F-15 fighter aircraft to Saudi Arabia, and after the 30-day congressional review period expired, the sale proceeded.

Congress has found it necessary to maintain close supervision to prevent sales, particularly to Middle Eastern countries, that it did not approve. In some cases its actions had the effect of halting sales, and it has frequently brought about changes in proposed arms sales packages.[31] In 1985 Congress passed a joint resolution (P.L. 99-162) prohibiting a proposed sale of certain advanced aircraft and air defense systems

---

[29]Foreign Operations Appropriations Act, Title I, P.L. 102-391, signed Oct. 5, 1992.

[30]P.L. 102-391, signed Oct. 6, 1992.

[31]For further information see Grimmett, Richard F. Executive-Legislative Consultations on U.S. Arms Sales. U.S. Congress. House. Committee on Foreign Affairs. Committee Print, December 1982. 39 p. See also Arms Sales, Congressional Review Process, by Grimmett, Richard F. CRS Report for Congress 96-971F. 6p.

to Jordan prior to March 1, 1986, unless direct and meaningful peace negotiations between Israel and Jordan were underway. After the date passed, the Administration did not propose the sale, apparently in the belief it would be disapproved by Congress. In 1986 both Houses passed a joint resolution disapproving a sale of advanced missiles to Saudi Arabia, and the President vetoed the resolution; the Senate sustained the veto by a 66-34 vote, but only after the Administration removed Stinger (hand-held) missiles from the package.

Since the 1980s various Administrations have used their authority to establish regulatory guidelines for the export of U.S.-origin dual-use technologies. In the case of exports to China since the 1989 Tiananmen Square crackdown, U.S. law has required that China cannot obtain commercial satellites or related technology from the United States unless the President issues a waiver of this restriction, on a case-by-case basis, on the grounds that such a transaction is in the U.S. national interest or because China has made reforms in its human rights or political practices. In March of 1996, President Clinton transferred authority for issuing export licenses from the State Department to the Commerce Department. Subsequently, when it was discovered that two U.S. companies had shared technical information regarding the cause of an explosion of a Chinese rocket launching a U.S. commercial satellite, without having secured a license to do so from the State Department, a Justice Department investigation was launched. In the wake of the controversy over this transfer of technical information regarding satellites to China and charges that insufficient scrutiny was being given to security issues involved in such prospective transfers, Congress by an amendment to the FY1999 National Defense Authorization Act (P.L. 105-261), transferred authority to license commercial satellite and related data exports from the Commerce Department back to the State Department, effective in March 1999.

Independent Action

Occasionally the President undertakes a dramatic or sudden foreign policy action before Congress is fully informed about it. Congress then is faced with the dilemma of supporting the action or being charged with undercutting the President before the world. Congress usually supports the President, but on occasion it tries to halt or reverse the policy or pass legislation to restrain the President from similar actions in the future.

When President Reagan launched a military invasion of Grenada on October 24, 1983, Congress essentially supported the President in his stated effort to prevent the formation of a Communist foothold there. Although both Houses of Congress passed separate measures that would invoke the War Powers Resolution, neither measure was passed by both Houses.[32] Congressional leaders apparently received assurances

---

[32]The War Powers Resolution, P.L. 93-148, was passed over the veto of President Nixon in November 1973 to assure that both the President and Congress participate in decisions that might involve the United States in war. It requires the President to consult with Congress in every possible instance prior to the introduction of armed forces into hostilities or situations of imminent hostilities, and establishes a time limit of 60-90 days for U.S. forces to remain

(continued...)

from the White House that the troops would be out within 60 days, and public opinion strongly supported the action. Congress also supported the President's action by approving $15 million for grant economic assistance programs to Grenada.

Similarly, when President Reagan ordered the bombing of Libya on April 15, 1986, to counter state-supported terrorism, and when President Bush ordered the invasion of Panama on December 20, 1989, to apprehend General Manuel Noriega, most Members supported the President's effort. Widespread public support greeted the President's action and was also a factor in determining the congressional response.

In another instance, President Clinton addressed a financial crisis in Mexico, after a devaluation of the peso in late December 1994. In an effort to prevent Mexican default on billions of dollars worth of debt obligations, in early 1995, the President's economic advisors crafted a package of support for Mexico that did not require a Congressional vote on the controversial proposal. This action was taken when it appeared possible that Congress would not enact the Administration's legislation to deal with the crisis. The independent initiative by President Clinton included $20 billion in credits from the Exchange Stabilization Fund (ESF) of the Treasury Department, which is normally used to stabilize the U.S. dollar's value; $10 billion in credits from the Bank for International Settlements, and $17.8 billion from the International Monetary Fund (IMF). The Clinton Administration's independent intervention in the Mexican peso crisis led to significant criticism in Congress, but efforts to modify or block it were either defeated or abandoned.[33]

Occasionally, however, Congress significantly refines or alters a policy independently undertaken by the President. This was the case in the 1979 policy change toward the People's Republic of China and Taiwan. On December 15, 1978, President Carter announced suddenly that the United States would establish diplomatic relations with the People's Republic of China on January 1, 1979, and terminate the defense treaty with the Republic of China on Taiwan after the one year's notice required by the treaty. The Administration also submitted legislation to govern future relations with Taiwan.

While few Members of Congress opposed the establishment of relations with China, a move anticipated since President Nixon's trip to China in 1972, many Members sought to modify the practical implications of the new policy and reassure allies in the Pacific. Congress added sections to the Taiwan Relations Act to affirm that the United States would consider any nonpeaceful effort against Taiwan as a threat to the Western Pacific and would provide Taiwan with defensive arms to maintain a sufficient self-defense capability. Congress also made modifications in the

---

[32](...continued)
in such situations without congressional authorization.

[33]For background see Storrs, K. Larry. Mexico-U.S. Relations: Issues for Congress. Issue Brief 97028, and "Clinton Leads Mexico Bailout Effort," Congressional Quarterly Almanac 1995, pp. 10-16 and 10-17.

legislation aimed at continuing economic ties and placing Taiwan-U.S. relations on a firmer legal basis.[34]

Senator Barry Goldwater and other Members of Congress filed suit against the President for terminating the security treaty with the Republic of China without the approval of two-thirds of the Senate or a majority of both Houses of Congress. Senator Goldwater also introduced legislation to bar the President from terminating other defense treaties without congressional participation. While neither effort was successful, they illustrated that in undertaking independent action, the President risks punitive action by Congress that may reduce future flexibility in foreign policy actions.

The Congress as Initiator

Following are six basic ways in which Congress can originate or shape foreign policy. In these circumstances, the executive branch is put in the position of responding positively to the congressional initiative or seeking to adjust or reverse its impact on the course of foreign policy.

Resolutions and Policy Statements

Every year Members of Congress introduce large numbers of simple or concurrent resolutions stating the sense of the House, Senate, or Congress on foreign policy, and many such resolutions are adopted. Many observers are skeptical about the effectiveness of these sense of the House, Senate, or Congress resolutions. Like Presidential policy statements, they express the policy of a single branch of government, but their effect is often weaker because Congress does not execute policy. Since simple and concurrent resolutions are not legally binding, the executive branch often ignores them in carrying out foreign policy.

Nevertheless, sometimes such resolutions play a significant role in foreign policy by launching a new idea or promoting a new policy. S. Res. 264, introduced by Senator A. S. Mike Monroney, and adopted July 23, 1958, led to the establishment of the International Development Association as an affiliate of the World Bank designed to make low-interest, long-term loans. In 1973 the Senate adopted S. Res. 71, introduced by Senator Claiborne Pell, calling for an international agreement "prohibiting environmental or geophysical modification activity as a weapon of war." Such an agreement was subsequently negotiated and ratified by the United States in 1979. In 1979 the House passed H. Res. 321 urging the United Nations to convene an emergency session of the General Assembly to deal with the refugee crisis in Southeast Asia. This added to other calls for such a conference and subsequently a United Nations Conference was convened in July 1979. H.Con. Res. 248, adopted September 17, 1990, called for a higher priority for environmental concerns and urged increased attention to the linkage between the environment and national security.

---

[34]For further discussion see Sutter, Robert. Congress and U.S. Policy in Asia: New Relationships with China and Taiwan. In Congress and Foreign Policy, 1979, p. 54-71, and Executive-Legislative Consultations on China Policy, 1978-1979. House Foreign Affairs Committee Print, June 1980. 42 p.

Holding hearings on resolutions has occasionally given impetus to a policy even though the resolution itself did not pass. In 1967 Senator Pell introduced S. Res. 172 relating to international regulation of ocean activities. The Administration opposed the resolution and it was not adopted, but later the concept came to fruition in the seabed arms control treaty of 1971.

Simple and concurrent resolutions also serve as a channel of communication between Congress and foreign countries. While often the communications to foreign governments are formal messages of sympathy, congratulations, and appreciation, at other times they are more substantive. H. Con. Res. 484 of August 8, 1988, called on President Zia of Pakistan, consistent with his pledge of May 29, 1988, to hold free and fair elections not later than November 16, 1988. H. Con. Res. 136 of May 24, 1989, called on the Chinese Government to resolve the political crisis in China without violence. Congress annually passed resolutions calling for Baltic Freedom and commemorating "Captive Nations Week" from 1959 until independence was achieved by Lithuania, Latvia, and Estonia in 1991.

Sense of the Congress resolutions also provide a vehicle for support or advice to the President on foreign policy. After the U.S. military intervention in the Dominican Republic in 1965, for example, the House passed H. Res. 560 supporting the President in any action he deemed necessary to prevent Communist subversive aggression in the Western Hemisphere.[35] On May 5, 1986, the House adopted H. Res. 424 supporting the President's policy in Libya by expressing gratitude to the United Kingdom for allowing U.S. bombers stationed there to participate in the April 14, 1986, raid aimed at terrorist bases in Libya.

Congressional concerns over United States involvement in the developing internal conflicts in former Yugoslavia—Bosnia and Kosovo in particular—led to passage of sense of the Congress resolutions. Section 8100 of the Defense Appropriations Act for fiscal year 1995 (P.L. 103-335, signed September 30, 1994) stated the sense of Congress that DoD funds should not be made available for the purpose of deploying U.S. armed forces to participate in implementation of a peace settlement in Bosnia, unless previously authorized by Congress. On March 11, 1999, the House passed H.Con. Res. 42 by a vote of 219-191, expressing the sense of Congress that the President was authorized to deploy U.S. troops to Kosovo as part of a NATO peacekeeping operation, subject to conditions and various reporting requirements. On March 23, 1999, the Senate by a vote of 58-41 passed S. Con. Res. 21 expressing the sense of the Congress that the President was authorized to conduct "military air operations and missile strikes in cooperation with our NATO allies against the Federal Republic of Yugoslavia (Serbia and Montenegro). This Senate concurrent resolution was passed in reaction to the Serbian military actions in Kosovo and President Clinton's request, on March 23, 1999, for "legislative support" of his actions to deal with the Kosovo crisis. Subsequently, on April 28, 1999, the House

---

[35]For additional information see: Hutchinson, Martha Crenshaw. The Dominican Republic Intervention in 1965: A Case Study of the Congressional Information Problem. In U.S. Congress. House. Committee on Foreign Affairs. Executive-Legislative Consultation on Foreign Policy: Strengthening Foreign Policy Information Sources for Congress. Committee Print, February 1982. Washington, G.P.O., 1982. p. 73-84.

by a tie vote of 213-213 defeated S.Con. Res. 21, as well as a joint resolution, H.J. Res. 44, declaring war against Yugoslavia. Through these votes at least one house of the Congress indicated its skepticism of current Administration policy toward resolving the Kosovo conflict[36]

Legislative Directives

Congress sometimes initiates a foreign policy by using legislation to establish a new program, set objectives and guidelines, authorize and direct the executive branch to undertake specified activities, and by earmarking appropriations to be used in a specified way. The executive branch influences this kind of policy initiative because Members regularly seek Administration views in the process of formulating legislation, the President must approve legislation unless it is passed over a Presidential veto, and the executive branch implements the legislation.

As examples, in 1991 Congress took the lead in using defense funds to provide assistance to the former Soviet Union, authorizing and appropriating funds to dismantle Soviet nuclear weapons and provide military transportation for humanitarian assistance.[37] In 1992 Congress placed new sanctions and controls against Iran, Iraq, and nations or persons who assisted them in acquiring weapons of mass destruction.[38]

In 1997 and 1998, Congress was principally responsible for advancing legislation aimed at elevating the importance of combating religious persecution worldwide among U.S. foreign policy objectives. On October 27, 1998, the International Religious Freedom Act was signed into law (H.R. 2431, P.L. 105-292). This act established within the State Department an Office of International Religious Freedom headed by an Ambassador at Large, subject to confirmation by the Senate. This Ambassador is charged with , among other things, recommending appropriate U.S. government responses where the right to religious freedom abroad is violated, including preparing an annual report on country practices regarding religious freedoms. This law specifies sanctions against countries if they are determined to have engaged in or tolerated particularly severe violations of religious freedom.[39]

---

[36]For background see: Kim, Julie and Steven J. Woehrel. Bosnia-Former Yugoslavia and U.S. Policy. CRS Issue Brief 91089 and Woehrel, Steven and Julie Kim. Kosovo and U.S. Policy. CRS Issue Brief 98041. U.S. Congress. Congressional Record, Senate, March 23, 1999, p.S3101 and Congressional Record, House, April 28, 1999, pp. H2440-H2441, H2451-H2452 (daily edition).

[37]Conventional Armed Forces in Europe Treaty Implementation Act, P.L. 102-228, December 12, 1991. For case study, see Congress and the Transformation of the Soviet Union, by Nichol, James P. in Congress and Foreign Policy, 1991, p. 55-81.

[38]Iran-Iraq Arms Non-Proliferation Act of 1992, Title XVI of National Defense Authorization Act for Fiscal Year 1993, P.L. 102-484, signed October 23, 1992.

[39]For background see: Bite, Vita. Religious Persecution Abroad: Congressional Concerns and Actions. CRS Report 97-968F.

Legislative Pressure

Sometimes Congress pressures the executive branch into a new direction in foreign policy by threatening to pass legislation, even though the legislation is not enacted, or by continuing to exhort a policy through many means.

An example is the congressional effort in the 1980s to pass legislation imposing economic and other sanctions against South Africa. The effort was widely seen to have prodded the Reagan Administration to establish limited economic sanctions. Dissatisfied with the Administration's policy of "constructive engagement" and quiet diplomacy to bring an end to apartheid in South Africa, the House in 1983 approved legislation applying sanctions against South Africa as part of an extension of the Export Administration Act, but the bill was rejected by the Senate. Toward the end of 1984, American civil rights leaders began daily protests at the South African Embassy in Washington to focus greater attention on racial violence in South Africa and the repressive policies of the white minority government in South Africa. In June 1985 the House passed H.R. 1460 imposing sanctions and threatening a future cutoff of U.S. investment. The Senate followed with S. 995 providing military sanctions. The conference report called for a compromise that included a ban on U.S. import of South African Krugerrands. Before the Senate voted on the final bill, on September 9, 1985, President Reagan issued an executive order imposing sanctions that banned computer sales to the South African police and military and other government agencies that enforce apartheid, exports of nuclear technology to South Africa, and further bank loans to the South African Government. Later the President banned the importation of South African Krugerrands. Nonetheless in 1986 Congress enacted comprehensive sanctions against South Africa over the veto of President Reagan.[40]

Congress for several years pressured President Bush to take a greater leadership role in protecting the international environment. In 1989 many Members criticized the President for not leading a world effort to deal with global warming. After numerous congressional efforts to persuade the administration, including letters, hearings, and a Senate amendment calling for a global conference on the environment in 1989, the President offered to host an international meeting as a step toward negotiations on an international agreement to deal with global warming. Congress also pressed other countries to take environmentally beneficial action in foreign aid legislation.[41]

On June 9, 1998, Congress passed the Iran Missile Proliferation Sanctions Act (H.R. 2709) which would have imposed various sanctions on foreign entities that aided Iran's efforts to develop ballistic missiles. This legislation was vetoed by President Clinton on June 23, 1998. Nevertheless, passage of this bill may have

---

[40]Comprehensive Anti-Apartheid Act of 1986, P.L. 99-440, signed October 2, 1986. See The 99th Congress and South African Sanctions, by Shepard, Robert B. in Congress and Foreign Policy, 1985-86, p. 13-36.

[41]See Congress and International Environmental Issues in 1989, by Tarnoff, Curt in Congress and Foreign Policy, 1989, p. 121-139.

induced the Clinton Administration to act more forcefully with Russia in order to get it to curtail its technological assistance to Iran's ballistic missile program.[42]

Another example of legislative pressure is the reaction of various Senators to the Kyoto Protocol to the United Nations Framework Convention on Climate Change. This protocol is the implementation vehicle for the Climate Change Convention. The Kyoto Protocol was concluded on December 10, 1997 by delegates of 161 nations and sets binding targets for reduction of emissions of greenhouse gases by developed nations. The United States signed it on November 12, 1998, but it has not been submitted to the Senate for its advise and consent, as of this writing, due, in part, to indications given by some Senators that it would be rejected unless their key concerns are addressed first. The Clinton Administration has been attempting to secure actions from various nations that would assist in convincing the Senate that the Kyoto Protocol should be approved.[43]

Legislative Restrictions/Funding Denials

Congress has been most visible in its foreign policy role when it has placed legislation prohibitions or other limitations on the President's freedom of action in foreign affairs. Often these measures have been amendments to legislation authorizing or appropriating funds that the President was unlikely to veto. The use of funding restrictions or denials by Congress is a classic illustration of the "power of the purse" under the Constitution. Unlike other legislative action by Congress, its use is not subject to serious challenge by the President as an unconstitutional infringement on the President's foreign policy powers. Major legislative-executive confrontations have occurred when such restrictions have been passed despite the opposition of the President. Some examples follow.

On January 23, 1973, President Nixon announced the signing of the Paris peace accords to end U.S. involvement in the Vietnam war, but attacks by the Khmer Rouge in Cambodia continued and the United States resumed bombing in Cambodia. The Administration wanted to maintain freedom of U.S. action if North Vietnam or its Communist associates violated the accords. But Congress effectively halted such military action when it passed over the President's opposition amendments to funding legislation stating that after August 15, 1973, no funds under any legislation could be used to finance combat activities by United States military forces in, over, or from off the shores of North Vietnam, South Vietnam, Laos or Cambodia.[44]

---

[42]For background see: Katzman, Kenneth. Iran: Current Developments and U.S. Policy. CRS Issue Brief 93033.

[43]For background see: Fletcher, Susan R. Global Climate Change Treaty: The Kyoto Protocol. CRS Report for Congress 98-2ENR; Ackerman, David M. Global Climate Change: Selected Legal Questions About the Kyoto Protocol. CRS Report for Congress 98-349A; Morrissey, Wayne A. and John R. Justus, Global Climate Change. CRS Issue Brief 89005 by and Fletcher, Susan R. Global Climate Change Treaty: Negotiations and Related Issues. CRS Report for Congress 97-1000ENR.

[44]For further discussion see chapter, The Legislated Peace, in Franck, Thomas M. and Edward Weisband. Foreign Policy by Congress. New York, Oxford University Press, 1979.

(continued...)

In 1974 the Nixon Administration was pursuing a policy of normalizing trade relations with the Soviet Union as part of the broader policy of detente. Against the wishes of the Administration, Congress passed amendments to the Trade Act of 1974 which limited the amount of Export-Import Bank credits to the Soviet Union to $300 million and made the granting of most-favored-nation treatment conditional upon Soviet adoption of more liberal emigration policies. Subsequently the Soviet Union stated that because of such restrictions it would not put into force the trade agreement which the United States signed in 1972.

In early 1976, when the United States was supplying covert assistance through the Central Intelligence Agency to factions in Angola against an Angolan movement supported by Cuban troops and Soviet military assistance, Congress prohibited any kind of U.S. assistance to Angola unless expressly authorized by Congress.[45] This provision, known as the Clark amendment, forced the Administration to end U.S. aid. Congress repealed the amendment in 1985.

Throughout the Reagan Administration, Congress legislated numerous restrictions and limitations on military assistance to Central American countries. In 1983, for example, it limited the amount that could be spent on U.S. intelligence activities supporting military or paramilitary activities in Nicaragua.[46] In 1987, after the Central American governments signed a peace accord, Congress cut off military assistance to the Nicaraguan Contras (anti-Sandinista guerillas), and in 1988 permitted only non-lethal assistance.[47]

In 1992, Congress prohibited the testing of any nuclear weapon until July 1, 1993, and permitted using funds for nuclear tests after that time only in accord with strict guidelines and conditions, including a plan for achieving a multilateral comprehensive test ban.[48]

In 1993, Congress established a deadline for U.S. troops to leave Somalia. No funds could be used for military action after March 31, 1994, unless the President requested an extension from Congress and received legislative authority.[49]

---

[44](...continued)
p. 13-33.

[45]See chapter, Teaching the President a Lesson: Angola. In Franck, Thomas M., and Edward Weisband. Foreign Policy by Congress. New York, Oxford University Press, 1979. p. 46-57.

[46]See chapter, Congress and the Central American-Caribbean Region, in Congress and Foreign Policy, 1983.

[47]See Congress and Policy Toward Central American and Panama, by Taft-Morales, Maureen and Mark P. Sullivan, in Congress and Foreign Policy, 1988, p. 51-87.

[48]Section 507, Energy and Water Development Appropriations Act, 1993, P.L. 102-377, signed October 2, 1992.

[49]107 Stat. 1476, sec. 8151(b)(2)(B) (1993).

On March 12, 1996, President Clinton signed into law, H.R. 927, the Cuban Liberty and Democracy Solidarity Act (P.L. 104-114), often referred to as the Helms-Burton Act. This legislation, among other things, codifies all existing Cuban embargo Executive orders and regulations. This law does not provide for a Presidential waiver of any of these codified embargo provisions. The legislation also allows U.S. nationals to sue for money damages in U.S. Federal Court those persons that traffic in property confiscated in Cuba. The President can waive this provision for six month periods of time. The legislation further denies admission to the U.S. of aliens involved in the confiscation of U.S. property in Cuba or in the trafficking of confiscated U.S. property in Cuba. The Helms-Burton legislation has a direct and important effect on U.S. Cuban policy and was strongly opposed by the Clinton Administration prior to its enactment.[50]

In 1996, Congress passed H.R. 3107, legislation that would impose U.S. sanctions on foreign companies that invested in energy production in Libya or Iran, or sold certain products to Libya. The legislation, the Iran and Libya Sanctions Act of 1996, was signed into law by President Clinton on August 5, 1996 (P.L. 104-172).[51]

Informal Advice

Often Members of Congress shape foreign policy by providing advice to the executive branch in informal contacts. Such advice can also be given at meetings between the President and Members where no formal decision-making is contemplated, but where general reactions to prospective policy initiatives may be solicited by the President.

An example is President Eisenhower's decision not to intervene militarily in Indochina in 1954. At a meeting on April 3, 1954, Secretary of State Dulles and other executive branch officials met with congressional leaders including Senate Majority Leader William Knowland, Minority Leader Lyndon Johnson, Speaker Joseph Martin, Jr. and Minority Whip John McCormack. Secretary Dulles said a unanimous congressional opinion developed in the meeting that there should be no congressional action on a resolution to support involvement until commitments for support were obtained from other nations. Without assurance of either congressional or allied support, President Eisenhower decided against intervention.[52]

Another example is the proposal for U.S.-Soviet nuclear risk reduction centers. The idea had been advanced by Senators Henry Jackson, John Warner, and Sam Nunn in 1980, and Congress had endorsed the concept in the 1985 defense authorization

---

[50]For background see: Sullivan, Mark P. Cuba: Issues for Congress. CRS Issue Brief 94005 and Congressional Quarterly Almanac 1996, pp. 9-6, 9-7 and 9-8.

[51]For background see: Katzman, Kenneth. Iran: Current Developments and U.S. Policy. CRS Issue Brief 93033 and Congressional Quarterly Almanac 1996 pp. 9-5 and 9-6.

[52]For further discussion see: Gibbons, William. The Government and the Vietnam War, Executive and Legislative Roles and Relationships, Part I, 1945-1961. Senate Print 95-185 Pt. 1. Washington, G.P.O., 1984. p. 175-227.

act. Senators Warner and Nunn apparently persuaded President Reagan to bring up the idea at the summit conference of 1985 with Soviet Secretary General Gorbachev, and the two leaders agreed to negotiations on the subject. An agreement on nuclear risk reduction centers was signed September 15, 1987.

Congressional letters helped bring about a change in U.S. policy toward Cambodia. 162 House Members and 26 Senators wrote Secretary of State Baker a letter on November 29, 1989, questioning administration policy on Cambodia. On July 24, 1990, 66 Senators wrote President Bush taking issue with past U.S. support for representatives of three resistance groups including the Khmer Rouge to be the legitimate representative of Cambodia in the United Nations. Congressional critics also contended that the administration was placing too much emphasis on the need for compromise by the Vietnamese and the State of Cambodia, and not enough on restricting the Khmer Rouge. As a result of congressional pressure, administration officials stressed more their opposition to the Khmer Rouge, and the aid program was changed from a covert to an overt one which could be more openly debated.[53]

Oversight of Policy

Congress shapes foreign policy through regular oversight of executive branch implementation of foreign policy. This involves such mechanisms as hearings and investigations. In particular, hearings on annual authorizations and appropriations of funds for executive branch agencies carrying out foreign policy provide an opportunity for committee members to question and influence activities and policies. The Senate Foreign Relations and House International Relations Committees oversee the Department of State and other foreign affairs agencies; the Armed Services Committees oversee the Defense Department; the Intelligence Committees oversee the Central Intelligence Agency, and other parts of the intelligence community.

Hearings and investigations may be on any subject within a committee's jurisdiction and raise questions about policy for public discussion. Senate Foreign Relations Committee hearings on the Vietnam War and national commitments in the late 1960s and early 1970s, for example, contributed to public opinion against continued U.S. participation in the war. In 1987 special House and Senate committees investigated revelations that staff of the National Security Council had entered secret negotiations that linked the sale of U.S. arms to Iran with the release of American hostages, and that part of the proceeds from the sale had been used to assist the Nicaraguan rebels known as "Contras."[54]

Other frequently used oversight mechanisms are reporting requirements and requirements that certain decisions or international agreements be submitted to Congress in advance of the date they would be effective. The Freedom Support Act of 1992, for example, required several annual reports, including one on the effectiveness of the assistance provided to each of the independent states of the

---

[53]See Support for Third World Resistance Movements: Changing Priorities, by Copson, Raymond W.and Robert G. Sutter, in Congress and Foreign Policy, 1990, p. 77-107.

[54]See Congress and the Iran-Contra Affair, by Woldman, Joel M. in Congress and Foreign Policy, 1987, p. 15-33.

former Soviet Union, an analysis of programs to assist U.S. companies in transacting business with the independent states, and the activities of the Democracy Corps. It required semiannual reports on Soviet weapons destruction and numerous one-time reports. It also required reports of proposed obligations of funds for nonproliferation activities in advance of actual obligation, and a certification that a state was meeting certain criteria, such as forgoing excessive military modernization, prior to obligating funds for nonproliferation and disarmament programs.[55]

Since the early 1970s, Congress has used oversight mechanisms to advance human rights as an important factor in U.S. foreign policy. The House International Relations and Senate Foreign Relations Committees have held hearings on human rights in various geographic regions and specific countries, and cases involving violations of human rights of individuals in foreign countries. In 1975, Congress established machinery in the State Department to carry out the human rights policy and required annual reports from the Department on human rights observance by each recipient of U.S. foreign aid. In 1979 it required that the report cover all members of the United Nations. Congress has monitored the reports and executive branch policies toward countries with poor human rights records, frequently inserting in legislation conditions or restrictions aimed at improving human rights policies. The foreign operations appropriation act for FY1993, for example, prohibited aid to Zaire because of continued reports of human rights abuses in that country.[56]

In the mid-1990s, the Indonesian government's use of military force to deal with internal political dissension in East Timor, a province it took over by force from Portugal in the mid-1970s, led to criticism in the Congress of Indonesia's human rights practices. This led to inclusion of a restriction in the Foreign Operations Appropriation Act for FY1995 (P.L. 103-306, signed August 23, 1994) against the sale or licensing of "small or light arms and crowd control items" by the U.S. for Indonesia, pending a report to the Appropriations Committees of Congress by the Secretary of State that there had been significant progress made on human rights practices in East Timor and elsewhere in Indonesia. Funding for grant military assistance training of the Indonesian military was also denied in this legislation. The restriction on funding for participation in grant military funding for the Indonesian military has also been placed in recent appropriations acts.[57]

Conclusion

The practices illustrated in this report show that making U.S. foreign policy is a complex process. Both the legislative and executive branches play important roles; the roles are different, although frequently overlapping. Both branches have

---

[55]P.L. 102-511, signed October 24, 1992.

[56]P.L. 102-391, signed October 5, 1992. See House Committee on Appropriations Report 102-108, June 12, 1991, p. 39.

[57]Foreign Operations, Export Financing and Related Appropriations Act, FY1998 (P.L. 105-118, November 26, 1997. Omnibus Consolidated and Emergency Supplemental Appropriations Act, FY1999. (P.L. 105-277, October 21, 1998).

continuing opportunities to initiate and change foreign policy, and the interaction between them continues indefinitely throughout the life of a policy.

The President as the chief spokesman of the Nation, directs Government officials and machinery in the daily conduct of diplomacy, and has the principal responsibility for taking action to advance U.S. foreign policy interests. Congress in its oversight responsibility can affect the course of policy through enactment of legislation governing foreign relations and through the appropriation or denial of funds. Experience has shown that cooperation between the two branches is necessary for a strong and effective U.S. foreign policy.

Appendix: Division of Foreign Policy Powers between the President and Congress

Excerpts from the Constitution

ARTICLE I. Section 7. All Bills for raising Revenue shall originate in the House of Representatives, but the Senate may propose or concur with Amendments as on other Bills....

Section 8. The Congress shall have Power To lay and collect Taxes, Duties, Imposts, and Excises, to pay the Debts and provide for the common Defense....

To regulate Commerce with foreign Nations...

To establish an uniform Rule of Naturalization...

To coin Money, regulate the Value thereof, and of foreign Coin...

To define and punish Piracies and Felonies committed on the high Seas, and Offences against the Law of Nations;

To declare War, grant Letters of Marque and Reprisal, and make Rules concerning Captures on Land and Water;

To raise and support Armies, ...To provide and maintain a Navy;...

To make Rules for the Government and Regulation of the land and naval Forces;

To provide for calling forth the Militia to execute the Laws of the Union, suppress insurrections and repel invasions;....

To make all Laws which shall be necessary and proper for carrying into Execution the foregoing Powers, and all other Powers vested by this Constitution in the Government of the United States, or in any Department or Officer thereof....

Section 9. No Money shall be drawn from the Treasury, but in Consequence of Appropriations made by law;....

ARTICLE II. Section 1. The executive Power shall be vested in a President of the United States....

Section 2. The President shall be Commander in Chief of the Army and Navy of the United States, and of the Militia of the several States, when called into the actual Service of the United States;....

He shall have Power, by and with the Advice and Consent of the Senate, to make Treaties, provided two thirds of the Senators present concur; and he shall nominate, and by and with the Advice and Consent of the Senate, shall appoint Ambassadors, other public Ministers and Consuls,....and all other Officers of the United States, whose Appointments are not herein otherwise provided for....

Section 3. ...he shall receive Ambassadors and other public Ministers; he shall take Care that the Laws be faithfully executed, and shall Commission all the Officers of the United States. ....

Foreign Policy of the United States
Volume 1

NATIONAL INTEREST AND U.S FOREIGN POLICY

Mark M. Lowenthal

SUMMARY

The phrase "national interest" is used with increasing frequency in debates over U.S. foreign policy in the post-Cold War world. Neither the term "national interest" nor its usage in connection with foreign policy debates is new, but the current range of views as to what constitutes national interest and how it should be determined has increased sharply.

"National interest" as a concept dates back to the emergence of modern states in the 16th and 17th century. The Founding Fathers used it frequently in the late 18th century. In the 20th century, analysts of the term were divided between those who held that national interests were firm and could be objectively determined and those who felt that these interests change over time.

The first defined U.S. national interest was a desire to keep distant from involvement in European conflicts. Both Washington's "Farewell Address" (1797) and the Monroe Doctrine (1823) stated these goals. This meant, in practical terms, taking steps to secure (and expand) U.S. borders and to limit European involvement in the Western Hemisphere. The emergence of the United States as a world power in 1898 saw a shift to a national interest in the international *status quo*, which also required the maintenance of a balance of power in Europe and Asia -- despite a deep-rooted American antipathy to this concept. This basic interest remained constant, however, through the end of the Cold War.

The concept of national interest remains a highly individual and perceptual one, beyond the core interests of security and defense. Efforts by the Bush and Clinton Administrations to redefine U.S. national interests in the post-Cold War world have not been very successful. Doing so is more difficult in the late 20th century for a number of reasons:

- The U.S. public is somewhat weary of international involvement;

- It is more difficult conceptually to garner strong support for programs or policies crafted to support a favorable *status quo* when there are no evident major threats to it;

- It is also difficult to defend a *status quo* some of whose major strains and stresses come from relations with allies and friendly nations who share our broader values and perhaps interests;

- The President remains predominant in stating U.S. national interests, but this now involves greater consultation with Congress and more concern over public opinion. It also requires devoting attention to broader foreign policy issues rather than individual crises. Finally, to be successful, defining national interests requires some set of policies or programs to defend or advance these interests. All of this comes at a time when the domestic agenda is again predominant.

INTRODUCTION

The phrase "national interest" is used with increasing frequency in debates over U.S. foreign policy in the post-Cold War world. Although neither the term "national interest" nor its use in connection with foreign policy debates is new, the current range of views as to what constitutes national interest and how it should be determined has increased significantly. This is a reflection of the more confusing and still-emerging post-Cold War international order, as well as the absence of a strong consensus as to the proper role that the United States should play internationally.

This debate over the future of post-Cold War U.S. foreign policy and U.S. national interests is unlikely to reach any firm consensus in the near future. Policy makers may find it useful as part of this ongoing debate to examine the origins and past use of "national interest" in U.S. foreign policy debates, and also the ways in which this concept has been and is being defined by policy makers in the Executive and Congress.

THE CONCEPT OF "NATIONAL INTEREST" AS USED IN FOREIGN POLICY

"National interest," under various guises and names, dates back to the emergence of modern states in the 16th and 17th centuries.[1] In the late 18th century, the Founding Fathers frequently referred to "the national interest" in their debates and discussions. The *Federalist Papers* have repeated references to this concept; it was also central to President Washington's discussion of foreign policy in his Farewell Address.[2]

Statesmen continued to use the concept during the 19th century, most famously in the words of Lord Palmerston, the British Foreign Secretary:

---

[1] See Beard, Charles A. *The Idea of National Interest.* (New York, 1934; reprinted by Greenwood Press, Westwood, CT, 1977), pp. 23-24. Some of the earlier terms used to express essentially the same concept were "will of the prince," "dynastic interests," or "*raison d'etat.*"

[2] *Ibid.*, pp. 33-39, 44. For the "Farewell Address," see Commager, Henry Steele, ed. *Documents of American History.* 9th edition. (Englewood, NJ, 1973), pp. 169-75, especially pp. 173-74. See also, Gilbert, Felix. *To the Farewell Address.* (Princeton, NJ, 1970), *passim*, which discusses the European intellectual antecedents of the concept as used by Washington.

> We have no eternal allies and we have no perpetual enemies.
> Our interests are eternal and perpetual, and these interests
> it is our duty to follow.[3]

It was during the mid-20th century, however, that the term "national interest" became a key component in debates over and analyses of foreign policy. Historians of the concept describe two broad groups of "national interest" analysts: (1) those who held that national interest was fairly constant and could be objectively determined; and (2) those who held that national interest changes as the values, preferences, etc. of the public change. Either view -- steadfast interests or changeable ones -- has been subject to rather severe limitations as an analytical tool given the absence of firm criteria or general agreement as to what these interests should be.[4] Nonetheless, "national interest" continues to be widely used in policy debates as a generally agreed upon notion, albeit undefined and subject to fairly broad differences of view.

NATIONAL INTEREST AND U.S. FOREIGN POLICY

The first great defined national interest in U.S. foreign policy was the desire -- if not necessity -- to be as far removed as possible from involvement in European conflicts during a period in which the nation was perceived as being vulnerable. This was a central point in the foreign policy portion of the Farewell Address.[5] This meant, in practical terms, taking steps to secure current U.S. borders and to limit European involvement in the Western Hemisphere.

---

[3] Palmerston said this in 1848, during the House of Commons debate over the Polish question.

[4] See Rosenau, James N. "National Interest," in David L. Sills, ed., *The International Encyclopedia of the Social Sciences* (New York, 1968), pp. 34-40, especially pp. 35-36. Hans J. Morgenthau (*Politics Among Nations: The Struggle for Power and Peace*, 1948; and *In Defense of the National Interest: A Critical Examination of American Foreign Policy*, 1951) is among the most cited of the first view. Richard C. Snyder (*Decision-making as an Approach to the Study of International Politics*, co-author, 1954), is among those holding the second view.

[5] Washington wrote:
> Europe has a set of primary interests which to us have none
> or a very remote relation....
> Our detached and distant situation invites and enables us to
> pursue a different course. If we remain one people, under an
> efficient government, the period is not far off when we may defy
> material injury from external annoyance;...when belligerent
> nations...will not lightly hazard the giving us provocation;...

See Commager, *Documents of American History*, p. 174.

There were two major initial manifestations of this national interest. First, there was a concentrated period of contiguous acquisition and expansion (1803-53). This expansion eliminated all proximate European colonies (except for Canada) and overran the northern portion of Mexico, resulting in borders that the United States acknowledged as permanent and pacific. Second, there was the promulgation of the Monroe Doctrine (1823), proclaiming the closure of the hemisphere to further colonization but also pledging not to interfere with existent colonies.

An important, albeit unspoken aspect of the Monroe Doctrine was the fact that U.S. ideology and values were not then seen as major spurs to national interests. Indeed, the American Revolution stands in stark contrast to the French and Russian Revolutions as being non-proselytizing. It was not until 1913, under President Wilson, that shared values or the imposition of U.S. political values became an important component of U.S. foreign policy. This component grew in significance during World War II and the Cold War, both of which had strong ideological components.

Abrogation of the second tenet of the Monroe Doctrine (non-interference with exiting colonies), by virtue of U.S. involvement in Cuba against Spain in 1898, also signalled the arrival of a profoundly different U.S. national interest. The removal of Spain from the hemisphere left only minor and more distant European colonies at a time when U.S. predominance and safety within the hemisphere was no longer in doubt. The acquisition of an overseas empire also marked the United States as both a world power and one with an acknowledged interest in the international *status quo*.[6]

This did not mean a dogged and static defense of all current global conditions. Indeed, maintaining a balance of power for prolonged periods usually requires changes in the *status quo*. For example, in the post-World War II period, the United States opposed reimposition of British and French rule over a number of colonies that had been overrun by Japan. The U.S. interest in the *status quo* meant an interest in the general balance of power in Europe and Asia. This interest was rarely stated overtly, as U.S. policymakers and politicians traditionally have eschewed the concept of a balance of power as something European and therefore alien, if not corrupt. However, such a

---

[6] To some extent, this was not markedly different from the Monroe Doctrine, which sought to preserve the *status quo* in the Western Hemisphere and was based, in large measure, on the fact of a similar British interest and the implicit support of the Royal Navy.

balance and its preservation was, in essence, a key to U.S. interests and policy.[7]

A profound U.S. national interest in the preservation of the international *status quo* also ran counter to the U.S. preference to avoid involvement in "foreign" (*i.e.*, beyond the Western Hemisphere) conflict. Still, the United States intervened -- reluctantly -- in both World Wars and then undertook the prolonged and eventually global policy of containment against the Soviet Union.

The use of "national interest" during the World War II-Cold War period became somewhat confused by the concurrent and increased use of the parallel terms "national security" or "national security interest."[8] Despite the similarity, these latter terms are not seen as being identical with the broader concept of "national interest," of which national security is a part.

In the aftermath of the Cold War, the U.S. interest in preserving the *status quo* presumably has not changed. However, it becomes more difficult to envisage threats to the *status quo* on the scale of those encountered from 1917 to 1990, again reflecting the confusion between "national interest" and "national security." Thus, although preserving the *status quo* remains an interest, preserving it against "what" poses a vexing question.[9]

Initial efforts to review, if not redefine U.S. national interests in the aftermath of the Cold war have been limited. President Bush's "new world order" broke little new ground, restating the U.S. interest in international peace, security, freedom, the promotion of democracy and the rule of law.[10] Similarly,

---

[7] On the early roots of this changed emphasis in U.S. foreign policy, see Beale, Howard K. *Theodore Roosevelt and the Rise of America to World Power*. (Baltimore, 1956), pp. 336, 456-58; and Kissinger, Henry A. *Diplomacy*. (New York, 1994), pp. 38-40, 50. On the U.S. antipathy towards "balance of power" politics, see Kissinger, *Diplomacy*, 19-20, 51, 226. Kissinger, like many others before him, sees Theodore Roosevelt and Woodrow Wilson as representing the two opposite conceptual poles of U.S. foreign policy in the 20th century.

[8] On the origin and use of "national security" see Lowenthal, Mark M. *"National Security" as a Concept: Does It Need To Be Redefined?* Washington: Congressional Research Service. CRS Report No. 93-12 S, January 7, 1993. Intellectually, "national security" derived from a concern over potentially hostile control of Eurasia and the inevitable threat this posed to the United States, even at a distance, via economic means.

[9] See Sloan, Stanley R. *The U.S. Role in the Post-Cold War World: Issues for a New Great Debate*. Washington: Congressional Research Service. CRS Report No. 92-308 S, March 24, 1992. pp. 14-16.

[10] Sloan, Stanley R. *The U.S. Role in a New World Order: Prospects for George Bush's Global Vision*. Washington: Congressional Research Service. CRS Report No. 91-294 RCO, March 28, 1991, p. 21.

in presenting its new policy of "enlargement," the Clinton administration spoke of "protect[ing] American interests," without further defining them.[11]

U.S. NATIONAL INTERESTS: ASSUMED OR DECLARED?

Nations rarely offer precise statements as to all of their national interests. Many are posited by the nation's very existence (external and internal security, safe borders, etc.) and do not need to be stated. It can be assumed that these are inherent to any state and are understood by all. Other interests, however, may require precise and public definition because they go beyond these shared core interests and very likely may involve territory, resources, people, values, etc. beyond the nation's borders.[12] This second set of interests is, in effect, non-existent unless it is brought to the attention of other states. Without doing so, these interests may serve as a source of misunderstanding if not gross miscalculation.[13] Also, such public declarations may be more necessary in a democracy as a means of rallying support in the legislative branch and among the public.

The course of U.S. national interests outlined above follows this pattern. Washington and Monroe each publicly stated their views on U.S. national interests, although, during this period, the United States had few means to defend them. Indeed, the geographic separation from Europe and Europe's own internal rivalries were more important factors in securing these interests than was any nation's respect for U.S. interests or U.S. ability to defend them.

However, the longstanding U.S. interest in the international *status quo* that began in 1898 was more often unstated, in part for the philosophical reasons noted above. It only became an overt and publicly acknowledged interest with the formation of the containment strategy and all that followed from it (the

---

[11] Secretary of State Warren Christopher said that protecting American interests was the central purpose of U.S. foreign policy in a speech at Columbia University on September 20, 1993, which was reprinted in the *Congressional Record*, September 20, 1993, p. S11964. See also Lowenthal, Mark M. *The Clinton Foreign Policy: Emerging Themes*. Washington: Congressional Research Service. CRS Report No. 93-951 S. pp. 2, 9.

[12] Among the distinctions that have been made between types of national interests are: Vital vs. Secondary; Permanent vs. Temporary; Specific vs. General; Complementary vs. Conflicting. Obviously, any national interest is likely to exhibit at least two, if not more, of these traits at any given time. See Roskin, Michael G. *National Interest: From Abstraction to Strategy*. (U.S. Army War College; Carlisle, PA; May 20, 1994) pp. 6-8.

[13] A classic example was Britain's failure in 1914 to make clear to Germany the strong British interest in Belgium's neutrality, thus contributing to an already confused and rapidly deteriorating diplomatic situation. Some German decisionmakers did not believe that Britain would go to war for "a mere scrap of paper" -- *i.e.*, the 1839 treaty establishing a neutral Belgium.

Truman Doctrine, the Marshall Plan, NATO) during the early years of the Cold War.

WHO DEFINES NATIONAL INTEREST?

Although the creation of U.S. foreign policy is shared by the Executive and Congress, the predominance of the President has meant that the Executive has largely been the source of defining national interest. The Executive has the inherent advantage of speaking with fewer (although not always one) voices in foreign policy than the Congress. Although Congress has many levers with which to influence foreign policy, only the President is seen as "speaking for the United States."[14]

Arguably, the primacy of the President's role has become more difficult in the 20th century. Washington's Farewell Address was, in part, a plea to avoid partisan wrangling over foreign policy; Monroe was addressing foreign powers more than the American population. U.S. interests in the two World Wars became evident to most people only over time. Moreover, U.S. policies were in part dictated by the actions of others (Germany's 1917 policy of undeclared submarine warfare, and Japan's attack in 1941).

The early prosecution of the Cold War stands out as a very different example, in that the threat was not as obvious or direct as were the two World Wars, and yet it required a massive mobilization of resources abroad and at home. Indeed, it could be argued that defining a national interest is meaningless if not dangerous unless there is also a plan for advancing or defending that interest. Thus, it becomes a two-fold process, involving: (1) defining the interest and defending it conceptually in public policy debates; and (2) implementing programs by which the defined interest is given shape and support. This also involves public debate as well as a legislative program. There is also a reverse effect, especially in democracies, as declared or generally accepted national interests tend to serve as a barometer of public opinion as well.[15]

U.S. NATIONAL INTEREST IN THE POST-COLD WAR WORLD

The international *status quo* is, arguably, more favorable to the United States today than it has been since prior to the outbreak of World War I. The

---

[14] Presidents have taken actions regarding fairly well-agreed national interests that have run contrary to the popular sentiment. Two pertinent examples are: (1) President Cleveland's refusal, in 1893, to annex Hawaii following a coup led by Americans, despite widespread support in the United States for annexation; and (2) President McKinley's initial reluctance, in 1898, to succumb to the pressure in favor of war with Spain.

[15] I am indebted to Robert G. Sutter, Senior Specialist in International Affairs, CRS, for this concept.

trend toward more nations that seek to be democratic and to have some version of free market economies represents not only a victory for U.S. values but also the basis of a world that is presumably less hostile to U.S. interests.[16]

At the same time, the end of the Cold War has seen a reversion to political issues that have long been problematic in the past, especially ethnic conflict, albeit on a more widespread basis, occurring in Europe, Africa and parts of what was the Soviet Union. There are also greater internal and external economic tensions within the group of stable democracies. Policy makers tend to list other issues -- that tend to be transnational or subnational, such as terrorism, proliferation, ecology, health concerns -- but, while problematic, these tend not to threaten the broader *status quo*.·

As noted, both the Bush and Clinton Administrations have evidently felt that U.S. national interests needed to be redefined in the aftermath of the Cold War, albeit with limited success in both cases. In the absence of some broad, easily grasped concept, the debate over U.S. post-Cold War national interest has been held over the individual areas of engagement -- successfully in the Gulf War, ultimately unsuccessful in Somalia, and diffidently in Rwanda and Haiti. It could be argued that it is much more difficult to have a meaningful debate over individual engagements when the larger framework remains so uncertain.

To a very great degree, the concept of national interest remains a highly individual and perceptual one, beyond those core interests of security and defense. As noted, in the past, U.S. national interests have largely been defined by successive Presidents, with remarkable consistency and few changes over 200 years. Doing so is more difficult in the late 20th century for a number of reasons:

- The U.S. public is somewhat weary of international involvement after over half a century of both involvement and leadership, from World War II through the end of the Cold War.

- It is more difficult conceptually to urge strong support for a favorable *status quo* when there are no evident major threats to it, and when there continues to exist a deep-rooted American antipathy to the concepts of the *status quo* and balance of power.

---

[16] According to National Security Adviser Anthony Lake (speech at Johns Hopkins University, Nitze School of Advanced International Studies, September 21, 1993), this is based on the belief that
    ...democracies tend not to wage war on each other or to sponsor terrorism. They are more trustworthy in diplomacy and do a better job of respecting the human rights of their people.
See *Congressional Record*, September 29, 1993, p. E2294.
    This view about the more pacific nature of democracies towards one another first became popular in policy debates during the Bush Administration.

- It is also difficult to defend a *status quo* some of whose major strains and stresses come from relations with allies and friendly nations whose broader values and perhaps interests are not very different from our own.

- Although the President remains predominant in stating U.S. goals and national interests, this involves greater consultation with Congress and more concern over public opinion than was the case during the early years of the Republic. It also requires devoting attention to broader foreign policy issues rather than individual crises. Finally, to be successful, defining national interests requires some set of policies or programs to defend or advance these interests. All of this comes at a time when the domestic agenda is again predominant.

Foreign Policy of the United States
Volume 1

THE U.S. ROLE IN THE WORLD: INDISPENSABLE LEADER OF HEGEMON?

Stanley R. Sloan

Summary

In the early 1990s, many friends and allies of the United States worried that the United States was turning inward. In recent years, however, international concern has focused more on what is perceived as unilateralist or "hegemonic" U.S. international behavior. The expressions of alarm from many U.S. friends and allies have been echoed prominently by less sympathetic powers and leaders. Some major powers, including Russia and China, have over time tried to reduce what they see as excessive U.S. influence on issues affecting their interests. One major U.S. ally, France, has traditionally sought to limit U.S. influence on its policies. President Clinton has claimed that the United States is the "indispensable power" in the international system but wishes to share leadership burdens and responsibilities with others. However, some U.S. actions have provided ammunition for those who claim that the United States is acting like a hegemonic power. These arguments and perceptions could increasingly undermine the U.S. ability to achieve its foreign policy objectives.

The U.S. Role in the World

Since the Cold War ended, there has been an ongoing elite debate about the role the United States should play in an international system that is no longer dominated by the bi-polar confrontation of two alliance systems led by the United States and the Soviet Union. That discussion may not have produced any clear consensus, but a definition of the U.S. role perhaps can be seen as emerging in U.S. foreign policy choices. President George Bush (1989-1993), who led the United States through the initial years of adjustment to a world in dramatic transition, clearly believed that the United States was required to play a strong international leadership role. Some of his advisers apparently thought the United States should use its position as the sole superpower to discourage challenges to that position, even among current allies. President Bush nonetheless accepted the importance

---

[1] Louis Golino and Marie Boyer provided research assistance for this report.

of building consensus in the United Nations and constructing coalitions to deal with international challenges (both illustrated by his orchestration of the response to Iraq's invasion of Kuwait). His strong interest in foreign affairs became a political liability in the 1992 elections, when many Americans apparently thought his approach was not sufficiently responsive to U.S. domestic problems.

In the first year of his presidency (1993), Bill Clinton and his foreign policy advisers experimented with a number of different approaches to U.S. foreign policy. President Clinton sought to convert his successful campaign slogan, "It's the economy, stupid," into a pillar of U.S. foreign policy. In part as a consequence of this philosophy, some Clinton Administration officials argued that Asia (rather than Europe) should be the central focus of U.S. foreign policy because of the opportunities presented by growing Asian markets. By the end of 1993, however, the Administration had moved to a posture emphasizing continuing U.S. political, economic, and strategic interests in Asia *and* Europe.

For most of President Clinton's first term, many observers saw the Administration as shifting between active internationalism and foreign policy reticence. But, campaigning in 1996 for a second term in office, President Clinton argued that the United States was the world's "indispensable power," suggesting that the international system required the active involvement of the United States to function effectively. Clinton maintained that such activism was in the U.S. interest. Throughout this period, debate over U.S. foreign policy among experts and editorialists included those who argued for a more restricted U.S. world role, and those who called for the United States to take full advantage of its position as the sole surviving superpower.[2] Public opinion polls suggest that the American people reject both options, and in fact favor an engaged U.S. world role based on sharing international burdens and responsibilities with other nations.[3]

Foreign Perceptions

At the start of the Clinton Administration, many traditional U.S. allies feared that the end of the Cold War, with all its benefits, might bring with it what they viewed as the undesirable consequence of a U.S. return to isolationism. European allies also worried the United States might shift the focus of its foreign policy toward Asia. Those concerns were heightened by the Clinton Administration's initial "tilt" toward Asia (1993), the U.S. reaction to the peacekeeping disaster in Somalia (1993), U.S. reluctance to become deeply involved in the conflict in former Yugoslavia (1991-1994), and an emerging tendency toward "self-deterrence," in which the United States appeared to be less and less inclined to risk the use of military force on behalf of international stability.[4]

---

[2]See, for example, CRS Report 92-308 S, *The U.S. Role in the Post-Cold War World: Issues for a New Great Debate*, by Stanley R. Sloan. March 24, 1992 and Stanley R. Sloan, *The U.S. Role in the 21ˢᵗ Century World: Toward a New Consensus?* Foreign Policy Association Headline Series No. 314. October 1997.

[3]See Steven Kull, I.M. Destler, and Clay Ramsay, *The Foreign Policy Gap, How Policymakers Misread the Public*. Center for International and Security Studies at the University of Maryland. October 1997.

[4]CRS Report 97-78 F, *The United States and the Use of Force in the Post-Cold War World:*
(continued...)

In recent years, that concern about incipient U.S. isolationism has diminished. In fact, as the United States took charge of the peace process in Bosnia in 1995 and began more actively to exert its influence in other ways, friends and allies became increasingly concerned about a U.S. tendency toward excessive unilateralism. Critics offered as evidence of this growing tendency:

- U.S. legislation (the Helms-Burton Act) seeking to impose sanctions on non-U.S. firms doing business with Cuba;
- Congressional insistence on specific reform of the United Nations before appropriation of monies to pay U.S. arrears to the organization;
- U.S. insistence on maintaining hard-line sanctions policies toward Iran, Iraq and Libya;
- U.S. refusal to give up NATO's Southern Command to a European officer, a condition sought by French President Jacques Chirac as a precondition for returning to NATO's integrated command structure;
- The Clinton Administration's approach to the (June 1997) Denver economic summit, seen by some summit participants as "in your face" bragging about the success of the U.S. economic model;
- Clinton Administration insistence on limiting the first group of candidates for NATO membership to three when many other allies supported one or two additional candidates;
- U.S. refusal to sign the treaty banning anti-personnel land mines;
- U.S. approaches to the global climate conference, seen by some as designed to protect U.S. economic advantages over other nations; and
- U.S. proposals in 1998 that NATO should be able to use force even when it is not possible to obtain a mandate from the UN security council.

Late in 1996, various observers in Europe and elsewhere began suggesting that the United States was acting like a classic, overbearing hegemonic power, using its position of supremacy in the international system to have its way at the expense of the interests and preferences of other powers. Some of the criticism came from traditional and predictable sources. The Russians complained that the United States was using its position to enlarge the NATO alliance. The Chinese continued their advocacy of a "multipolar" world and criticism of U.S. hegemony.

The United States Information Agency (USIA) concluded that some foreign analysts were becoming "almost paranoid about alleged U.S. intentions in the world," including commentators from Russia and China. According to USIA's media analysis, "They saw an `imperial' America bent on a relentless hegemonic drive and predicted dire consequences for the world. Beijing's official *China Daily* held that the U.S. constantly `ignores' other countries' sovereignty and uses its power to direct another country to do whatever (the U.S.) wants it to do."[5] In April 1997, Russian President Boris Yeltsin and

---

[4](...continued)
Away from Self-Deterrence? by Stanley R. Sloan. January 6, 1997.

[5]See, for example, USIA, Office of Research and Media Reaction, Foreign Media Reaction Daily Digest. "Trend Analysis: Mixed Assessments of U.S. `Undisputed' Role as Superpower," September 29, 1997.

Chinese leader Jiang Zemin, meeting in Moscow, agreed on a "strategic partnership" against those who would "push the world toward a unipolar order."

Leaders from two states currently suffering from U.S.-led sanctions, Cuba and Iraq, have emphasized the hegemony theme, apparently trying to play on divisions they perceived developing between the United States and its allies regarding U.S. foreign policy leadership. Cuba's Fidel Castro, in his opening speech to the Ibero-American summit in Venezuela in November 1997 warned that the world is being "led by a... crushing and brutal globalism under the sponsorship of the most powerful and selfish world power in history." Within a few days, Iraqi Deputy Prime Minister Tariq Aziz was beating the U.S. hegemony drum at the United Nations. Arguing for a relaxation of international sanctions imposed at U.S. initiative, Aziz claimed the United Nations Special Commission was "dominated by the Americans who are implementing the policy of their government" and that the ultimate "end users" of information gained by weapons inspectors in Iraq were the Pentagon, the CIA, and the U.S. State Department.

Over the course of 1997 and 1998, commentaries in newspapers across Europe, Asia, Africa and Latin America picked up the theme. Perhaps most serious, however, is the degree to which the critique has emanated from friendly nations and allied governments, on whose cooperation the United States counts in a wide range of issues. In the past year, officials of several friendly governments, while abstaining from use of words like "hegemony," have nonetheless privately expressed their concern about a growing U.S. tendency toward unilateral behavior.[6] Most U.S. allies in Europe and elsewhere broadly sympathize with the objectives of U.S. foreign policy but occasionally differ on specific policies and see the United States as insufficiently sensitive to their interests and domestic political requirements.

Among U.S. allies, only France was willing publicly to associate itself with the Russian and Chinese critiques of U.S. power. Ever since French President Charles de Gaulle identified American power as a threat to French sovereignty, French policies have been influenced by the concern that France's role in the world would be circumscribed by American leadership. During the first half of 1997, as France approached parliamentary elections, leading members of the opposition Socialist Party warned that President Chirac's attempt to negotiate a return to NATO's integrated command structure threatened France's independence and put France in danger of succumbing to U.S. hegemony. Once the Socialists and their allies on the left came to power following their electoral victory in June 1997, they reigned in their criticism and moderated their vocabulary, but still would like to circumscribe U.S. influence. For example, Socialist chairman of the defense committee in France's National Assembly, Paul Quiles, warned in December 1998 that the NATO 50th anniversary summit in Washington in April 1999 should not "set the seal on the United States' hegemony over the alliance.[7]

President Chirac has on several occasions formally aligned France with the hegemony critique. In May 1997, President Chirac joined the Chinese in a communique at the end of his state visit to Beijing praising the virtues of a "multipolar world"-- thin cover for

---

[6]Author's discussions with officials of allied governments, autumn 1997.

[7]Paul Quiles. "NATO Must Not Turn Into a 'Holy Alliance,'" *Le Monde*, Paris, December 1, 1998, p. 16 (as reported by the Foreign Broadcast Information Service, December 2, 1998).

criticism of U.S. hegemony. In June 1997, at the NATO summit meeting in Madrid, President Chirac, having failed to win acceptance of Romania and Slovenia as candidates for NATO membership, reacted by declaring that France would not help pay for the American policy goal of NATO enlargement. When Mr. Chirac visited Moscow in October, French commentators noted that Mr. Chirac failed to dispute Russian President Yeltsin's view of a Europe organized between Russia, France and other members of the European Union (recalling all too clearly old Soviet proposals for a "European house" excluding the United States).[8]

Implications for U.S. Interests

The United States did not by itself create the circumstances that have left it as the world's only surviving superpower. But it does face the challenge of dealing with this new reality. The Clinton Administration has for the most part pursued an activist international role. It has attempted to avoid policies that are, or could be perceived as, isolationist or unilateralist. But it has, on occasion, misjudged how its actions would be seen by its friends and allies. The Administration has also been pushed by the Congress in some directions that apparently would not have been its first choice - for example, on the issues of extraterritorial sanctions and non-payment of U.S. arrears at the United Nations. Recent Administration setbacks in the Congress concerning payment of U.N. arrears and "fast track" authorization for international trade negotiations, with roots more in domestic than international politics, may nonetheless be perceived abroad as additional signs of unilateralist tendencies.

Most U.S. allies have made it clear that they would far prefer to deal with a United States that is engaged internationally, putting up with a bull that occasionally breaks some dishes in the international china shop, than with a United States that has withdrawn from an active world role. European reactions to U.S. leadership may to some extent reflect cultural unease with a country that at once seems immature, idealistic, and impetuous from the perspective of experienced and once dominant "old world" powers. On some issues, the United States and its allies simply disagree or have different priorities. On balance, however, most see U.S. international engagement as "indispensable," even if, from time to time, the quality of U.S. leadership leaves something to be desired.

Part of the danger in this debate lies in the language that is used to discuss the issue. Not all foreign commentaries are benign, but many foreign observers do use "hegemony" as a descriptive, academic term intended to characterize the structure of current international power relationships. *Webster's New Collegiate Dictionary* defines "hegemony" as "preponderant influence or authority esp[ecially] of one nation over others." This presumably is a condition that can exist even if the country in question does not seek a hegemonic position. The American people and their leaders, however, do not perceive the United States as a hegemonic power and do not aspire to hegemony. "Hegemony," to the American ear, is an offensive term; it is recognized as the word that was appropriately used to describe the policies and practices of the Soviet Union during the Cold War. How, most Americans might wonder, can our friends use terminology to

---

[8]See, for example, Daniel Vernet. "Moscow's Double-Dealing With Europe and Washington," *Le Monde*, Paris, September 30, 1997, p. 18 (as reported by the Foreign Broadcast Information Service, October 2, 1997).

describe us that was once appropriate for an expansionist, dictatorial Communist regime? In the long run, continued use of this term by friendly countries could produce a backlash with the American people and with Members of Congress. A reaction could be expected in particular if regimes seen as unsympathetic to U.S. interests appear to benefit from associating themselves with anti-hegemony arguments of U.S. allies.

Beyond the reaction to the term, there are immediate and practical implications. If the United States appears to be overbearing in its relations with other countries, it may have difficultly in building international consensus on behalf of its policies. Late in 1997, one experienced U.S. diplomat observed to the author that he occasionally found it difficult to convince his host government to support some U.S. policies because they did not want to be seen as slavishly following U.S. desires.[9] There may be occasions on which the United States will choose to pursue a dominating line, even at the expense of dissonance with its allies, when it feels that important interests are at stake. But it is clear that there are costs associated with policies that build coalitions only by the use of overwhelming political force rather than by consultation, persuasion and compromise. The underlying reality — that the United States occupies a central and unmatched position in international politics — will not change in the foreseeable future. Even if the crisis in the Clinton presidency has weakened the President's hand, it does not change the fundamentals underlying the U.S. position in the world as the only global power and the international community's "indispensable leader."[10] This circumstance, points out one European analyst, cannot be seen simply in classic balance of power terms. He argues the United States is different from previous dominant powers: "It irks and domineers, but it does not conquer. It tries to call the shots and bend the rules, but it does not go to war for land and glory."[11] Further, he argues, the dominating U.S. position is based on "soft" as well as "hard" power: "This type of power — a culture that radiates outward and a market that draws inward — rests on pull, not on push; on acceptance, not on conquest."[12]

Under these circumstances, the United States faces the challenge of using its power in ways that reflect U.S. interests and draw on the American public's desire to cooperate with other countries while not inspiring opposition as a result of appearing too domineering. If U.S. allies still believe that U.S. leadership is essential on many international issues, as they apparently do, then their challenge is to express their criticism of U.S. leadership style in terms that are appropriate for frank and honest discussions among friends. If the United States and its allies do not manage this issue effectively, it could intrude dramatically on a wide range of issues in which their common interests are likely served by pragmatic cooperation rather than conflict inspired by current international power realities.

---

[9]Discussion with the author.

[10]CRS Report 98-828 F, *The Clinton Presidency in Crisis: Foreign Reactions and Policy Implications* by Stanley R. Sloan. October 6, 1998.

[11]Josef Joffe, "How America Does It," *Foreign Affairs*, September/October 1997, p. 16.

[12]*Ibid.*, p. 24.

Foreign Policy of the United States
Volume 1

FOREIGN POLICY AGENCY REORGANIZATION

Susan B. Epstein. Larry Q. Nowels, and Steven A. Hildreth

SUMMARY

Throughout 1995 and into 1996, both the Administration and Congress continued to consider options to re-organize the structure of U.S. government foreign policy agencies. At issue was how best to tighten the foreign policy budget while maximizing the effectiveness of interagency coordination, seeing that they all work toward common foreign policy goals in an ever-changing post-Cold War world. Three of the four agencies were created during the Cold War, and their usefulness as independent agencies was questioned by some in the 104th Congress. Critics of U.S. foreign policy management practices charged that these agencies at times maintain conflicting agendas, house duplicative functions and bureaus, and often do not give proper emphasis to national priorities, such as U.S. economic opportunities abroad.

On March 15, 1995, Senator Helms announced a plan to reorganize the U.S. foreign policy agency structure. The original Helms plan would have eliminated the U.S. Information Agency (USIA), the U.S. Agency for International Development (USAID), and the Arms Control and Disarmament Agency (ACDA). According to Senator Helms, it would have created a "new," more effective State Department with some of the functions of the eliminated agencies merged into it. An "America Desk" would have been established in the State Department to ensure that all U.S. foreign policy contributes to American national interests. It also would have required the President to draft a report assessing the merits of having a core foreign service that would combine all foreign service officers from USIA, USAID, USDA, and Commerce.

The Senate Foreign Relations Committee marked up and ordered reported its version (S. 908) of the consolidation bill on May 17, 1995. Senate Democrats, however, blocked debate of the legislation. After several months of negotiations, Senate leaders reached agreement (which was adopted by the full Senate on December 14, 1995) on a compromise proposal to consolidate U.S. foreign affairs agencies. The agreement did not require the Administration to abolish agencies, but mandated $1.7 billion budget savings in program and operating expenses.

The House reorganization bill (H.R. 1561) was introduced by Representative Gilman and passed by the House June 8. It would have abolished USAID, USIA, and ACDA, folding their functions into State with newly-created Under Secretary positions. Furthermore, the bill would have required that expenditures for any consolidated functions must be reduced by 20% in each of the two years following the implementation of the merger plan.

Conferees on H.R. 1561 reached agreement March 7, 1996, on a bill that would require the abolishment of one agency, to be selected by the President. The President also had to certify: 1) that his foreign policy consolidation plans would save $1.7 billion over four years, and 2) that the preservation of the remaining two agencies is important to U.S. national interests. Congress cleared the conference report on March 28. President Clinton, however, vetoed the bill because of agency consolidation and other objectionable provisions. The House failed to override the veto on April 30. Although the issue did not re-emerge in FY1996, it may be the subject of debate in the 105th Congress.

INTRODUCTION

The 104th Congress considered within the context of the foreign relations authorization legislation proposals to eliminate three foreign policy agencies -- U.S. Information Agency (USIA), the Agency for International Development (USAID),[1] and the Arms Control and Disarmament Agency (ACDA) -- and merge their functions into the State Department. The congressionally passed Foreign Relations Authorization Act (H.R. 1561), however, was vetoed by the President (with a veto override vote failing in the House). The issue has been temporarily set-aside in Congress. Nevertheless, the State Department, USIA, USAID, and ACDA continue to pursue management reforms and downsize as they adjust to operating expense reductions enacted in FY1996 and funding cuts projected for the future. The State Department's FY1996 appropriations decreased from FY1995 levels by 6%, USIA's by 20%, USAID development funds and operating budget by 17%, and ACDA's by 30%. Subsequent reductions-in-force (RIFs) have been instituted at USIA and USAID. Further budget cuts are anticipated for these four agencies in FY1998. Although the second session of the 104th Congress did not consider legislation on foreign policy agency reorganization measures, consolidation objectives are expected to resurface in future appropriation and authorization legislation in the next Congress.

BACKGROUND AND ANALYSIS

The idea of reconfiguring U.S. foreign policy organizational structures has been raised on numerous occasions over the years and once again gained momentum in 1995. Recent interest in abolishing selected foreign affairs agencies and consolidating their responsibilities more centrally under the Secretary of State appear to have been driven by three key concerns:

(1) **Have foreign policy agencies adjusted their missions to the post-Cold War world?** In general, many foreign policy experts concur that the U.S. Information Agency (USIA), the U.S. Agency for International Development (USAID) and the Arms Control and Disarmament Agency (ACDA) were designed largely to counter communist expansion during the Cold War. Critics assert that these organizations, along with the State Department, have not sufficiently modified their mission responsibilities to reflect profound global changes and

---

[1] State Department, USIA, and ACDA funding is in the Commerce, Justice, State Department and related agencies appropriations; USAID funding is in Foreign Operations Appropriations (H.R. 3540).

newly emerging U.S. national interests. Some argue, for example, that the State Department continues to focus on security and political matters while failing to address what they see as the more potent foreign policy challenge of international economic competition facing the United States today. Others believe the need for a separate arms control agency has faded because the strategic nuclear threat posed by the Soviet Union has ended. The prudence of continuing USIA-operated surrogate broadcasting activities aimed largely at the communist world is similarly challenged. Finally, although critics acknowledge that USAID has established a new rationale for foreign aid based on the strategy of sustainable development, they disagree that it serves the highest U.S. interests or that aid is allocated in places that warrant U.S. financial support.

(2) **Are foreign policy agencies organized efficiently?** Some observers, including some former Secretaries of State, contend current U.S. foreign policy lacks focus, caused to some degree by individual foreign affairs agencies pursuing their own agendas that do not always correspond to White House or State Department policy priorities. In short, critics say, the Secretary of State does not have under his direct control all assets to conduct a cohesive, effective U.S. foreign policy. Moreover, they note that each foreign affairs agency maintains offices conducting similar functions, such as country desks and regional bureaus, legislative and public affairs offices, administrative departments, legal specialists, and separate inspectors general.

(3) **Can administrative and organizational reforms save money?** Consolidation proponents believe agency streamlining initiatives can reduce staff size and significantly decrease the number of U.S. personnel posted abroad. The basis of their argument is that, with the end of the Cold War, the United States does not need such a large overseas presence in which USAID, for example, maintains a mission in every country, or even in most countries. Some contend that, with the strong likelihood of declining foreign policy budgets in the future, administrative savings can free up funds for high priority international programs, domestic needs, or deficit reduction.

Similar themes were articulated during Bush Administration studies of foreign policy agency reorganization. Then Secretary of State, James Baker III, for example, commissioned an effort to analyze the U.S. foreign policy mechanism and recommend changes. *State 2000, A New Model for Managing Foreign Affairs*, prepared by the State Department in December 1992, concluded that unless the United States integrates its foreign policy, there is the risk of "incoherent, even contradictory policy," that could threaten our "preeminent position in the world." The report also accused the State Department of being dominated by a "Cold War political-military view" of the world.

In a separate move, Congress mandated the creation of a presidential commission, appointed by President Bush (known as the Ferris Commission, named for its chairman, George Ferris), to examine management problems at USAID. In a series of reports issued throughout 1992, the Ferris Commission recommended, among other things, that USAID be merged into the State

Department and reconstituted within the office of a new Under Secretary for Development.

The Clinton Administration itself raised the issue of consolidation in late 1994 and early 1995 as part of a broader examination of federal agency organization and the second phase of the Vice President's National Performance Review (NPR). Responding to a White House call for organizational options, Secretary of State Warren Christopher submitted a plan for merging USIA, USAID, and ACDA into the State Department. (State Department officials assert that the Secretary regarded this plan as a series of ideas and that he never endorsed any specific option.) Following weeks of an intensive interagency debate, Vice President Gore concluded in late January 1995 that greater efficiency and effectiveness could be achieved by keeping the current foreign affairs organizational structure intact, while pursuing additional management reforms and downsizing each agency.

Congressional interest in this reorganization question materialized at about the same time as the Administration's study. In December 1994, Senator McConnell, the soon-to-be Chairman of the Senate Foreign Operations Appropriations Subcommittee, outlined a foreign aid reform initiative (formally introduced on February 15, 1995, as S. 422) that included eliminating USAID and transferring its responsibilities to the State Department. Senator Helms, Chairman of the Foreign Relations Committee (the committee of jurisdiction over the State Department), announced on February 14 his intention to seek a comprehensive consolidation effort along the lines of that proposed by Secretary Christopher. More details of the Helms proposal came in a March 15 press conference in which he proposed eliminating USIA, ACDA, and USAID and creating a "new" State Department that would administer most of those agencies' foreign policy functions. On May 3, Representative Gilman introduced the House version of foreign policy reform (H.R. 1561), which also would eliminate USIA, ACDA, and USAID and transfer those functions into the State Department.

The Administration stood by the Vice President's NPR plans to pursue further reforms under the current organizational configuration and rejected the congressional proposals. Nevertheless, outside supporters and opponents expressed various perspectives during hearings in early 1995. For example, some of the strongest support for the Helms initiative came from former senior U.S. foreign policy officials, including former Secretaries of State Lawrence Eagleburger, George Shultz, and James Baker, and former National Security Advisor Brent Scowcroft. Critics of the consolidation plans included a variety of groups, non-governmental and private voluntary organizations, some of which implement U.S. aid programs, and former foreign affairs officials like McGeorge Bundy. Organizations representing Foreign Service Officers -- personnel that would be directly affected by these proposals -- appeared somewhat divided. The Senior Foreign Service Association supported the consolidation concept, but the American Foreign Service Association (which represents members in all five agencies) took a more cautious approach, calling for an in-depth study before taking action.

THE CURRENT FOREIGN POLICY ORGANIZATION

Although the State Department has existed since 1789, USAID, ACDA, and USIA were created during the Cold War era. All four agencies have distinct missions, all of which contribute to U.S. foreign policy objectives, and operate under the policy guidance of the Secretary of State.

The State Department's mission is to advance and protect the worldwide interests of the United States and its citizens. Currently, the State Department represents American interests of 50 U.S. government agencies and organizations operating at 250 posts around the world. It has a staff of about 9,369 in Washington, D.C., and 15,700 employees overseas. Of the overseas total, approximately 6,200 are Americans and 9,500 are foreign nationals.

USAID promotes long-term, sustainable development abroad, helping countries grow economically, strengthen democratic institutions, protect the environment, stabilize population growth, and deal with disasters and other humanitarian requirements. Currently, USAID has programs in 103 countries, although the Agency has recently announced plans to reduce to 75 by the year 2000 the number of countries in which it maintains activities. Agency staff totals 8,653, down from over 10,700 in 1993. The current level includes 2,725 American direct hires, about 1,000 of which work overseas, and roughly 500 foreign national direct hires. In addition, USAID has 5,400 American and foreign national contractors. USAID expects to continue to reduce its staff size, projecting a work force of less than 8,000 by the year 2000. USAID has instituted a reduction-in-force of 200 of its American direct-hire employees.

ACDA's mission is designed to strengthen U.S. national security by advocating, formulating, negotiating, implementing, and verifying sound arms control, nonproliferation, and disarmament policies and agreements. It is the only U.S. government agency dedicated solely to this mission. As the smallest of the foreign policy agencies, ACDA maintains a staff of about 255.

USIA's mission is to understand, inform, and influence foreign publics as a means of promoting U.S. national interests and dialogue between Americans and their institutions and their counterparts abroad. USIA employs 7,055; 3,442 work in the United States and 3,613 are employed overseas.

CONGRESSIONAL ACTION

The 104th Congress considered several different proposals to reorganize and consolidate U.S. foreign affairs agencies. The first detailed initiative was unveiled by Senator Helms in March, 1995. His plan (as outlined in March and later incorporated into S. 908 when it was reported by the Foreign Relations Committee in June) sought to eliminate and consolidate a total of ten agencies—the three mentioned above plus seven smaller entities. According to Senator Helms, it would create a new State Department that would incorporate most of the administrative and program functions of the three large agencies in an effort to eliminate duplication and bring all policy tools directly under the control of the Secretary.

Although the Administration continued to flatly reject all congressional consolidation proposals, Senators Helms and Kerry stated they could agree on a plan to proceed with debate on a foreign policy reorganization bill. Following months of negotiations over an acceptable "managers amendment," Senators Helms and Kerry announced on December 7, 1995, an agreement that departed significantly from the original Helms plan set out in March.

Highlights of Original Helms Proposal

- Eliminate USIA, USAID, and ACDA. Move some functions into the State Department. Close all USAID overseas missions.

- Create an "America Desk" within the State Department to coordinate policy efforts and solve problems that cut across Department bureaucratic structures.

- Require a Presidential report regarding the effectiveness U.S. Government export promotion activities with a plan for improvement.

Senator Helms claimed that the Congressional Budget Office (CBO) had estimated, that when fully implemented, his plan would save more than $3.5 billion over 4 years. He claimed that his proposal would reduce overlapping geographical and functional bureaus by two-thirds, eliminate 40% of senior level positions, consolidate three foreign services (State, USAID, USIA) into one unified system, consolidate three inspectors general into one location and ten legislative affairs offices into three, and consolidate and coordinate within State more than 100 international exchange programs currently administered by over 25 agencies.

The proposal did not explicitly require the termination of any agency but instead required the Administration to reduce administrative and program costs of the foreign affairs agencies by $1.7 billion over five years, using FY1995 levels as the baseline. Two additional requirements put pressure on agency operations: 1) program funds, such as USAID development assistance, could only account for 30% of the savings, and 2) the State Department would absorb only 15% of the total cuts. The Senate passed the amended S. 908 on December 14, 1995, by a vote of 82 to 16.

A second initiative came from Representative Gilman, incorporated as Division A in H.R. 1561, and passed by the House on June 8, 1995. The Gilman plan did not create a new State Department, but it did abolish USAID, ACDA, and USIA and merge them into the existing State Department, creating new under secretary positions to administer the merged functions. The Gilman plan, as amended, required those functions merged into the State Department to be reduced by 20% in FY1998 and FY1999. It offered the Administration greater flexibility than the original Helms proposal in determining the organization of the State Department and where the various functions fit, but offered less flexibility than the Senate-passed version because it mandated the termination of the three agencies. Reportedly, the Congressional Budget Office estimated that Gilman's consolidation proposal would save up to $3 billion over five years. Reorganization would take effect no later than March 1, 1997.

In conference, House and Senate negotiators agreed to a modified arrangement incorporating aspects of both the Helms/Kerry and Gilman initiatives. H.R. 1561, as reported March 8, 1996, and agreed to by the House (March 12) and the Senate (March 28), required the President to abolish all three agencies, but permitted him to waive the termination for two of the agencies. In order to exercise the waiver, the President would certify to Congress by October 1, 1996, that his foreign policy agency reorganization plan would achieve $1.7 billion in budget savings over four years and adhere to operating expense reductions specified in the bill and that the preservation of the remaining two agencies was important to U.S. national interests. Many congressional observers believed that ACDA, because it is the smallest and possibly the easiest agency for the State Department to absorb, would be terminated if H.R. 1561 was enacted into law. The legislation required whichever agency was selected to be terminated by March 1, 1997.

The $1.7 billion savings requirement, like the Helms/Kerry plan, limited to 30% the amount of savings that could be achieved from program funds, with the rest coming from operating budgets of the agencies. Savings would be measured against appropriated levels for FY1995. A new feature in the conference agreement, however, was the inclusion of specific operating expense authorities for State, USIA, USAID, and ACDA through FY1999. The USAID operations budget, for example, would fall from $515 million in FY1995 to $435 million by FY1999, contributing a total of $305 million in savings against the FY1995 baseline. Likewise, USIA operation costs would drop from $476 million to $399 million by the end of the century. By doing this, the conference measure locked in at least $1.774 billion in program and operation savings **and** specified exactly which agencies would absorb the reductions. Some agency consolidation supporters had criticized the earlier Helms/Kerry $1.7 billion savings requirement for not identifying exactly where costs would be cut, arguing that executive branch officials could have met the savings requirement without streamlining and downsizing agency operations as intended by Congress.

THE ADMINISTRATION'S POSITION

Prior to House consideration of the conference report, the Administration notified Congress that the President would veto H.R. 1561 because of the agency consolidation plan, as well as other foreign policy provisions opposed by the White House. Following through on that statement, the President vetoed the legislation on April 12, 1996 and returned it to Congress. (The House failed to override the President's action in an April 30 vote.) This position was consistent with Administration statements during earlier House and Senate debates on other versions of the bill, although officials said in December 1995 that they could accept the Helms/Kerry package approved by the Senate. Under the Vice President's NPR, the Administration asserted that it was already achieving millions of dollars of savings by reorganizing and downsizing the agencies, while keeping them independent. "We believe that these missions are best pursued by lean, effective organizations operating under the foreign policy guidance of the Secretary of State, not as part of a mega-bureaucracy." On mission focus, Administration officials argued that they were maintaining an effective and well-coordinated foreign policy team over which Secretary Christopher remained squarely in charge. They further contended that ongoing NPR activities would result in eliminating duplicative functions and would improve the management structures of the four major agencies. In some cases, they moved forward with efforts similar to those proposed by Senator Helms and Representative Gilman, such as consolidating the functions of congressional relations, public affairs, politico-military policymaking, as well as merging State and USIA inspectors general.

Moreover, Clinton Administration officials pointed out that the reinventing government efforts resulted in the closing of 17 State Department posts, 27 USAID missions that saved nearly $30 million annually prior to FY1996, savings of more than $400 million by consolidating overseas broadcasting, and elimination of hundreds of high-level positions. They believed that any additional savings under the Helms or Gilman plans would not be significant. In addition, the Administration asserted that conducting foreign policy is the prerogative of the President, a principle that it would continue to protect. Further, officials argued, major government reorganizations are usually initiated by the executive branch, with consultation and review from Congress; they are normally not imposed on the President over his strong objections.

KEY POLICY QUESTIONS

THE "NEW" STATE DEPARTMENT AND FOREIGN POLICY MANAGEMENT

Many officials, including Senator Helms, former Secretary of State Eagleburger, and former National Security Advisor Scowcroft have criticized the State Department for having 1) poor management structures with too many layers that impede efficient policymaking, 2) too many disputes funneling directly to the Secretary of State, creating decisionmaking overload at the highest level, and 3) a lack of coordination in regional and functional bureaus that undermines consistent policy direction. Many on both sides on the consolidation proposal agree that the Department suffers from weak management and has thus far been unable to divest itself of Cold War operational standards and adopt a revised set of mission priorities. While the State Department has made some foreign policy downsizing efforts in response to FY1996 budgetary pressures, the changes have been mostly quantitative with little noticeable change in State's policy direction or management structure.[2]

Critics of merging other agencies into the Department claim that well-functioning organizations should not be moved into what they view as a dysfunctional agency; that only after the State Department fully implements NPR reforms and integrates new policy priorities should the idea of a "super"

---

[2] Diplomatic Disorder, by Roger Sperry, *Government Executive*, July 1996.

State Department be given serious consideration. Senator Helms and his supporters disagree, saying that the continuing independence of key foreign affairs agencies contributes to the fractured decisionmaking process and weakened position of the Secretary of State and ambassadors around the world. Moreover, they believe that the consolidation of external agency responsibilities into the Department will force State to incorporate "non-traditional" yet important foreign policy initiatives into its priorities. For these reasons, Senator Helms had endorsed (with his original consolidation bill) not only abolishing USIA, ACDA, and USAID, but in effect abolishing the State Department as it is currently conceived and reconstituting it with a "new" organization.

The conference committee agreement, although quite different from Senator Helms' original proposal, still would have required some tightening of State's budget and increased cooperation with the other three agencies. Even though the conference arrangement would not have abolished all three agencies, it would have directed that certain functions common to all be transferred to the State Department: non-specialized procurement, travel and transportation, facilities management, and security operations. Further, the legislation would have abolished the Inspector Generals of ACDA and USIA, folding their functions into the State Department's IG office. Other objectives of Senator Helms' original reorganization proposal, including the goal to streamline the U.S. foreign policy apparatus, bring all policy tools directly under the control of the Secretary, and have the foreign policy agencies adjust their missions to the post-Cold War world, had been dropped.

Despite the failure of Congress to make the reorganization legislation law, the Department of State has carried out tightening measures. From FY1994 to the end of FY1996, State closed 25 overseas posts (14 of which closed in FY1996), reduced the size of the agency's workforce by 1,900 positions (about 8%), eliminated one in four deputy assistant secretary positions, and reduced the size of the Senior Foreign Service by 15%. As a result of the FY1996 appropriations law (P.L. 104-134), USIA's Office of Inspector General was merged into State's IG Office to conduct oversight for USIA, in addition to ACDA and State. The Department is continuing its efforts to implement a new overseas administrative support system and improve U.S. border security.

AGENCY FOR INTERNATIONAL DEVELOPMENT AND U.S. ECONOMIC AID POLICY

USAID is the central U.S. government institution responsible for administering most (about $5.9 billion currently) bilateral economic assistance. The agency was founded in 1961 in an effort to integrate into a single organization several U.S. aid programs underway at that time. It has maintained an independent and somewhat ambiguous relationship with the State Department, although the USAID Administrator operates under the foreign policy guidance of the Secretary of State.

Underlying congressional proposals to terminate USAID is the view that as an independent agency, USAID lies outside the core foreign policy establishment. As such, its programs cannot always be utilized effectively by the Secretary of State as a tool promoting the highest U.S. national interests. Moreover, the agency, from this perspective, is a maze of bureaucratic regulations that impedes the implementation of sustainable development projects by private and non-governmental organizations. Further, Senator Helms believes that the mission of USAID could be pursued with a much smaller staff in Washington; his original plan called for the elimination of all 75 USAID missions and representational offices around the world, staffed by nearly 1,000 Americans. With a $159,000 average cost of posting each U.S. direct hire abroad, the amount of savings could be substantial.

Consistent with the results of its policy review in January 1995, the White House opposed the consolidation of USAID into the State Department. Backing arguments made by USAID, Vice President Gore acknowledged the unique mission of the agency in constructing and implementing U.S. sustainable development programs. The Administration noted the different nature of the State Department and USAID: State more often focuses on resolving short-term crises through diplomacy and political government-to-government relations. Sustainable development, however, requires an integrated, long-term strategy to achieve results, it said, that would be compromised by merging some USAID programs into the State Department. USAID officials further noted that for nearly three years the agency has been heavily engaged in organizational reforms and participating as an "experimental laboratory" in the Vice President's NPR. USAID is nearing the end of a process to close 27 overseas aid missions, terminating relations with governments that are uncooperative development partners, and establishing a results-oriented accountability system against which the agency and Congress will be able to measure results. Because of enacted and projected budget reductions, the agency further plans to close additional missions, lowering the total of full overseas offices within a few years to 30. (USAID maintained 70 missions in 1993.) Moreover, USAID officials argued that multiple coordinating mechanisms exist between the agency and State Department/White House policymakers, both in Washington and in the field, that adequately ensure the implementation of cohesive policy.

Original House and Senate congressional initiatives potentially would have had a substantial impact not only on foreign aid organizational structures but also on policy priorities and program implementation. With USAID moved into the State Department, as Representative Gilman proposed, for example, the role of regional bureau Assistant Secretaries in influencing aid policy would have been strengthened. Each Assistant Secretary would have been required to approve all aid projects carried out in their area of jurisdiction, an authority they do not currently have. Further, one of the major challenges for the Department in shaping such a plan would have been the integration of the functions performed by three senior officials, the USAID Administrator, the Under Secretary for Global Affairs, and the Under Secretary for Economic, Business, and Agricultural Affairs, into a single entity and deciding how much weight to assign each of the various policy responsibilities of the new Under Secretary.

Other key questions raised by the year-long congressional debate over the consolidation initiative include:

- Can the United States construct a consistent, integrated, and comprehensive bilateral economic assistance strategy in the absence of a single bilateral aid agency and the diffusion of responsibilities within and without the State Department? Currently, U.S. development aid goals and integrated country strategies are built largely by USAID but with considerable input from the State Department (particularly the Under Secretary for Global Affairs) and the White House. The Gilman plan established the Under Secretary for Development as the senior policy-making official but required approval of regional Assistant Secretaries for project implementation, a situation that might lead to frequent disputes taken to the Secretary. A related concern of some is that with State Department regional bureaus exerting more influence over long-term development activities, resources would be diverted away from these projects to deal with short-term, crisis situations -- a fear that development aid would become more a political tool of U.S. foreign policy.

- Would the proposal shift the development policy emphasis of the Clinton Administration away from population and environment objectives? The Gilman plan did not alter the President's policy focus directly, but other parts of H.R. 1561 slashed development aid funding by one-third to a level the Administration argued would be impossible to conduct its sustainable development agenda. Development aid authorization levels in the conference agreement on H.R. 1561, however, were dropped from the bill. A related question is, with the creation of an Under Secretary for Development and Economic Affairs, would U.S. economic aid goals take on an orientation aimed more at export promotion?

- How would the operating expense (OE) savings required in the conference agreement affect USAID's efforts to work worldwide? There are multiple ways in which the Administration could implement the requirement to save the mandated cuts of $305 million over 4 years. Congress reduced the Agency's OE budget for FY1996 by about 10% and subsequently, USAID announced that it would have to RIF about 200 personnel by the beginning of FY1997 and start phasing down programs in more countries. The $435 million level mandated in FY1999 would be 15% lower than USAID operations last year. Moreover, in real terms, the cut would be far greater -- about 5% annually due to cost-of-living increases, currency exchange rate fluctuations and overseas inflation, and other uncontrollable costs. Under this scenario, USAID would almost certainly have to cut its staff considerably more and shut down additional foreign missions. But, as noted above, the Agency itself has began to take similar steps in the direction of downsizing envisioned in the legislative proposals.

- Do the cost efficiencies of closing USAID missions, as suggested by Senator Helms and a possible outcome if H.R. 1561 was enacted, outweigh the advantages of having an in-country presence? Many regard these missions as one of the strongest and most unique features of the U.S. aid program. A key question is whether adequate accountability and oversight of U.S.-financed projects and economic reforms can be maintained without a mission staff. Senator Helms believes that adequate oversight at a much reduced cost can be achieved by embassy personnel.

ARMS CONTROL AND DISARMAMENT AGENCY AND INTERNATIONAL SECURITY

Statutorily, ACDA has primacy over the U.S. arms control agenda. Founded in 1961 as an independent advocate for arms control in the federal government, ACDA's record, however, is mixed. Its supporters point to a number of significant arms control accomplishments for the United States; critics argue that in some of those instances, ACDA's role was limited. Over the past several years, legislative and executive efforts have been made to strengthen the agency, but critics continue to assert that ACDA has not adapted to the new arms control environment of the post-Cold War era and therefore its responsibilities should be subsumed within the State Department.

Two of the strongest arguments that have been made for merging ACDA's functions into the State Department were its projected cost savings and the necessity to streamline government operations. Some congressional estimates of annual savings ran as high as the agency's total annual budget, and an early, internal State Department proposal suggested significant cost savings and important streamlining benefits. But both of these arguments were scrutinized by the Executive Branch, which concluded there would be little if any cost savings, and that the need for an independent arms control advocate outweighed the relatively little actual overlap in arms control responsibilities between State and ACDA. ACDA's supporters in Congress similarly agreed and to a large extent prevailed over the views of others who insisted on the contrary.

At stake in the proposed merger of arms control responsibilities was the issue of who have primacy over the arms control policy agenda? ACDA was established in 1961 as a quasi-independent agency and given a close bureaucratic relationship with the State Department. The agency was created because prior to 1961, the United States had approached arms control in an *ad hoc* manner and the government saw a need for a more coherent national arms control policy. ACDA's mandate was to be "the central organization charged by statute with primary responsibility" for arms control under the direction of the President and Secretary of State (P.L. 87-297; 75 STAT 631). ACDA's Director was also designated the principal adviser to the President, the Secretary of State, and the National Security Council (NSC) on arms control issues. The Director thus was to be an independent advocate for arms control in the government.

But, as mentioned earlier, ACDA's performance has often come under scrutiny, especially over the past decade. (See, for example, CRS Report 93-443F, *ACDA: Abolition, Reorganization, Cost, and Other Issues*.) Among other things, critics accused ACDA of lackluster performance and charged that the agency had often been shut out of major arms control decisions, shunted aside, and failed to exercise its independence sufficiently, due, in part, to executive choice. (See also, CRS Report 95-692F, *Arms Control and Disarmament Agency: Background and Current Issues*.) Some of these charges persist today. For example, in the July/August 1996 issue of *Foreign Affairs*, former Secretary of State Eagleburger argues that arms control expertise is still vital in the post-Cold War era, but that a separate agency for it is no longer justified.

As to arms control decisionmaking, most critics and proponents of ACDA agree that ACDA's lead in arms control has not been realized. Most observers also agree that in actuality the arms control role played by the ACDA Director has been determined by the Director's personal relationship with both the President and the Secretary of State, and not by what may be directed statutorily. Interagency disagreements with ACDA opposing the State Department have resulted in those disagreements being elevated to the NSC and the President for resolution.

Original House and Senate initiatives sought to provide unified support for arms control policy within the Department of State before going to the NSC and the President. Such legislation would not ensure, however, unified arms control positions with the other major arms control players, such as the Departments of Defense and Energy, the Intelligence Community (IC), or the Joint Chiefs of Staff. Critics of these initiatives argued that legislation passed in 1994 with the broad support of Congress to revitalize ACDA was intended to resolve previous Agency inadequacies and should have been given a chance to prove itself (P.L. 103-236, Arms Control and Nonproliferation Act of 1994). The Administration believes that ACDA was strengthened because of this Act. Additionally, a recent report by State and ACDA outlined a number of steps taken by each agency independently and in collaboration with the other to reduce unnecessary duplication and streamline the arms control process. Among other things, it was concluded there was actually little bureaucratic overlap; State and ACDA performed complementary supporting functions. Also, a number of mid-level and other State Department positions are being eliminated.

Also at stake in the proposed legislative merger was the substance and direction of arms control policy itself. Abolishing ACDA and merging its functions into State Department would eliminate an independent advocate for arms control within the federal government at the level of NSC principals. Arms control advocacy thus would compete with other voices within the State Department. Sometimes these interests would complement other U.S. foreign policy objectives and other times they would be at odds. For example, the issue of ensuring compliance with various arms control agreements can easily be at odds with U.S. international economic or diplomatic interests. Under the proposed legislation, resolution of those issues would be resolved by the Secretary of State, and any independent arms control advocacy would not necessarily be shared with the President. Whether this is desirable policymaking is the subject much debate.

ACDA supporters thus believe that the U.S. arms control agenda would suffer as a result. Arms control advocacy could become muffled in pursuit of other and larger State Department interests, as well as those of the Department of Commerce, for example, as it relates to the control of dual-use and high technology exports. Hence, some facets of arms control could become increasingly less important.

The congressional debate over consolidating the arms control responsibilities of State and ACDA raised key questions:

> In the post Cold War era, what role should arms control issues play in foreign policy and national security decisionmaking? Should those interests be more important than others? What priorities should there be? Besides the President, who should establish those priorities? How important are arms control interests compared to other U.S. security, diplomatic, and commercial interests? Does the federal government need an independent advocate for arms control at the level of NSC principals? Can the Secretary of State sufficiently advocate arms control goals? Do arms control issues *per se* automatically merit presidential attention? How would arms control interests be made fully known to the President and the National Security Council on a sustained basis for determining U.S. policy?

> Where competition exists, how would U.S. commercial and nonproliferation interests be reconciled? What mechanism would ensure that the President was presented with the best options? Where arms control noncompliance is identified, would U.S. foreign policy and arms control interests compete with each other, especially if treaty noncompliance might adversely affect other diplomatic or military relations? How would difficulties be resolved?

U.S. INFORMATION AGENCY AND PUBLIC DIPLOMACY

The U.S. Information Agency was established in 1953 to help present the American culture and U.S. government policy to foreign publics. In 1978 Congress merged the State Department's Bureau of Education and Cultural Affairs (which was responsible for international exchange programs and tours) into the USIA (which primarily focused on international broadcasting). The argument for consolidating the two functions was that public diplomacy should be administered consistent with, but separate from, the conduct of the Nation's official diplomacy. The goal of the 1978 reorganization, in part, made the Washington administration of the programs consistent with their administration abroad. (Both sets of programs were run overseas by USIA officers, but were administered in Washington by different bureaucracies that mistrusted each other.)

The original Helms bill would have eliminated USIA and merged its functions into the Department of State. The conference agreement on H.R. 1561, however, would not have abolished the agency, but would have decreased USIA and international broadcasting operating expenses to $399 million and $315 million, respectively, by FY1999. For USIA the cut would have amounted to about 18% from last year's level.

Despite the failure of H.R. 1561 to become law, USIA sent out about 100 RIF notices in the spring of FY1996 and closed 10 overseas posts in that fiscal year alone. Furthermore, USIA is conducting several internal changes, including reorganizing and downsizing two bureaus -- the Bureau of Management and the Bureau of Education and Cultural Affairs. A third bureau was dismantled from which the USIA established an entirely new Bureau of Information that is 30% smaller.

Throughout the reorganization debate in Congress, some questioned whether international broadcasting would be able to maintain its present level of credibility with foreign publics in promoting democracy and the U.S. perspective if it were to be administered by the State Department. Proponents of public diplomacy argued that broadcasting is an inexpensive and safe way to promote democracy around the world. Maintaining its credibility under USIA is required, they claimed. On the other hand, supporters of the consolidation proposals believed that putting international broadcasting in the State Department would strengthen the link between broadcasting and U.S. foreign policy objectives. Similarly, some questioned whether international exchange programs, if placed within the Department of State, would continue to emphasize cross-cultural understanding or whether they would be used to promote political-military goals of U.S. foreign policy.

Responding to the view that consolidation into State would reduce expensive duplication and increase the effectiveness of remaining exchange programs, USIA continues to assert that consolidation would be detrimental to the effectiveness of its programs. Administration officials claim that such consolidation initiatives simply would move existing coordination authorities to the Secretary of State. USIA views its role as an "honest broker" whose programs respond to a broad range of concerns of numerous agencies. USIA contends it has already undergone a massive restructuring and streamlining effort in FY1994, FY1995 and FY1996, particularly with the consolidation of international broadcasting.

EXPORT PROMOTION AND U.S. ECONOMIC INTERESTS

Currently, the United States conducts export promotion through the Export-Import Bank, the Overseas Private Investment Corporation, the Trade and Development Agency, USDA's Foreign Agricultural Service and Commerce's Foreign Commercial Service. The Trade Promotion Coordinating Committee is an interagency committee that coordinates the various government trade activities, including those of the above mentioned agencies. Many in the business community and the Administration support the current system of government export promotion with coordination of it under the Trade Promotion Coordinating Committee (TPCC).

Early congressional efforts to reorganize foreign affairs agencies also included export promotion elements in their plans. The original Helms proposal, for example, would have merged the Foreign Commercial Service and Foreign Agricultural Service into a unified Foreign Service within the State Department. It also would have created an Under Secretary of State for Export, Trade, Economics, and Business. The Gilman plan as passed the House, would have required the TPCC to report by March 1, 1996, to specified congressional committees on what is being done to improve accessibility and coordination, and what will be done to improve efficiency among all trade promotion organizations and agencies. In addition, the President would have been given authority to privatize OPIC. Neither the Senate-passed bill nor the conference agreement included language on export promotion reporting requirements or consolidation.

LEGISLATION

H.R. 1561 (Gilman)

Foreign Affairs Agencies Consolidation Act of 1995. (Division A of H.R. 1561, American Overseas Interests Act of 1995). Introduced May 3, 1995; referred to Committee on International Relations. Reported to House (H.Rept. 104-128, Part 1) May 19, 1995; passed House, amended, June 8 (222-192). The Senate, after deleting the House text and inserting the text of S. 908, approved H.R. 1561 on December 14, 1995. Conference report filed March 8, 1996 (H.Rept. 104-478); passed the House March 12 (226-172); passed the Senate March 28 (52-44). Vetoed by the President April 12. The House failed to override the President's veto on April 30 (234-188).

S. 422 (McConnell)

The International Partnership and Prosperity Act, 1995. Among other things, eliminates USAID and merges its functions into State Department. Consolidates OPIC and TDA. Introduced February 15, 1995; referred to Committee on Foreign Relations.

S. 908 (Helms)

Foreign Relations Revitalization Act of 1995. (Division B). Abolishes USAID, ACDA, and USIA. Transfers their functions to State: ACDA by October 1, 1996; USAID and USIA by March 1, 1997. Reorganizes State Department by creating new Under Secretary positions to administer abolished agencies' functions. Markup of Chairman's mark May 17, 1995. Ordered reported May 17 by 10 to 8 vote (S.Rept. 104-95). Laid before the Senate July 28. Senate failed to invoke cloture on July 28 and August 1, 1995. Returned to Senate calendar. Senate agreed to a compromise amendment and passed S. 908 on December 14, 1995, by a vote of 82 to 16. See H.R. 1561, above, for conference action.

S. 1441 (Helms)

Foreign Relations Revitalization Act of 1995 (a slightly revised version of S. 908). Introduced November 30, 1995.

Foreign Policy of the United States
Volume 1

Most-Favored-Nation (Normal-Trade-Relations) Policy of the United States

Vladimar N. Pregelj

Most Recent Developments

In 1998, legislation was enacted to replace the term "most-favored-nation" in certain U.S. statutes by a less misleading term "normal trade relations" or another appropriate expression. Also in 1998, the President issued the initial Jackson-Vanik waiver for Vietnam, but the completion of a trade agreement with Vietnam (which will require approval by a joint resolution of Congress) has been delayed by Vietnam.

Vietnam's and Belarus' waivers were renewed in mid-1999; joint resolutions to disapprove the former, introduced in both houses, were not passed, and the waiver has remained in force. The President reported to Congress, in January 2000, continued full compliance with the requirements of the Jackson-Vanik amendment by 11 former Soviet republics.

Legislation to extend permanent MFN status to Mongolia has been enacted and implemented in July 1999, and measures to extend permanent MFN status to Albania and Kyrgyzstan, introduced in both houses, were passed by the Senate in November 1999. Also being contemplated (as yet without any introduced legislation) is permanent restoration of the MFN status to Armenia, Georgia, Laos, and Moldova. Bills introduced to reform unilateral economic sanctions legislation provide for impairment or denial of nondiscriminatory treatment as a sanction measure; also being considered is the withdrawal (as a sanction) of the MFN status of Lebanon and Syria.

CONTENTS

SUMMARY

The United States accords general most-favored-nation (nondiscriminatory) treatment as a matter of statutory policy to all trading partners except those whose MFN tariff status has been suspended by specific legislation. Virtually all such suspensions have been carried out under the mandate of the Trade Agreements Extension Act of 1951.

MFN tariff status, however, can be restored to and retained temporarily by most of these countries under Title IV of the Trade Act of 1974 if they conclude with the United States a trade agreement, containing a reciprocal MFN clause, and if they are (and remain) in compliance with the requirements of the Act's free-emigration provision (Jackson-Vanik amendment).

The trade agreement must be approved by a joint resolution, and the required presidential semiannual reports with respect to full compliance with the free-emigration provision, or annual recommendations for extensions of the authority to waive it, are annually subject to possible disapproval by joint resolution. Trade agreements are triennially self-renewable, but their renewal is also subject to presidential confirmation.

MFN status of a country can also be changed by specific legislation.

In 19 instances, MFN status has been restored to the suspended countries under the waiver provisions of Title IV; in 17 of these cases, restoration under the waiver was changed to one under the determination of full compliance and, in five cases, such restoration was later made permanent. Permanent MFN status was restored directly to four former non-MFN countries, while six countries are still denied it.

Legislation to extend permanent MFN status to Mongolia has recently been enacted and implemented, and permanent extension of MFN status to Albania and Kyrgyzstan was approved by the Senate in November 1999.

In 1998, legislation was enacted to replace in U.S. statutes the misleading term "most-favored-nation" with "normal trade relations" or another appropriate term.

Impairment or denial of MFN status is provided as a measure in bills to reform unilateral economic sanctions legislation. The sanction of withdrawing the MFN status would also be applied to Lebanon and Syria.

BACKGROUND AND ANALYSIS

What is Most-Favored-Nation Treatment?

Although legislation has been enacted to replace the term "most-favored-nation" treatment in existing and future legislation with the term "normal trade relations" or another appropriate expression, the former term is still used in this issue brief for reasons of historical continuity and because of its continued universal use in international trade relations as well as in several U.S. bilateral trade treaties.

In international trade, the expression "most-favored-nation," usually abbreviated "MFN," status (or treatment) has a specific meaning quite at variance with what it appears to mean. While suggesting special and exclusive privileges granted to one country, it means in reality equal treatment of all countries. More precisely, it denotes the extension by a country of any concessions, privileges, or immunities granted, or yet to be granted, in a trade agreement to one country that is, or would be, the "most favored" in this respect, to all countries to which it accords MFN treatment. As a consequence, all countries to which a country extends MFN treatment are, or would be, treated equally by the extending country. Most-favored-nation treatment in fact means equal treatment, and the terms "most-favored-nation" and "nondiscriminatory" are often used interchangeably.

In practice, the principal benefit a country gains from being accorded MFN status by another country is that the latter's imports from the former are dutied at concessional (often referred to as "MFN", and listed in the tariff schedules as "General") rather than full rates. Thus, the extension of MFN treatment to a country can often mean a significantly lower cost and, hence, greater competitiveness of its products in the extending country's markets.

U.S. Most-Favored-Nation Policy

There are three basic, often overlapping, ways in which the United States accords general MFN treatment to its trading partners. One is by means of a bilateral compact (e.g., a "friendship, commerce, and navigation" or similar treaty, or an executive trade agreement) in which MFN status is accorded reciprocally. Another, much broader in its reach, is through being a member of the World Trade Organization (WTO), which, as a rule, carries with it the obligation of according MFN treatment to all other members.

In addition, the United States specifically accords to all foreign countries any concession on tariffs or other import restrictions agreed to in reciprocal negotiations with any trading partner by its own law, first enacted in 1934 and now contained in Section 126 of the Trade Act of 1974 (19 U.S.C. 2136). U.S. legislation provides no specific procedure for extending MFN status to a country (except in the case of restoration of the status mentioned below) nor is there an official list of countries with MFN status. All countries other than those to which MFN treatment is specifically denied by law have MFN status.

The policy of general application of MFN treatment was modified when the President, as required by Section 5, Trade Agreements Extension Act of 1951 (65 Stat. 73), suspended, in 1951 and 1952, the application of MFN tariff rates to the Soviet Union and to all countries or areas under the control of international communism (in practice, the suspension applied to all countries of the then Sino-Soviet bloc but not to Yugoslavia). This action resulted in the increase of customs duties assessed on the U.S. imports from the countries involved from the concessional levels resulting from trade agreements with third countries to considerably higher levels as enacted by the highly protectionist Tariff Act of 1930.

The countries and areas initially denied MFN tariff treatment under Section 5 were: Albania, Bulgaria, China (any part under Communist domination or control), Czechoslovakia, Estonia, Germany (Soviet Zone and Soviet Sector of Berlin), Hungary, Indochina (any part of Cambodia, Laos, or Vietnam under Communist domination or control), Korea (any part under Communist domination or control), Kurile Islands, Latvia, Lithuania, Outer Mongolia, Poland and areas under Polish domination or control, Rumania, Southern Sakhalin Island, Soviet Union, Tanna Tuva, and Tibet.

Subsequently, Poland's MFN tariff status was restored in December 1960, while Cuba's was suspended in May 1962. Also in 1962, a list of "Communist countries" (all "Section 5" countries except Poland), to which MFN tariff status was being currently denied, was included in the newly revised Tariff Schedules of the United States, enacted by the Tariff Classification Act of 1962.

Section 231 of the Trade Expansion Act of 1962 (P.L. 87-794; 76 Stat. 876) applied the Section 5 suspension to "any country or area dominated by Communism" and thereby placed in jeopardy MFN status of Yugoslavia as well as Poland. The implementation of this directive was delayed and the law was later amended by allowing any country with MFN status at the time of its enactment (December 16, 1963) to retain it if the President determines it to be in the national interest. Such determination was made on March 26, 1964, for both countries.

The Trade Expansion Act of 1962 also made impossible the restoration of MFN status to a country subject to Section 5 suspension except by legislation. Such a law was enacted as part of the Trade Act of 1974, which in its Section 401 requires the continuation in force of the then existing suspensions of MFN tariff status, but also, in the remainder of its Title IV, authorizes the President to restore MFN status to a "nonmarket economy" (NME) country and maintain it in effect. The restoration may take place if (1) the President determines and reports initially and then semiannually to Congress that such country is not in violation of the requirements of the freedom-of-emigration ("Jackson-Vanik") amendment, or if he waives full compliance with such requirements under specified conditions, and his waiver authority and the existing waivers are renewed annually in mid-year; and (2) the country has concluded with the United States a trade agreement providing for reciprocal MFN treatment and containing other provisions as required by law, and the agreement is approved by a joint resolution enacted under a specific fast-track procedure.

The President's initial and any year-end report of full compliance with (no violation of) the free-emigration requirements or his annual mid-year recommendation of renewal of the waiver authority can be disapproved by a fast-track enactment of a joint resolution. A trade agreement with an NME country remains in effect for 3-year periods and is extended automatically under its own terms unless denounced; each such extension also requires a presidential determination of satisfactory reciprocation of the benefits extended by the United States under its MFN policy to the NME country. Triennial extensions do not require congressional approving action.

Poland's MFN tariff status was suspended again in October 1982 after the Polish martial-law government increased its repressive measures, but was restored in February 1987, after most such measures had been repealed. In January 1986, Afghanistan's MFN status was suspended by specific law; it can be restored, under specified conditions, by executive action without congressional involvement. In 1989 the designation "Communist countries" was omitted from the title of the list of countries denied MFN tariff treatment in the newly enacted Harmonized Tariff Schedule of the United States and the designation of the countries themselves was streamlined to reflect the actual World War II border changes, except for Estonia, Latvia, and Lithuania, which remained listed individually, since their incorporation into the USSR had not been recognized by the United States. The suspension of East Germany's MFN tariff status automatically ended with the unification of the two Germanies on October 3, 1990. By the end of 1990, MFN status had been restored under the waiver provisions of Title IV to Romania (1975), Hungary (1978), China (including Tibet) (1980), and Czechoslovakia (1990). Romania, however, in 1988, renounced the continuation of its MFN tariff status subject to the conditions of Title IV.

Much activity related to MFN tariff status of U.S. trading partners took place during the 102nd through 105th Congresses (1991-1998).

The status was restored temporarily under the waiver provision of Title IV to Bulgaria and Mongolia in November 1991, and permanently by law in December 1991 to previously non-MFN countries Estonia, Latvia, and Lithuania, after they declared their independence from the Soviet Union, and, in April 1992, to Czechoslovakia (later split into the Czech

Republic and Slovakia) and Hungary (both of which already had MFN status under Title IV). After the dissolution of the Soviet Union in late December 1991, the suspension of MFN tariff status continued in force individually with respect to its other 12 former constituent republics. Most of these had their MFN status restored within the next two years under the waiver provision of Title IV and by acceding to the U.S.-Soviet Union trade agreement of June 1, 1990, modified to apply to each individual republic. Thus MFN status was restored to Armenia in April 1992, Russia and Ukraine in June 1992, Moldova in July 1992, Kyrgyzstan in August 1992, Belarus and Kazakhstan in February 1993, Georgia in August 1993, Turkmenistan in October 1993, Tajikistan in November 1993, and Uzbekistan in January 1994. Azerbaijan was the only former Soviet republic whose restoration of MFN status under Title IV was still awaiting at the end of 1994 (since April 1993) the approval of that country's parliament.

During the same period, MFN tariff status also was regained under Title IV waiver provision by Albania (November 1992) and Romania (November 1993, following the September 1992 refusal of the House to restore it). MFN status of Bulgaria and the Russian Federation, restored earlier under the waiver provision, was continued in force by presidential determinations of full compliance with the freedom-of-emigration requirements (made, respectively, in June 1993 and September 1994).

Although President Bush issued in October 1992 a notice of intention to restore MFN status to Afghanistan, no action to that effect has as yet been taken.

Also in October 1992, legislation was enacted to withdraw MFN tariff status from Serbia and Montenegro (constituent republics of Yugoslavia in its reduced size). The status may be restored by the President to either republic 30 days after he certifies to the Congress that it had ceased its warlike activities in the former Yugoslavia.

In April 1995, MFN tariff status was extended to Azerbaijan under the Jackson-Vanik waiver provision, and permanent and unconditional MFN tariff status was restored in late 1996 by specific law to three countries: Bulgaria, and Romania (both of which at the time already had MFN status under the full-compliance provision of the Jackson-Vanik amendment), respectively in October and November, and Cambodia (then a non-MFN country) in October.

Measures introduced to restore MFN tariff status, either temporarily or permanently, to a number of other countries were not given further consideration, nor were measures denying or restricting MFN status of certain countries in a variety of circumstances. The Senate did approve, however, a bill to substitute in all U.S. statutes the often misunderstood term "most favored nation treatment" with "normal trade relations;" a similar House bill, using the term "standard trade relations," remained pending.

In 1996, the President renewed his determinations of full compliance with the Jackson-Vanik amendment requirements for Bulgaria, Romania (both since granted permanent MFN status), and Russia, and made the initial determination for Mongolia. The President also confirmed 3-year extensions of trade agreements with 10 NME countries.

During the 105th Congress, several bills affecting the MFN status of U.S. trading partners were introduced, but none enacted. Most legislative action involved bills permanently restoring MFN tariff status to Mongolia (passed by the House and favorably reported in the Senate) and Laos (favorably reported in the Senate). Introduced but not further considered was a bill granting permanent nondiscriminatory status to Kyrgyzstan and one that would grant, under certain conditions, permanent MFN status to any country still without it. On the other hand, bills also were introduced which would withdraw MFN tariff treatment from certain countries.

The President, at the appropriate times, extended all the existing Jackson-Vanik waivers, determined full compliance with the free emigration requirements by all but two (Belarus, and China) countries then still subject to the waiver, and subsequently reconfirmed such compliance. The President also issued, in April 1998, a Jackson-Vanik waiver for Vietnam. Joint resolutions to disapprove this waiver were introduced in both houses and reported unfavorably, whereupon the House resolution was defeated, allowing Vietnam's waiver to remain in force.

During the entire period since mid-1989, the most controversial issue of the U.S. MFN policy has been the MFN status of China. Yet, despite strong opposition in Congress to the President's annual renewals of China's Jackson-Vanik waiver and MFN status, joint resolutions introduced every year since the June 1989 Tiananmen Square events to disapprove such renewals have not been adopted. Legislation to subject China's MFN status to additional restrictions, passed by both sessions of the 102nd Congress, was vetoed by the President and the veto was upheld by the Senate. Similar legislation as well as joint resolutions disapproving China's waiver in subsequent Congresses have not reached enactment

Without actually affecting the practical application of MFN tariff treatment, legislation was enacted in 1998 (Section 5003 of the Internal Revenue Service Restructuring and Reform Act of 1998) to replace the term "most-favored-nation" in seven specific statutes with "normal trade relations" or another appropriate term.

In view of the, then prospective, accession of the Kyrgyz Republic to the World Trade Organization (which eventually took effect on December 20, 1998) and the obligation of a WTO member to accord permanent and unconditional most-favored-nation treatment to all WTO members, the United States on October 12, 1998, invoked Article XIII of the WTO Agreement. The article allows the nonapplication of the entire WTO Agreement (and not merely of one part of it) between any current WTO member and the acceding member, upon written notice to the WTO by either, before the latter's accession. Without invoking Article XIII, the United States would be in violation of its WTO obligation toward the Kyrgyz Republic because of the latter's MFN status being subject to the Jackson-Vanik amendment. (Identical action had been taken in similar circumstances on July 11, 1996, with respect to Mongolia, then a candidate for WTO membership. After Mongolia's accession to the WTO (January 29, 1997) and the extension of permanent MFN status to Mongolia by the United States (see next page), U.S. recourse to Article XIII was rescinded by the United States with respect to Mongolia on July 7, 1999).

Developments during the 106th Congress

In the 106th Congress, legislation to extend permanent MFN status to Mongolia has been enacted. Measures, introduced in both houses, to extend permanent MFN status to Albania and Kyrgyzstan were passed by the Senate in November 1999. Legislation to disapprove the mid-1999 renewals of Vietnam's (and China's) waivers failed to be enacted, while several measures to reform unilateral economic sanctions legislation (including MFN policy) are under consideration.

Extension of permanent MFN tariff status to Mongolia was the subject of several legislative measures, identical in their operative provisions: **Section 2424** of the Miscellaneous Trade and Technical Corrections Act of 1999 (**H.R. 326, H.R. 435,** and **S. 262**); and **S. 354**; of these, S. 262 has been reported favorably in the Senate, and H.R. 435 has been enacted (P.L. 106-36) and MFN tariff status extended to Mongolia by Presidential Proclamation 7207 (July 1, 1999).

S. 332 and **H.R. 1318,** authorizing the extension of permanent MFN tariff status to Kyrgyzstan, were introduced, respectively, January 28 and May 25, 1999, and referred, respectively, to the Senate Finance, and the House Ways and Means Committees. A provision to extend permanent MFN status to Kyrgyzstan is included as **Section 702** in the Senate-amended version of **H.R. 434,** passed by the Senate November 3, 1999.

Authorization for extending permanent MFN status to Albania is contained in **H.R. 2746,** introduced on August 5, 1999, and referred to the Committee on Ways and Means, and in **S. 1957,** introduced September 29, 1999, and referred to the Committee on Finance. A provision to extend permanent MFN status to Albania is included as **Section 701** in the Senate-amended version of **H.R. 434,** passed by the Senate November 3, 1999.

(The extension of permanent and unconditional MFN status to either country by H.R. 434, however, is subject to the provisions of **Section 722** of **H.R 434,** as added by the Senate, which denies *any* benefits of H.R. 434 to any country that does not meet and enforce the standards of child labor set by the ILO Convention for the Elimination of the Worst Forms of Child Labor.)

Three bills to reform unilateral economic sanctions legislation (**H.R. 1244, S.757,** and **S. 927**), introduced, respectively, March 24, March 25, and April 29, 1999, provide for impairment or denial of nondiscriminatory treatment as a sanction measure; referred, respectively, to the House Committees on International Relations, Ways and Means, and Banking and Financial Services, and to the Senate Finance Committee.

H.R. 2056, introduced June 8, 1999, and referred to the Committees on International Relations, Ways and Means, and Banking and Financial Services, would, among other sanctions aimed at Lebanon and Syria, withdraw their nondiscriminatory treatment.

On February 2, 1999, the President determined and transmitted to Congress the 1998 end-year report (H.Doc. 106-16) that Albania continues to be in full compliance with the free-emigration requirements of the Jackson-Vanik amendment, and, on February 11, 1999, transmitted an identical report on Mongolia (H.Doc. 106-19). On June 3, 1999, the President recommended one-year extensions of Jackson-Vanik waivers for Belarus, China, and Vietnam, triggering the introduction of joint resolutions disapproving the extension for China (H.J.Res. 57 and S.J.Res. 27) and Vietnam (**H.J.Res. 58** and **S.J.Res. 28**). A hearing on H.J.Res. 58 was held by the Ways and Means Trade Subcommittee; H.J.Res. 58 was reported adversely August 2, 1999 (H.Rept. 106-282), and failed to pass August 3, 1999 (130 - 297).

Apparently in preparation for the introduction of legislation for this purpose, the Trade Subcommittee of the House Ways and Means Committee solicited, on July 29, 1999, public comments on granting permanent nondiscriminatory status to Laos with September 10, 1999, as the deadline.

The President also renewed the semiannual determination of full compliance with the Jackson-Vanik requirements for 11 former Soviet Union republics (July 2, 1999, and January 7, 2000) and Albania (July 19, 1999).

As in the case of the Kyrgyz Republic, the United States, on September 30, 1999, invoked the nonapplication provision (Article XIII) of the WTO Agreement with respect to Georgia, whose accession to the WTO has been approved by the WTO but is still waiting for the approval by the country itself and entry into force.

Present Status

In view of the statutory general applicability of MFN status to U.S. trading partners under Section 126 of the Trade Act of 1974, there is no official specific list of countries with MFN status; all countries other than those to which MFN tariff status has been specifically denied by law or extended conditionally under Title IV of the Trade Act of 1974, have permanent and unconditional MFN status.

Countries to which, at present, MFN tariff status is denied are Afghanistan, Cuba, Laos, North Korea, Vietnam, and Yugoslavia (Serbia and Montenegro).

Countries to which MFN tariff status is at present being extended after having been conditionally restored temporarily under the provisions of Title IV of the Trade Act of 1974 are:

(1) under the presidential waiver of Jackson-Vanik amendment requirements, which must be renewed annually and is subject to disapproval by joint resolution of Congress: Belarus, and China (with Tibet). (A waiver is also in effect for Vietnam, but the restoration of MFN tariff status is still contingent on the conclusion of a bilateral trade agreement, which has been reached in principle on July 25, 1999, but whose signing has been delayed by Vietnam. The agreement also has to be approved by the enactment of a joint resolution of the U.S. Congress and ratified by Vietnam's National Assembly

(2) under the presidential determination of full compliance with the Jackson-Vanik amendment requirements, which, after the initial one, must be repeated semiannually and is subject to disapproval by joint resolution of Congress at the time of year-end renewal: Albania, Armenia, Azerbaijan, Georgia, Kazakhstan, Kyrgyzstan, Moldova, Russia, Tajikistan, Turkmenistan, Ukraine, and Uzbekistan.

Restoration of permanent MFN status to Mongolia has been enacted and implemented by Presidential Proclamation 7207, effective July 1, 1999, and restoration of permanent MFN status to Albania and Kyrgyzstan has been approved by the Senate, albeit under restrictive conditions. Legislation awaits conference action.

MFN status can be restored to Afghanistan and Yugoslavia — countries not subject to the Jackson-Vanik amendment — by executive action under conditions specified in the legislation suspending the status.

Presidential determinations of satisfactory reciprocity, which the law requires for extending the triennial terms of bilateral trade agreements with NME countries, have in recent years been published with delays or, in one instance, not at all. The only published determination still in effect is the one for China; there are no extant published determinations extending the agreements with the rest of NME countries, whose terms have all expired (12 recently, 1 several years ago). This omission apparently does not in practice affect the MFN status of the latter countries, since they are all still treated as having MFN status.

Legislation to replace the term "most-favored-nation" in existing and future legislation with "normal trade relations" or another appropriate term has been enacted.

LEGISLATION

(For legislative activity with respect to China's most-favored-nation status, please see CRS Report RL30225, *Most-Favored-Nation Status of the People's Republic of China*.)

H.J.Res. 58 (Rohrabacher)/S.J.Res. 28 (Bob Smith)
Disapproves the extension of the Jackson-Vanik waiver for Vietnam. H.J.Res.58 introduced June 9, 1999, referred to Committee on Ways and Means; a hearing by Ways and Means Trade Subcommittee on U.S.-Vietnam trade relations, including Jackson-Vanik waiver, held June 17, 1999. S.J.Res. 28 introduced June 7, 1999, referred to Committee on Finance. H.J.Res. 58 reported adversely June 30, 1999 (H.Rept. 106-282); failed of passage (130 - 297) August 3, 1999. Motion to discharge S.J.Res. 28 rejected (5 - 94) July 20, 1999.

Section 2424 of H.R. 326 (Archer), H.R. 435 (Archer), S. 262 (Roth), and S. 354 (Thomas)
Authorizes the President to extend permanent nondiscriminatory treatment to Mongolia. H.R. 326 introduced Jan. 19, 1999, H.R. 435 introduced Feb. 2, 1999, both referred to Committee on Ways and Means; S. 262 introduced Jan. 20, 1999, S. 354 introduced Feb. 3, 1999, both referred to Committee on Finance; S. 262 favorably reported Feb. 3, 1999 (S.Rept. 106-2). H.R. 435 passed the House (414-1) Feb. 9, 1999, and Senate (by unanimous consent, amended) May 27, 1999; Senate amendments agreed to by the House (375 - 1) June 17, 1999; signed into law June 25, 1999 (P.L. 106-36). Permanent nondiscriminatory treatment extended to Mongolia by Pres. Proclamation 7207 of July 1, 1999 (64 F.R. 36549).

H.R. 1244 (Crane); S. 757 (Lugar); S. 927 (Dodd)
Includes among the authorized sanction measures "the imposition of increased tariffs on, or other restrictions on imports of, products of a foreign country or entity, including the

denial, revocation, or conditioning of nondiscriminatory (most-favored-nation) trade treatment." H.R. 1244 introduced Mar. 24, 1999; referred to the Committees on International Relations, Ways and Means, and Banking and Financial Services; S. 757 introduced Mar. 25, 1999, S. 927 introduced Apr. 29, 1999, both referred to the Committee on Foreign Relations.

H.R. 1318 (Dunn)/S. 332 (Brownback)/Sec. 702, H.R. 434 (as amended; Roth/Moynihan)

Authorizes the President to extend permanent nondiscriminatory treatment to Kyrgyzstan. S. 332 introduced Jan. 28, 1999; referred to Committee on Finance; H.R. 1318 introduced Mar. 25, 1999; referred to Committee on Ways and Means; Sec. 702, proposed as Senate amendment SP2325 to H.R. 434 Oct. 27, 1999, passed Nov. 3, 1999, subject to a restriction.

H.R. 2056 (Forbes)

Lebanon Independence Restoration Act of 1999. Along with the imposition of other sanctions, withdraws nondiscriminatory treatment from products of Lebanon and Syria until Syria withdraws all of its and its proxies' forces from Lebanon and full democracy and stability is restored in Lebanon, as certified by the President to the Congress. Introduced June 8, 1999; referred to the Committees on International Relations, Ways and Means, and Banking and Financial Services.

H.R. 2746 (Engel)/Sec. 701, H.R. 434 (as amended; Roth/Moynihan)

Trade and Development Act of 1999. Authorizes the President to extend permanent nondiscriminatory treatment to Albania. H.R. 2746 Introduced Aug. 5, 1999; referred to the Committee on Ways and Means; Sec. 701, proposed as Senate amendment SP2325 to H.R. 434 Oct. 27, 1999, passed Nov. 3, 1999, subject to a restriction.

CHRONOLOGY

01/07/00 — The President determined and reported to Congress that 11 former Soviet Republics (all except Belarus) continue to be in full compliance with the Jackson-Vanik requirements.

11/03/99 — H.R. 434 (amended and renamed "Trade and Development Act of 1999"), in added Secs. 701 and 702 extending unconditional normal trade relations (MFN status), respectively, to Albania and Kyrgyzstan, passed by the Senate (76 yeas - 19 nays).

10/27/99 — Substitute amendment SP2325 to H.R. 434, authorizing unconditional normal trade relations (MFN status) with Albania and Kyrgyzstan, proposed.

09/30/99 — The United States invoked the nonapplication provision (Article XIII) of the WTO Agreement with respect to Georgia..

09/29/99 — S. 1657 to extend permanent nondiscriminatory treatment to Albania introduced.

08/05/99 — H.R. 2746 to extend permanent nondiscriminatory treatment to Albania introduced.

08/03/99 — H.J.Res. 58, disapproving the extension of Vietnam's waiver, failed of passage (130 - 29), thereby continuing in force Vietnam's waiver.

08/02/99 — H.J.Res. 58 reported adversely (H.Rept. 106-282).

07/29/99 — Presaging legislative action on the subject, the Trade Subcommittee of the House Ways and Means Committee solicits public comments on the extension of permanent nondiscriminatory treatment to Laos.

07/20/99 — Motion to discharge Senate Finance Committee from further consideration of S.J.Res. 28 rejected (5-94).

07/19/99 — President determined and reported to Congress that Albania continues to be in full compliance with the Jackson-Vanik requirements (H.Doc. 106-98).

07/07/99 — United States rescinded the invocation (July 11, 1996) of the nonapplication provision (Article XIII) of the WTO Agreement with respect to Mongolia.

07/02/99 — The President determined and reported to Congress that 11 former Soviet Republics (all except Belarus) continue to be in full compliance with the Jackson-Vanik requirements (Weekly Compilation of Presidential Documents, v. 35, No. 27, p. 1281).

07/01/99 — Permanent nondiscriminatory status extended to Mongolia by Presidential Proclamation 7027 (64 F.R. 36549) (see preceding entry).

06/25/99 — The President signed H.R. 435, containing the authority to extend by proclamation permanent nondiscriminatory treatment (NTR) to the products of Mongolia.

06/17/99 — Hearing on U.S.-Vietnam trade relations, including Jackson-Vanik waiver for Vietnam, held by Ways and Means Subcommittee on Trade.

06/09/99 — H.J.Res. 58 to disapprove the extension of the Jackson-Vanik waiver for Vietnam introduced.

06/08/99 — H.R. 2056 (Lebanon Independence Restoration Act of 1999) introduced, among other sanctions, withdrawing Lebanon's and Syria's MFN treatment.

06/07/99 — The House agreed (375 - 1) to H.R. 435, as amended by the Senate, approving the extension of permanent MFN tariff status to Mongolia.
  — S.J.Res. 28 to disapprove the extension of the Jackson-Vanik waiver for Vietnam introduced.

06/03/99 — The President issued Presidential Determinations 99-26 and 99-27, extending for one year Jackson-Vanik waivers, respectively, for Belarus and Vietnam (H.Docs. 106-76 and 106-78).

05/27/99 — The Senate amended and passed H.R. 435 by unanimous consent.

04/29/99 — S. 927 (Sanctions Rationalization Act of 1999) introduced; provides for denial or restriction of MFN status as an economic sanction.

03/25/99 — H.R. 1318 to extend permanent nondiscriminatory treatment to Kyrgyzstan introduced.

       — S. 757 (Sanctions Policy Reform Act) introduced; provides for denial or restriction of MFN treatment as an economic sanction.

03/24/99 — H.R. 1244 (Enhancement of Trade, Security, and Human Rights through Sanctions Reform Act) introduced; provides for denial or restriction of MFN status as an economic sanction.

02/11/99 — The President determined and reported to Congress that Mongolia continues to be in full compliance with the Jackson-Vanik requirements (H.Doc. 106-19).

02/09/99 — The House passed H.R. 435 (Miscellaneous Trade and Technical Corrections Act of 1999) on a roll-call vote (414 - 1); Section 2424 authorizes the President to extend permanent nondiscriminatory treatment to Mongolia.

02/03/99 — S. 262, in Section 2424 authorizing the extension of permanent nondiscriminatory treatment to Mongolia, reported favorably (S.Rept. 106-2).

       — S. 354 to extend permanent nondiscriminatory treatment to Mongolia, introduced.

02/02/99 — H.R. 435 (Miscellaneous Trade and Technical Corrections Act of 1999) introduced; Section 2424 authorizes the President to extend permanent nondiscriminatory status to Mongolia.

       — The President determined and reported to Congress that Albania continues to be in full compliance with the Jackson-Vanik requirements (H.Doc. 106-16).

01/28/99 — S. 332 to extend permanent nondiscriminatory treatment to Kyrgyzstan introduced.

01/20/99 — S. 262 (Miscellaneous Trade and Technical Corrections Act of 1999) introduced as an original Committee bill; Section 2424 authorizes the President to extend permanent nondiscriminatory treatment to Mongolia.

01/19/99 — H.R. 326 (Miscellaneous Trade and Technical Corrections Act of 1999) introduced; Section 2424 authorizes the President to extend permanent nondiscriminatory status to Mongolia.

12/29/98 — The President determined and reported to Congress that 11 former Soviet Republics (all except Belarus) continue to be in full compliance with the Jackson-Vanik requirements (H.Doc. 106-5).

10/20/98 — H.R. 4856 (Miscellaneous Trade and Technical Corrections Act), in Section 2424 extending permanent nondiscriminatory treatment to Mongolia, introduced, called up under suspension of the rules, and passed by the House.

10/12/98 — H.R. 4807 to extend permanent nondiscriminatory to Mongolia introduced.

— The United States invoked Article XIII of the WTO Agreement against the application of the Agreement between the United States and the Kyrgyz Republic.

09/22/98 — H.R. 4606 to extend permanent nondiscriminatory status to Kyrgyzstan (identical with S. 2363) introduced.

07/31/98 — S. 2400 (Trade and Tariff Act of 1998), extending in Title VI, Subtitle A, permanent normal trade relations (MFN) treatment to Mongolia, reported favorably as an original Finance Committee bill (S.Rept. 105-280).

07/30/98 — H.J.Res. 120, disapproving the extension of Vietnam's Jackson-Vanik waiver, defeated in a yea-nay vote (163-216).

07/29/98 — H.J.Res. 120, disapproving the extension of Vietnam's Jackson-Vanik waiver, reported unfavorably (H.Rept. 105-653)

07/28/98 — S. 2363 to extend permanent nondiscriminatory treatment to Kyrgyzstan introduced.

07/22/98 — Internal Revenue Service Restructuring and Reform Act of 1998 enacted (P.L. 105-206), containing in Section 5003 the language of H.R. 2316, requiring replacement of the term "most-favored-nation" with "normal trade relations."

07/16/98 — President Clinton reported to Congress Albania's continued full compliance with the Jackson-Vanik amendment requirements (H.Doc. 105-285).

07/10/98 — S.J.Res. 47 reported unfavorably without written report.

07/09/98 — President Clinton reported to Congress continued compliance with the Jackson-Vanik amendment requirements by 11 former Soviet republics (H.Doc. 105-298).

07/07/98 — Hearing on S.J.Res. 47 held by Senate Finance Committee.

07/01/98 — President Clinton reported to Congress Mongolia's continued full compliance with the Jackson-Vanik amendment requirements (H.Doc. 105-283).

06/24/98 — Language of H.R. 2316, requiring replacement of the term "most-favored-nation" with "normal trade relations" in U.S. statutes added in conference (H.Rept. 105-599) as Section 5003 to Internal Revenue Service Restructuring and Reform Act of 1998.

06/18/98 — Hearing on H.J.Res. 120 held by House Ways and Means Trade Subcommittee.

06/04/98 — Joint resolutions to disapprove the extension of the Jackson-Vanik waiver for Vietnam introduced (H.J.Res. 120; S.J.Res. 47).

06/03/98 — The President issued Presidential Determinations 98-27 and 98-28, extending for one year Jackson-Vanik waivers, respectively, for Vietnam and Belarus, together with messages to Congress (H.Doc. 105-263 and -264) .

04/07/98 — The President issued Executive Order 13079 granting a Jackson-Vanik waiver for Vietnam (63 FR. 17309).

03/09/98 — The President notified Congress of his determination (Pres. Det. 98-17) that a Jackson-Vanik amendment with respect to Vietnam will substantially promote the objectives of the amendment (H.Doc. 105-227; 63 F.R. 14329).

01/21/98 — The President determined and reported to Congress that Albania continues to be in full compliance with the Jackson-Vanik requirements (H.Doc. 105-210).

01/20/98 — The President determined and reported to Congress that Mongolia continues to be in full compliance with the Jackson-Vanik requirements (H.Doc. 105-196).

Chronology for earlier years can be obtained from the author of the Issue Brief (phone 7-7747).

CONGRESSIONAL HEARINGS, REPORTS, AND DOCUMENTS

NOTE: For hearings, reports, and documents relating to MFN status of China, see CRS Report RL30225.

U.S. Congress. House. Committee on Ways and Means. Disapproving extension of waiver authority under Section 402(c) of the Trade Act of 1974 with respect to Vietnam; adverse report (to accompany H.J.Res. 120). Washington, U.S. Govt. Print. Off., July 29, 1998. 7 p. At head of title: 105th Congress, 2d Session. H.Rept. 105-653.

—— Subcommittee on Trade. Written comments on extension of unconditional most-favored-nation treatment to Mongolia and Laos. Washington, U.S. Govt. Print. Off., August 28, 1997. 15 p. At head of title: 105th Congress, 1st session. Committee print WMCP: 105-5.

—— Subcommittee on Trade. Written comments on the extension of normal trade relations to the Kyrgyz Republic. Washington, U.S. Govt. Print. Off., February 10, 1999. 6 p. At head of title: 105th Congress, 2nd session. Committee print WMCP: 105-12.

—— Subcommittee on Trade. Written comments on the extension of unconditional normal trade relations to the Kyrgyz Republic. Washington, U.S. Govt. Print. Off., November 4 1999. 11 p. At head of title: 106th Congress, 1st session. Committee print WMCP: 106-5.

—— Subcommittee on Trade. Written comments on the extension of normal trade relations to the Lao People's Democratic Republic. Washington, U.S. Govt. Print. Off., November 4, 1999. 44 p. At head of title: 106th Congress, 1st session. Committee print WMCP:106-6.

U.S. Congress. Senate. Committee on Finance. Miscellaneous Trade and Technical Corrections Act of 1999; report (to accompany S. 262). Washington, U.S. Govt. Print. Off., February 3, 1999. 81 p. [p. 73]. At head of title: 106th Congress, 1st session. S.Rept. 106-2.

—— Trade and Tariff Act of 1998; report (to accompany [S.]2400). Washington, U.S. Govt. Print. Off., July 31, 1998. 82 p. At the head of title: 105th Congress, 2d session. S.Rept. 105-280.

U.S. President, 1993- (Clinton). An update on the emigration laws and policies of Albania; communication from the President of the United States... Washington, U.S. Govt. Print Off., 1999. 3 p. (106th Congress, 1st session. H.Doc. 106-16). Communication dated February 2, 1999.

—— A report on most-favored-nation status; communication from the President of the United States... [on Armenia, Azerbaijan, Georgia, Kazakhstan, Kyrgyzstan. Moldova, the Russian Federation, Tajikistan, Turkmenistan, Ukraine, and Uzbekistan]. Washington, U.S. Govt Print. Off., 1999. 6 p. (106th Congress, 1st session. H.Doc. 106-5). Communication dated December 29, 1998.

—— Emigration laws and policies of Albania; communication from the President of the United States... Washington, U.S. Govt. Print. Off., 1998. 3 p. (105th Congress, 2d session. H.Doc. 105-210). Communication dated January 21, 1998.

—— Emigration laws and policies of Albania; message from the President of the United States... Washington, U.S. Govt. Print. Off., 1998. 3 p. (105th Congress, 2d session. H.Doc. 105-285). Message dated July 16, 1998.

—— Emigration laws and policies of Albania; message from the President of the United States... Washington, U.S. Govt. Print. Off., 1999. 3 p. (106th Congress, 1st session. H.Doc. 106-98). Message dated July 19, 1999.

——Emigration laws and policies of Armenia, Azerbaijan, Georgia, Kazakhstan, Kyrgyzstan, Moldova, the Russian Federation, Tajikistan, Turkmenistan, Ukraine and Uzbekistan; communication from the President of the United States... Washington, U.S. Govt. Print. Off., 1998. 9 p. (105th Congress, 2d session. H.Doc. 105-298). Communication dated July 9, 1998.

—— Emigration laws and policies of Mongolia; communication from the President of the United States ... Washington, U.S. Govt. Print Off., 1998. 3 p. (105th Congress, 2nd session. H.Doc. 105-196). Communication dated January 20, 1998.

—— Emigration laws and policies of Mongolia; communication from the President of the United States ... Washington, U.S. Govt. Print Off., 1998. 3 p. (105th Congress, 2nd session. H.Doc. 105-283). Communication dated July 1, 1998.

—— Emigration laws and policies of Mongolia; communication from the President of the United States ... Washington, U.S. Govt. Print Off., 1999. 3 p. (106th Congress, 1st session. H.Doc. 106-19). Communication dated February 11, 1999.

—— Extension of waiver authority for the Republic of Belarus; message from the President of the United States... Washington, U.S. Govt. Print. Off., 1998. 5 p. (105th Congress, 2d session. H.Doc. 105-264). Message dated June 3, 1998.

—— Extension of waiver authority for Vietnam; message from the President of the United States... Washington, U.S. Govt. Print. Off., 1998. 5 p. (105th Congress, 2d session. H.Doc. 105-263). Message dated June 3, 1998.

—— Presidential determination with respect to Vietnam; message from the President of the United States... Washington, U.S. Govt. Print. Off., 1998. 3 p. (105th Congress, 2nd session. H.Doc. 105-227). Message dated March 9, 1998.

——A report to Congress concerning the extension of waiver authority for Belarus; communication from the President of the United States... Washington, U.S. Govt Print. Off., 1999. 4 p. (106th Congress, 1st session. H.Doc. 106-76). Communication dated June 3, 1999.

——A report to the Congress concerning the extension of waiver authority for Vietnam; communication from the President of the United States... Washington, U.S. Govt. Print. Off., 1999. 6 p. (106th Congress, 1st session. H.Doc. 106-78). Communication dated June 3, 1999.

Foreign Policy of the United States
Volume 1

TERRORISM, THE FUTURE, AND U.S. FOREIGN POLICY

Raphael F. Perl

CONTENTS

SUMMARY

International terrorism threatens U.S. foreign and domestic security and compromises a broad range of U.S. foreign policy goals. This issue brief examines emerging international terrorist threats and the U.S. policy response. Available policy options range from diplomacy, international cooperation and constructive engagement to economic sanctions, covert action, physical security enhancement and military force.

Throughout successive administrations, a key element of stated U.S. policy has remained: no concessions to terrorism. Recent willingness by such groups as the PLO, and IRA to moderate behavior may indicate success of this policy. In this context, current U.S., British, and Israeli policies of engagement with such groups is supported by some as a response to changing circumstances.

Dramatic events, such as the Oklahoma City, World Trade Center, and U.S. Embassy bombings in Kenya and Tanzania, as well as the Tokyo subway gas attack, have brought the issue of terrorism to the forefront of American public interest. These specific occurrences raise questions whether U.S. policy and organizational mechanisms are adequately focused to combat what may be a new brand of terrorist: one who does not work for any established organization and who is not an agent of any particular state sponsor, yet has access to the most lethal weaponry.

Formal definitions of terrorism do not include terrorist activity for financial profit or terrorists motivated by religious goals. Non-traditional harm such as computer "violence" is excluded as well. Such activity may well be on the rise, and policy and organizational mindsets geared to deal with terrorism as politically motivated and violent behavior may limit our ability to combat new and expanding forms of terrorism.

Terrorist access to chemical, biological, or nuclear weaponry raises the specter of mass-casualty attacks. Faced with such prospects, governments are increasingly likely to consider utilizing covert operations to protect their citizenry.

In light of the shifting nature and enhanced intensity of the new terrorist threat, some analysts believe a comprehensive review of U.S. terrorism policy, organizational structure, and preparedness to respond to major terrorist incidents in the United States is desirable. PDD 62, which established a terrorism coordinator at the National Security Council (NSC), may take much of the terrorism decisionmaking process out of the realm of congressional oversight as NSC members do not generally testify on the Hill.

Radical Islamic fundamentalist groups pose a major terrorist threat to U.S. interests and friendly regimes. Potential "hot spots" include Bahrain, Jordan, Pakistan, and Saudi Arabia. One of the seven states on the State Department's terrorism list, Iran, continues to be a major source of state sponsored terrorism, although the State Department no longer lists Iran as the most active state sponsor. Iran has been aggressively seeking nuclear weapons technology. Sanctions have not deterred such activity to any meaningful degree. Some see utility in an informal "watch-list" of nations not currently qualifying for inclusion on the terrorism list. See also: CRS Report 98-733F, *Terrorism: U.S. Response to Bombings in Kenya and Tanzania: A New Policy Direction?*

MOST RECENT DEVELOPMENTS

On April 30, 2000, the Department of State is expected to release its annual Patterns of Global Terrorism report. Data is expected to show an increase in the number of terrorist incidents worldwide in 1999 [about 1/3] as compared to 1998, including those in the Mid-East. Total numbers of casualties and total number of reported deaths are down significantly, due in large part to an absence of major incidents. The main area of U.S. policy focus continues to be terrorism by non state actors. A heavy area of focus remains the ability of terrorists to raise funds through non-state sources-often through charitable contributions, kidnaping, and drug trafficking. Concerns that the Northern Ireland peace process may unravel highlighted by disputes over the decommissioning of weapon held by IRA splinter groups such as the "real IRA" remains an important area of concern.

On March 17, 2000, Secretary of State Albright announced suspension of a ban on imports of Iranian pistachio nuts, caviar, and carpets – a move seen as a gesture to Iranian reformers and their supporters.

BACKGROUND AND ANALYSIS

In recent years, terrorism has been primarily viewed as an international and foreign policy issue. Numerous acts of state-sponsored terrorists and of foreign-based groups have given support to this notion. While U.S. policies, citizens and interests are prime targets for international terrorism — in 1998, approximately 40% — up from 33% in 1997 — of all terrorist incidents worldwide were committed against U.S. citizens or property according to the U.S. Department of State— the vast majority of those acts took place on foreign soil. Although terrorism may be internationally motivated, financed, supported or planned, on the receiving end all terrorism is local. Thus, U.S. public perception of terrorism as primarily an overseas issue may be changing with the bombings of the Trade Center in New York and the Federal Building in Oklahoma City. The predominant method of attack during 1998 was bombing [three-fifths of all incidents]; the most common targets were business related.

On April 30, 1999, the Department of State released its Patterns of Global Terrorism report. In 1998 casualties associated with terrorism worldwide were significantly up from 1997 data. The report indicates that worldwide deaths from terrorist incidents are up roughly threefold from 1997 [from 221 to 741] and the number of wounded was up roughly eightfold from 693 to 5,952. In terms of deaths by region, Africa ranked first; Asia, second; and Latin America, third. In terms of wounded by region, Africa ranked first, Western Europe, second, and Asia, third. In 1997, the Middle East was highest in both the number of dead and wounded by terrorism; Asia was in second place. In contrast to reports of previous years, Iran was not cited as the most active state sponsor of international terrorism.

Both timing and target selection by terrorist groups has produced significant political and economic impact on phenomena such as the Middle East peace process and tourism in nations such as Egypt. Some analysts have expressed concern that radical Islamic groups may seek to exploit economic and political instabilities in Saudi Arabia. Other potential target nations of such groups include Algeria, Bahrain, Egypt, India, Jordan, Turkey, and Pakistan. In 1998, Africa replaced the Middle East as the region with the highest casualty levels.

The April 1999 report retained Syria on the list of states supporting terrorism and listed Iran as a continuing active supporter of international terrorism. The State Department data indicate that the number of international terrorist acts generally declined from 1987 through 1994: 322 in 1994, 431 in 1993, and 665 in 1987. From 1994 to the present the numbers are mixed. Incidents were up significantly in 1995 from 322 to 440, but down to 296 in 1996, slightly up in 1997 to 304, and down to 273 in 1998. International terrorist acts against U.S. interests rose from 66 in 1994 to 99 in 1995; were 73 in 1996, increased to 123 in 1997, and went down to 111 in 1998. The number of U.S. citizens killed rose from 4 to 12 in 1995; was 25 in 1996 and was down to 7 in 1997, and 12 in 1998. The percentage of anti-U.S. incidents rose from 25% in 1996 to 33% in 1997 to 40% in 1998.

On November 2, 1999, State Department Counter-terrorism Coordinator Michael A. Sheehan, in testimony before Congress, suggested that a decline in state sponsorship of terrorism has moved terrorism eastward — from Libya, Syria, and Lebanon — to South Asia. The result: more U.S. policy focus on Usama Bin Laden and the alliance of groups operating out of Afghanistan with the acquiescence of the Taliban.

The total number of terrorist related deaths in 1998 was up from 314 to 741 and the number of persons wounded increased dramatically from 693 to 5,952. The bombings of the N.Y. World Trade Center and the Jewish cultural center in Buenos Aires may indicate a trend to inflict higher casualties on what are generally less protected civilian targets. Access by terrorist groups to chemical, biological, or nuclear technology, and employment of such weapons, would raise casualty statistics even higher. It appears that state-sponsored terrorism is decreasing significantly as, in a post Cold War era, groups find it harder to obtain sponsors and rogue states are less willing to risk exposure to broad based and severe international sanctions. In this environment, access to private sources of funding for terrorist enterprises becomes critical. Finally, some see a trend by major organizations such as the PLO, and the IRA, to moderate their behavior, become legitimate, and pursue their goals through political negotiation, compromise, and other non-violent means.

International terrorism is recognized as a threat to U.S. foreign and domestic security; it also undermines a broad range of U.S. foreign policy goals. Terrorism erodes international stability — a major foreign and economic policy objective for the United States. Terrorist groups often seek to destabilize or overthrow governments, sometimes democratically elected — or friendly — governments, and such groups often draw their support from public discontent over the perceived inability of governments to deliver peace, security, and economic prosperity. Efforts by governments to enhance national or regional economic development and stability may become the object of particularly virulent attack. In this regard, and because of their avowed goals to overthrow secular regimes in countries with large Muslim populations, extremist Islamic fundamentalist groups, and Iran's support for such groups, are seen as a major threat to U.S. foreign policy goals and objectives.

Definitions

There is no universally accepted definition of international terrorism. One definition widely used in U.S. government circles, and incorporated into law, defines "international terrorism" as terrorism involving the citizens or property of more than one country. Terrorism is broadly defined as politically motivated violence perpetrated against noncombatant targets by subnational groups or clandestine agents. A "terrorist group" is defined as a group which practices or which has significant subgroups which practice terrorism (22 U.S.C. 2656f). One potential shortfall of this traditional approach is its focus on groups and group members and exclusion of individual (non- group organized) terrorist activity which has recently risen in frequency and visibility. Another possible weakness of these standard definitions is the criteria of violence in a traditional form. Analysts pointing to "virus" sabotage incidents warn that terrorists acts could include more sophisticated forms of destruction and extortion such as disabling a national infrastructure by penetrating vital computer software.

Current definitions of terrorism all share one common element — politically motivated behavior. Such definitions do not include violence for financial profit or religious motivation. The rapid growth of transnational criminal organizations and the growing range and scale of such operations could well result in their use of violence to achieve objectives with financial profit as the driving motivation. As an example, in the case of Islamic extremist groups, religious and political motivation may be inextricably intertwined. Thus, although the basic assumption today is that all terrorist acts are politically motivated, some are driven by other factors, and this number may grow in light of expanding international criminal activity and an increasing number of extremist acts carried out in the name of religious and cultural causes. More traditional mindsets may limit the ability of defenders to predict terrorist violence, confront it, and respond in appropriate terms. A new approach might focus more on defining terrorist acts, giving less emphasis to the motivation behind the acts.

U.S. Policy Response

Framework

Past administrations have employed a range of options to combat international terrorism, from diplomacy and international cooperation and constructive engagement to economic sanctions, covert action, protective security measures and military force. The application of sanctions is one of the most frequently used tools of U.S. policymakers. Governments supporting international terrorism (as identified by the Department of State) are prohibited from receiving U.S. economic and military assistance. Export of munitions to such countries is foreclosed, restrictions are imposed on exports of "dual use" equipment such as aircraft and trucks.

Throughout successive administrations, U.S. policy as publicly stated has remained: *no concessions to terrorists*, the U.S. government will not pay ransoms, release prisoners, change its policies, or agree to other acts that might encourage additional terrorism. Practice, however, has not always been so pure. The United States will also use most available resources to gain the safe return of American citizens who are held hostage by terrorists. U.S. policy is to encourage other nations to do likewise. Recent U.S. and Israeli overtures to the PLO, and recent U.S. and British approaches to the IRA clearly appear to reflect some change in approach as such groups begin to moderate their behavior. It has recently been noted that the 1994 capture by France of the notorious "Carlos" is unlikely to have occurred without some acquiescence from Sudan. Some, however, see engagement with such groups or their sponsors as softening of a long established principle of no concessions.

Most experts agree that the most effective way to fight terrorism is to gather as much intelligence as possible; disrupt terrorist plans and organizations before they act; and organize multinational cooperation against terrorists and countries that support them. The U.N.'s role in mandating sanctions against Libya for its responsibility in the 1988 Pan Am 103 bombing was significant as the first instance when the world community imposed sanctions against a country in response to its complicity in an act of terrorism. Several factors made the action possible. First, terrorism has touched many more countries in recent years, forcing governments to put aside parochial interests. (Citizens from over 30 countries have reportedly died in Libyan-sponsored bombings.) Second, the end of the Cold War has contributed to increased international cooperation against terrorism. And third, U.S. determination to punish terrorist countries, by military force in some instances, once their complicity was established, was a major factor spurring other countries to join U.N.-sponsored action.

In the past, governments have often preferred to handle terrorism as a national problem without outside interference. Some governments were also wary of getting involved in others battles and possibly attracting additional terrorism in the form of reprisals. Others were reluctant to join in sanctions if their own trade interests might be damaged or they sympathized with the perpetrators' cause. Finally, there is the persistent problem of extraditing terrorists without abandoning the long-held principle of asylum for persons fleeing persecution for legitimate political or other activity.

Dilemmas

In their desire to combat terrorism in a modern political context, nations often face conflicting goals and courses of action: (1) providing security from terrorist acts, i.e. limiting the freedom of individual terrorists, terrorists groups, and support networks to operate unimpeded in a relatively unregulated environment versus (2) maximizing individual freedoms, democracy, and human rights. Efforts to combat terrorism are complicated by a global trend towards deregulation, open borders, and expanded commerce. Particularly in democracies such as the United States, the constitutional limits within which policy must operate, are often seen to conflict directly with a desire to more effectively secure the lives of citizens against terrorist activity.

Another dilemma for policymakers is the need to identify the perpetrators of particular terrorist acts and those who train, fund, or otherwise support or sponsor them. Such relationships are by their nature clandestine. Moreover, as the international community has increasingly demonstrated its ability to unite and apply sanctions against rogue states, states will become less likely to formally support terrorist groups or engage in state sponsored terrorism.

Today a non-standard brand of terrorist may be emerging: individuals who do not work for any established terrorist organization and who are apparently not agents of any state sponsor. The worldwide threat of such individual or "boutique" terrorism or that of "spontaneous" terrorist activity such as the bombing of bookstores in the United States after Ayatollah Khomeini's death edict against Salman Rushdie, appears to be on the increase.

Thus, one likely profile for the terrorist of the 21st century may well be a private individual not affiliated with any established group. Another profile might be a group-affiliated individual acting independent of the group, but drawing on other similarly minded individuals for support. Because the current U.S. international counter-terrorism policy framework is sanctions-oriented, and has traditionally sought to pin responsibility on state-sponsors, some policy realignment may be required.

Another problem surfacing in the wake of the number of incidents associated with Islamic fundamentalist groups is how to condemn and combat such terrorist activity, and the extreme and violent ideology of specific radical groups, without appearing to be anti-Islamic in general. A desire to punish a state for supporting international terrorism may also be subject to conflicting foreign policy objectives. For example, many in the Administration and Congress who would seek to sanction Syria for its support of international terrorism would, at the same time, like to see Syria removed from the terrorist list to encourage and reward Syrian participation in the Middle East peace process. The State Department, however, has repeatedly stated that prior to removal from the list, Syria must first cease its terrorist support activities.

Policy Tools

The U.S. government has employed a wide array of policy tools to combat international terrorism, from diplomacy and international cooperation and constructive engagement to economic sanctions, covert action, protective security measures and military force.

Diplomacy/Constructive Engagement. Most responses to international terrorism involve use of diplomacy in some form as governments seek cooperation to apply pressure on terrorists. One such initiative was the active U.S. role taken in the March 1996 Sharm al-Sheikh peacemaker/anti-terrorism summit. Another is the ongoing U.S. effort to get Japan and major European nations to join in U.S. trade and economic sanctions against Iran. Some argue that diplomacy holds little hope of success against determined terrorists or the countries that support them. However, diplomatic measures are least likely to widen the conflict and therefore are usually tried first.

In incidents of international terrorism by subnational groups, implementing a policy response of constructive engagement is complicated by the lack of existing channels and mutually accepted rules of conduct between governmental entities and the group in question. In some instances, as was the case with the PLO, legislation may specifically prohibit official contact with a terrorist organization or its members. Increasingly, however, governments appear to be pursuing policies which involve verbal contact with terrorist groups or their representatives.

The media remain powerful forces in confrontations between terrorists and governments. Appealing to, and influencing, public opinion may impact not only the actions of governments but also those of groups engaged in terrorist acts. From the terrorist perspective, media coverage is an important measure of the success of a terrorist act or campaign. And in hostage type incidents, where the media may provide the only independent means a terrorist has of knowing the chain of events set in motion, coverage can complicate rescue efforts. Governments can use the media in an effort to arouse world opinion against the country or group using terrorist tactics. Public diplomacy and the media can be used to mobilize public opinion in other countries to pressure governments to take action against terrorism. An example would be to mobilize the tourist industry to pressure governments into participating in sanctions against a terrorist state.

Economic Sanctions. In the past, use of economic sanctions was usually predicated upon identification of a nation as an active supporter or sponsor of international terrorism On August 20, 1998, President Clinton signed an executive order freezing assets owned by bin Laden, specific associates, their self proclaimed Islamic Army Organization, and prohibiting U.S. individuals and firms from doing business with them. *Previously*, the Clinton Administration had frozen the assets of 12 alleged Middle East terrorist organizations and 18 individuals associated with those organizations. On October 8, 1997, the State Department released a list of 30 foreign terrorist organizations . The 1996 Antiterrorism and Effective Death Penalty Act makes it a crime to provide support to these organizations, and their members shall be denied entry visas into the United States.

On August 10, 1999, the United States froze the assets of Afghanistan's national airline under sanctions designed to punish the Taliban movement for harboring Saudi-born Islamic terrorist leader Osama Bin Laden. Apprehension of Bin Laden remains a publically announced top priority for the U.S. counter-terrorism community, despite suggestions from some that such policy focus overstates his importance, aids his recruitment efforts, neglects other foreign policy and national security priorities, and diverts resources from other counter-terrorism areas where they are badly needed. In related developments, on July 6, 1999, the United States banned trade with parts of Afghanistan controlled by the Taliban.

Economic sanctions fall into six categories: restrictions on trading, technology transfer, foreign assistance, export credits and guarantees, foreign exchange and capital transactions, and economic access. Sanctions may include a total or partial trade embargo, embargo on financial transactions, suspension of foreign aid, restrictions on aircraft or ship traffic, or abrogation of a friendship, commerce, and navigation treaty. Sanctions usually, require the cooperation of other countries to make them effective, and such cooperation is not always forthcoming.

The President has a variety of laws at his disposal, but the broadest in its potential scope is the International Emergency Economic Powers Act. The Act permits imposition of restrictions on economic relations once the President has declared a national emergency because of a threat to the U.S. national security, foreign policy, or economy. While the sanctions authorized must deal directly with the threat responsible for the emergency, the President can regulate imports, exports, and all types of financial transactions, such as the transfer of funds, foreign exchange, credit, and securities, between the United States and the country in question. Specific authority for the Libyan trade embargo is in Section 503 of the International Trade and Security Act of 1985, while Section 505 of the Act authorizes the banning of imports of goods and services from any country supporting terrorism.

Other major laws that can be used against countries sponsoring terrorism are the Export Administration Act, Arms Export Control Act, foreign assistance legislation. The Export Administration Act (Section 6(j)) allows the President to regulate export of dual use technology and prohibit or curtail the export of critical technology or other technological data. U.S. sales of technology, particularly high technology processes, have been considerable, and sales restrictions or prohibitions are known to have put pressure on states reluctant to control terrorism. Under this Act, exports of various sensitive articles to terrorism-list states are strictly controlled or prohibited because of their support of terrorism. The Arms Export Control Act authorizes the President to restrict the sale of defense articles and restrict or suspend defense services to states fostering terrorism. Foreign assistance authorization and appropriations acts deny foreign aid to countries supporting terrorism and require the U.S. to vote against loans to such countries in the multilateral developments banks. Country specific export control restrictions on munitions list items and dual use equipment apply to Iraq and Iran and are found in the Iraq Sanctions Act (Section 586 of P.L. 101-513). More recently, Executive Orders 12957 and 12959 prohibit U.S. development of Iran's oil industry and U.S. exports to — and imports from — Iran as well as third country reexport of U.S. products to the Islamic Republic. P.L. 104-172, the 1996 Iran Oil Sanction's Act prohibits U.S. trade with companies that invest more than $40 million in Iran's or Libya's petroleum development, or with companies not complying with U.N. mandated embargoes on sales of oil equipment to Libya.

On October 15, 1999, the U.N. security Council unanimously adopted a resolution imposing limited sanctions against the Taliban. The Council demanded that the Taliban turn over alleged Saudi terrorist suspect Usama bin Laden to a country where he will be effectively brought to justice. Sanctions called for include: (1) denying aircraft landing and takeoffs to and from Taliban controlled territory, and (2) freezing funds and financials resources from Taliban owned or controlled undertakings.

The United States can suspend airline service to and from a nation or deny entry to terrorists and their supporters. In 1978, the United States joined with West Germany, Canada, Britain, France, Italy, and Japan in declaring a willingness to suspend commercial airline service between any of those countries and any country harboring hijackers. Recently, efforts have been made to sanction third- countries for trading with an already sanctioned country.

Covert Action. Intelligence gathering, infiltration of terrorist groups and military operations involve a variety of clandestine or so called "covert" activities. Much of this activity is of a passive monitoring nature. A more active form of covert activity occurs during events such as a hostage crisis or hijacking when a foreign country may quietly request advice, equipment or technical support during the conduct of operations, with no public credit to be given the providing country.

Some nations have periodically gone beyond monitoring or covert support activities and resorted to unconventional methods beyond their territory for the express purpose of neutralizing individual terrorists, and/or thwarting preplanned attacks. Examples of activities might run the gamut *from* intercepting or sabotaging delivery of funding or weapons to a terrorist group *to* seizing and transporting a wanted terrorist to stand trial for assassination or murder. Arguably, such activity might be justified as preemptive self defense under Article 51 of the U.N. charter. On the other hand, it could be argued that such actions violate customary international law. Nevertheless, a July 1989 memorandum by the Department of Justice's Office of Legal Counsel advises that the President has the authority to violate customary international law and can delegate such authority to the Attorney General level, should the national interest so require.

Assassination is specifically prohibited by U.S. Executive Order (most recently, E.O. 12333), but bringing of wanted criminals to the United States for trial is not. There exists an established U.S. legal doctrine that allows an individual's trial to proceed regardless of whether he is forcefully abducted from another country, or from international waters or airspace. For example, Fawaz Yunis, a Lebanese who participated in the 1985 hijacking of a Jordanian airliner with two Americans among its 70 passengers, was lured aboard a yacht in international waters off the coast of Cyprus in 1987 by federal agents, flown to the United States for trial, and convicted.

Experts warn that bringing persons residing abroad to U.S. justice by means other than extradition or mutual agreement with the host country, i.e., by abduction and their surreptitious transportation, can vastly complicate U.S. foreign relations, perhaps jeopardizing interests far more important than "justice", deterrence, and the prosecution of a single individual. For example, the abduction of a Mexican national in 1990 to stand trial in Los Angeles on charges relating to torture and death of a DEA agent led to vehement protests from the government of Mexico, a government subsequently plagued with evidence of high level drug related corruption. Subsequently, in November 1994, the two countries signed a treaty to Prohibit Transborder Abductions. Notwithstanding the unpopularity of such abductions in nations that fail to apprehend and prosecute those accused, the "rendering" of such wanted criminals to U.S. courts is permitted under limited circumstances by a January 1993 Presidential Decision Directive issued under the Bush Administration, and reaffirmed by President Clinton. Such conduct, however, raises prospects of other nations using similar tactics against U.S. citizens.

Although conventional explosives —specifically car bombs—appear to be the terrorisn weapon of choice, the world is increasingly moving into an era in which terrorists may gain access to nuclear, chemical or biological weaponry. Faced with the potential of more frequent and higher conventional casualty levels, or a nuclear or biological holocaust, nations may be more prone to consider covert operations designed to neutralize such threats.

Rewards for Information Program. Money is a powerful motivator. Rewards for information have been instrumental in Italy in destroying the Red Brigades and in Colombia in apprehending drug cartel leaders. A State Department program is in place, supplemented by the aviation industry, offering rewards of up to $4 million to anyone providing information that would prevent or resolve an act of international terrorism against U.S. citizens or U.S. property, or that leads to the arrest or conviction of terrorist criminals involved in such acts. This program was at least partly responsible for the arrest of the unabomber, of Ramzi Ahmed Yousef, the man accused of masterminding the World Trade Center bombing and of the CIA personnel shooter, Mir Amal Kansi. The program was established by the 1984 Act to Combat International Terrorism (P.L. 98-533), and is administered by State's Diplomatic Security Service. Rewards over $250,000 must be approved by the Secretary of State. The program can pay to relocate informants, and immediate family who fear for their safety. The 1994 "crime bill" (P.L. 103-322) helps relocate aliens and immediate family members in the U.S. who are reward recipients. Expanded participation by the private sector in funding and publicizing such reward programs has been suggested by some observers.

Extradition/Law Enforcement Cooperation. International cooperation in such areas as law enforcement, customs control, and intelligence activities is an important tool in combatting international terrorism. One critical law enforcement tool in combatting international terrorism is extradition of terrorists. International extradition traditionally has been subject to several limitations, including the refusal to extradite for political or extraterritorial offenses and the refusal of some countries to extradite their nationals. The United States has been encouraging the negotiation of treaties with fewer limitations, in part as a means of facilitating the transfer of wanted terrorists. Because much terrorism involves politically motivated violence, the Department of State has recently sought to curtail the availability of the political offense exception, found in many extradition treaties, to avoid extradition.

Military Force. Although not without difficulties, military force, particularly when wielded by a superpower such as the United States, can carry substantial clout. Proponents of selective use of military force usually emphasize the military's unique skills and specialized equipment. The April 1986 decision to bomb Libya for its alleged role in the bombing of a German discotheque exemplifies use military force. Other examples are: (1) the 1993 bombing of Iraq's military intelligence headquarters by U.S. forces in response to Iraqi efforts to assassinate former president George Bush during a visit to Kuwait and (2) the August 1998 missile attacks against bases in Afghanistan and a chemical production facility in Sudan.

Concerns about the terrorist threat prompted an extensive buildup of the military's counter-terrorist organization. A special unit known as "Delta Force" at Fort Bragg, NC, has been organized to perform anti-terrorist operations when needed. Details about the unit are secret, but estimates are that it has about 800 assigned personnel. The failure of the April 1980 Iran rescue mission and the October 1983 bombing of the U.S. Marine headquarters in Beirut raised questions about the adequacy of the training and equipment of regular military units for use against terrorists.

Use of military force presupposes the ability to identify a terrorist group or sponsor and its location, knowledge often unavailable to law enforcement officials. For example, to date, those investigating the September 1995 wave of bombings in Paris as well as the rocket grenade attack on the U.S. embassy in Moscow, have not been able to link these incidents to a specific individual, group or state-sponsor. Moreover, such efforts, as in the case of the Pan-Am 103 bombing, may take up to a year or more, and still there will be those who cast doubt on the findings. Policymakers using military instruments seek public support. Such support tends to be strongest during or immediately after an incident when outrage is still widespread, emotional and hot. Risks include (1) military casualties or captives, (2) foreign civilian casualties, (3) retaliation and escalation by terrorist groups, (4) holding the wrong parties responsible, (5) sympathy for the "bullied" victim, and (6) perception that the U.S. ignores rules of international law.

P.L. 104-264 includes a sense of the Senate statement that if evidence suggests "beyond a clear and reasonable doubt" that an act of hostility against any U.S. citizen was a terrorist act sponsored, organized, condoned or directed by any nation, then a state of war should be considered to exist between the United States and that nation.

International Conventions. International conventions are considered an integral part of international law and as such contribute actively to the making and conduct of international policy. In the area of terrorism, such conventions define a consensus view of what constitute internationally recognized crimes; what obligations nations have to protect against and prosecute those committing those crimes; and what mechanisms and procedures shall be utilized to guarantee prosecution and enhance overall cooperation to achieve the goals of each specific convention. To date, the United States has joined with the world community in developing all of the major anti- terrorism conventions. These conventions impose on their signatories an obligation either to prosecute offenders or extradite them to permit prosecution for a host of terrorism-related crimes including hijacking vessels and aircraft, taking hostages, and harming diplomats. An important new convention not yet in force is the Convention for the Marking of Plastic Explosives. Implementing legislation is in P.L. 104-132.

Potential Tools

An International Court for Terrorism. Each year bills are introduced urging that an international court be established, perhaps under the U.N., to sit in permanent session to adjudicate cases against persons accused of international terrorist crimes. The court would have broad powers to sentence and punish anyone convicted of such crimes. Critics point out many administrative and procedural problems associated with establishing such a court and making it work, including jurisdictional and enforcement issues. An International Court of Justice in the Hague exists, but it deals with disputes between states and lacks compulsory jurisdiction and enforcement powers.

Media Self-Restraint. For some, the term "media self-restraint" is an oxymoron; the sensational scoop is the golden fleece and dull copy is to be avoided. While some of the media struggle to maintain objectivity, they are occasionally manipulated into the role of mediator and often that of publicist of terrorist goals. Though not an international incident, the publication of the unabomber's "manifesto" illustrated this. Notably, there have been attempts by the media to impose its own rules when covering terrorist incidents. Standards established by the Chicago Sun-Times and Daily News include paraphrasing terrorist demands to avoid unbridled propaganda; banning participation of reporters in negotiations with terrorists; coordinating coverage through supervising editors who are in contact with police authorities; providing thoughtful, restrained, and credible coverage of stories; and allowing only senior supervisory editors to determine what, if any, information should be withheld or deferred. Such standards are far from uniformly accepted. In an intensely competitive profession consisting of a multinational worldwide press corps, someone is likely to break the story. See CRS Report 97-960, *Terrorism, the Media, and the Government: Perspectives, Trends and Options for Policymakers.*

U.S. Organization and Program Response

The chain of command on anti-terrorism planning runs from the President through the National Security Council, a representative of which chairs a Senior Interagency Coordinating Group (ICG) on Terrorism. The State Department is designated the lead agency for countering terrorism overseas; the Justice Department's Federal Bureau of Investigation (FBI) is the lead agency for domestic terrorism; and the Federal Aviation Administration is the lead for hijackings when a plane's doors are closed. These roles were reaffirmed by Presidential Decision Directive (PDD) No. 39 in June 1995. PDD 62 (Protection Against Unconventional Threats) and PDD 63 (Critical Infrastructure Protection) of May 22, 1998: (1) established within the NSC a National Coordinator for Security, Infrastructure Protection, and Counterterrorism who also provides "advice" regarding the counterterrorism budget; (2)

established within the NSC two Senior Directors who report to the National Coordinator —one for infrastructure protection and one for counterterrorism; (3) established a new inter-agency working group primarily focused on domestic preparedness for WMD incidents; and (4) laid out the architecture for critical infrastructure protection. Intelligence information among the various agencies is coordinated by an Intelligence Committee, chaired by a representative of the CIA. An important policy question is whether current organizational structure brings excessive focus on state- sponsored actions at the expense of attention on so-called "gray area" terrorist activity (i.e. terrorist activity not clearly linked to any perpetrator, group, or supporting/sponsoring nation). In light of recent trends in terrorist activity, some suggest an independent comprehensive review of counter-terrorism policy, organizational structure, and preparedness to respond to major terrorist incidents in the United States is warranted. Whether PDD 62, by establishing a national terrorism coordinator at the NSC, takes too much of the terrorism decisionmaking process out of the realm of congressional oversight is another issue as NSC members generally do not testify before Congress.

A number of Administration programs focus specifically on combatting international terrorism. They include the Department of State's (1) Anti-Terrorism Assistance Program (ATA), (2) Counter-Terrorism Research and Development Program, and (3) Diplomatic Security Program. The DOD Authorization Act (Title XIV) for FY1997 (P.L. 104-201) seeks to ensure DOD assistance to federal, state, and local officials in responding to biological, chemical and nuclear emergencies..

On January 22, 1999, President Clinton announced a $10 billion initiative to address terrorism. Included are $1.4 billion to protect against chemical and biological terrorism and $1.46 billion to protect critical systems from cyber and other attacks.

Anti-Terrorism Assistance Program

The State Department's anti-terrorism assistance program provides training and equipment to foreign countries to help them improve their anti-terrorism capabilities. More than 16,000 individuals from 83 countries have received training since the program's inception in 1983 in such skills as crisis management, VIP protection, airport security management, and bomb detection and deactivation. The Administration's FY1998 $18 million request for this program was fully funded at $19 million; the FY1999 request totaled $21 million and was funded at $41 million (which included $20 million from a FY 1999 emergency security supplemental appropriations), and the FY 2000 request is $23 million.

Counter-Terrorism Research and Development Program

The State Department's Counter-Terrorism Research and Development Program, which is jointly funded by the Departments of State and Defense, constitutes a response to combat the threat posed by increasingly sophisticated equipment and explosives available to terrorist groups. Recent projects include detectors for nuclear materials, decontaminants for chemical and biological weapons, law enforcement and intelligence database software and surveillance technology. The State Department's FY1997- FY2000 budget requests for these programs totaled $1.8 million annually, down $2 million from FY1996. Congress appropriated the $1.8 million requested for FY1997-FY1999. DOD's FY1997 request for the counterterrorism technical support program totaled $16.5 million and P.L. 104-208 appropriated this amount plus an additional $6 million for pulse fast neutron analysis (PFNA) detection technology development. For FY1998 Congress appropriated $27.5 million and added $9 million for PFNA, facial recognition technology and anti-biological devices. The FY1999 DOD request was $35.8 million with $38.3 million appropriated plus an additional $2.5 million for facial recognition technology. The FY2000 request totaled $52.2 with a $54.8 million request projected for FY2001.

Diplomatic Security Program

The Diplomatic Security Program of the State Department is designed to protect U.S. personnel, information and facilities abroad. Providing security guards and counterintelligence awareness are important elements of the program. Detection and investigation of passport and visa fraud is another component of the program.

The Administration's FY 2000 request for the Diplomatic Security Program is $226.514 million which is roughly equal to the FY1999 request of $226.8 million which was funded at $215,132, and which is somewhat down down from the FY1998 request of $235.2 million which was funded at $217 million. One component of the broader program provides protection of international organizations, foreign missions and officials under the Foreign Missions Act of 1982. Security enhancement for U.S. embassies is funded through the "Acquisition and Maintenance of Buildings Abroad" account. For FY1998 $371.1 million was requested and $397.9 million was appropriated. The FY1999 request was $640.8 million with $1,030.6 million appropriated. The larger amount is attributable to the FY1999 Emergency Supplemental appropriations.

The State Department's FY 2000 request to Congress includes $568 million for embassy security (See: CRS Report No. 98-771 F: *Embassy Security: Background, Funding, and the FY2000 Budget*, by Susan B. Epstein). The Administration included in its State Department request an advance appropriation of $3 billion for FY 20001-FY 2005. Beginning with a FY 2001 baseline of $300 million, the Administration will allocate these funds in additional $150 million increments each year ending with $900 million for FY 2005.

Options for Program Enhancement

Numerous options have been proposed to improve the effectiveness of programs designed to combat terrorism. Some notable areas cited for improvement include contingency planning; explosives detection; joint or multinational research, operational and training programs/exercises; nuclear materials safeguarding; and disaster consequence management. Some have suggested that U.S. public diplomacy/media programs could be broadened to support anti-terrorism policy objectives. Cyber security remains an important area for program enhancement. On January 9, 2000, the Administration released a comprehensive plan to combat cyber-terrorism including $2 billion in proposed spending next year to make the nation's computer systems less vulnerable to attack. Plan elements include: (1) enhanced funding for research and development; (2) creation of an ROTC-type corps of information specialists; and (3) creation of a national institute charged with forging a research partnership with the private sector.

State-Supported Terrorism

The Secretary of State maintains a list of countries that have "repeatedly provided support for acts of international terrorism". Data supporting this list is drawn from the intelligence community. Listed countries are subject to severe U.S. export controls — particularly of dual use technology and selling them military equipment is prohibited. Providing foreign aid under the Foreign Assistance Act is also prohibited. Section 6(j) of the 1979 Export Administration Act stipulates that a validated license shall be required for export of controlled items and technology to any country on the list, and that the Secretaries of Commerce and State must notify the House Committee on Foreign Affairs, and both the Senate Committees on Banking, Housing, and Urban Affairs, and Foreign Relations, at least 30 days before issuing any validated license required by this Act. In addition, Section 509(a) of the 1986 omnibus anti-terrorism act (P.L. 99-399) bars export of munitions list items to countries on the terrorism list.

Adding and Removing Countries on the List

In late January each year, under the provisions of Section 6(j) of the Export Administration Act of 1979, as amended, the Secretary of Commerce in consultation with the Secretary of State provides Congress with a list of countries supporting terrorism. Compilation of the list is the result of an ongoing process. Throughout the year the Department of State gathers data on terrorist activity worldwide, and then beginning about November, the list is formally reviewed. Each new determination under Section 6(j) of the Act must also be published in the Federal Register.

Congressional report language provides guidelines to facilitate designation. A House Foreign Affairs Committee report approving the Anti-Terrorism and Arms Export Amendments Act of 1989 (H.Rept. 101-296) included as criteria (1) allowing territory to be used as a sanctuary; (2) furnishing lethal substances to individuals/groups with the likelihood that they will be used for terrorism; (3) providing logistical support to terrorists/groups; (4) providing safe haven or headquarters for terrorists/organizations; (5) planning, directing, training or assisting in the execution of terrorist activities; (6) providing direct or indirect financial support for terrorist activities; and (7) providing diplomatic facilities such as support or documentation to aid or abet terrorist activities. A Senate report had similar criteria (S.Rept. 101-173).

Paragraph 6(j)(4) of the Export Administration Act prohibits removing a country from the list unless the President first submits a report to the committees mentioned above. When a government comes to power (i.e., a government different from that in power at the time of the last determination), the President's report, submitted before the proposed rescission would take effect, must certify that (1) there has been a fundamental change in the leadership and policies of the government of the country concerned (this means an actual change of government as a result of an election, coup, or some other means); (2) the new government is not supporting acts of international terrorism; and (3) the new government has provided assurances that it will not support acts of international terrorism in the future. When the same government is in power, the President's report — **submitted at least 45 days before the proposed rescission would take effect** — must justify the rescission and certify that, (1) the government concerned has not provided support for international terrorism during the preceding 6-month period; and (2) the government concerned has provided assurances that it will not support acts of international terrorism in the future. Congress can let the President's action take effect, or pass legislation to block it, the latter most likely over the President's veto. To date Congress has passed no such legislation or resolution, although Syria would be the likely target of such endeavors, should the Administration prematurely seek its removal from the terrorism list.

Countries on the List

There are currently seven countries on the "terrorism list": Cuba, Iran, Iraq, Libya, North Korea, Sudan and Syria. (For further information on states sponsoring international terrorism, see *Patterns of Global Terrorism*, Department of State, April 1999.) Of the seven, five are Middle Eastern nations with predominantly Muslim populations. (See CRS Report 98-722, *Terrorism: Middle Eastern Groups and State Sponsors*.) Of these, Iran and Iraq could currently be characterized on one extreme as active supporters of terrorism: nations that use terrorism as an instrument of policy or warfare beyond their borders. Iran, Iraq, and Libya are major oil producers, holding 17% of the world's remaining oil and producing, in 1994, 5.5% of the world's oil supply, 31% of Europe's (OECD) oil consumption, and 9% of Japan's. Such dependence on oil complicates universal support for sanctions against these nations.

On the other extreme one might place countries such as Cuba or North Korea, which at the height of the Cold War were more active, but in recent years have seemed to settle for a more passive role of granting ongoing safe haven to previously admitted individual terrorists. Closer to the middle of an active/passive spectrum is Libya, which grants safe haven to wanted terrorists. Syria, though not formally detected in an active role since 1986, reportedly uses groups in Syria and Lebanon to project power into Israel and allows groups to train in territory under its control, placing it somewhere in the middle to active end of the spectrum. And Sudan, which allows sites for training, remains an enigma. Although Sudan has been considered primarily a passive supporter, charges have been made that Sudan was actively involved in a 1995 attempt to assassinate Egyptian President Hosni Mubarak.

A complex challenge facing those charged with compiling and maintaining the list is the degree to which diminution of hard evidence of a government's active involvement indicates a real change in behavior, particularly when a past history of active support or use of terrorism as an instrument of foreign policy has been well established. Removing a country from the list is likely to result in some level of confrontation with Congress, so the bureaucratically easier solution is to maintain the status quo, or add to the list, but not to delete from it.

Iran. The U.S. government no longer publically names Iran as the most active state sponsor of terrorism and the major state-sponsored threat to U.S. interests worldwide. Iran, however, continues to be deeply involved in the planning and execution of terrorist acts by its own agents and surrogate groups. It provides ongoing direction, safehaven, funding, training, weapons and other support to a variety of radical Islamic terrorist groups including Hizballah in Lebanon, as well as Hammas and Palestinian Islamic Jihad (PIJ) to undermine the Middle East peace process. There are press reports that Iran is building a terrorist infrastructure in the region by providing political indoctrination, military training, and financial help to dissident Shia groups in neighboring countries, including Kuwait, Bahrain, and Saudi Arabia. Iran has reportedly concentrated efforts to make Sudan a center for terrorist training and activities and reportedly continues to conduct assassinations of writers and political dissidents beyond its borders. Iran was placed on the terrorism list in January of 1984. President Clinton has halted U.S. trade with Iran and barred U.S. companies from any involvement in the Iranian oil sector.

The threat perceived from Iran as a leading supporter of terrorism is substantially raised by reports that Iran is acquiring nuclear technology and seeking nuclear weapons technology.

Iraq. On September 13, 1990, Iraq was placed once again on the terrorism list, after having been removed in 1982. Iraq's ability to instigate terror has been curbed by U.S. and U.N. sanctions which were imposed after the Kuwait invasion. Nevertheless, the State Department's 1999 global terrorism report indicates that Saddam Hussein's regime continues to murder dissidents and provide a safehaven for a variety of Palestinian rejectionist groups. There are numerous claims that the Iraqi intelligence is behind killings and at least one planned bombing during 1988. Moreover, the leader of the Abu Nidal organization may have relocated to Baghdad in late 1998. In the past, Iraq has temporarily expelled terrorists, only to invite them back later.

Libya. Libya has a long history of involvement in international terrorism. Libya was placed on the terrorism list when it was started in December 1979 and approximately $1 billion in bank deposits belonging to Libya are frozen by the United States. Libyan terrorism has been sharply reduced after imposition of U.N. sanctions in the wake of Libyan involvement in the bombings of Pan Am flight 103 and in the 1989 bombing of French UTA flight 772 which killed 170 persons including seven Americans. Evidence suggests Libya has not abandoned its support for international terrorism as an instrument of foreign policy, and it still refuses to hand over some accused of terrorist acts. Throughout 1998, Libya continued to support groups opposed to the Mid-East peace process that engage in violence. Nevertheless, the response of the international community and U.S. Congress (P.L. 104-172) seems to have been relatively effective in restraining the level of Libya's outlaw behavior and may provide one model for future international action. There is no evidence of Libyan involvement in recent acts of international terrorism.

Syria. Syria was placed on the first terrorism list in December 1979. It is generally believed within the western community that Syria has a long history of using terrorists to advance its own interests. The United States has said that it has no evidence of Syrian government direct involvement in terrorism since 1986. Informed sources suggest, however, that the Syrian government remains active, hiding behind the sophisticated operational level of their intelligence services and their ability to mask such involvement. Many major terrorist groups are known to maintain an active presence [including training camps and operational headquarters] in Syria or in Syrian-controlled Lebanon and Syria has allowed Iran to supply Hizballah with weaponry via Damascus. Providing such support and safe haven has caused prominent Members of Congress to contend that Syria should remain on the terrorism list, and Administration spokespersons have firmly maintained in testimony before Congress that until this problem is resolved, Syria will remain on the list. In contrast, many observers speculate that the Administration has made it clear to Syria that it will take steps to remove Syria from the list should a peace treaty with Israel be signed. Some observers argue that Syria should continue to be subject to U.S. sanctions because of involvement in drug trafficking by some of its ruling elites and their alleged involvement in counterfeiting of U.S. currency.

Sudan. Sudan was added to the terrorism list in August 1993. Sudan continues to harbor members of some of the world's most violent organizations and according to the State

Department's 1999 global terrorism report continues to serve as a refuge, nexus, and training hub for a number of terrorist organizations including, Hizballah, Hamas, and Bin Laden's al-Qaida organization. Egypt and Ethiopia have charged the Sudanese government with involvement in a failed assassination attempt against President Hosni Mubarak while in Ethiopia in June 1995. On September 11, 1995, the Organization for African Unity (OAU), in an unprecedented action criticizing a member, passed a resolution calling on Sudan to extradite to Ethiopia, three suspects charged in the assassination attempt. The U.N. Security Council has also demanded extradition of the three suspects. Sudan, continues to permit its territory to be used by Iran to transport weapons to Islamic extremist groups and as a meeting place for Iranian-backed terrorist groups.

Cuba. Fidel Castro's government has a long history of providing arms and training to terrorist organizations. A cold war carryover, Cuba was added to the 1982 U.S. list of countries supporting international terrorism based on its support for the M-19 guerrilla organization in Columbia. The 1999 State Department Global Terrorism report does not cite evidence that Cuban officials were directly involved in sponsoring an act of terrorism in 1998, but notes that Havana remains a safe haven to several international terrorists. The report noted that Cuba no longer actively supports armed struggles in Latin America or elsewhere. Nevertheless, Havana continues to maintain close ties to other state sponsors of terrorism and leftist insurgent groups in Latin America. Havana has not formally renounced political support for groups that engage in terrorism.

North Korea. North Korea was added to the "official" list of countries supporting terrorism because of its implication in the bombing of a South Korean airliner on November 29, 1987, which killed 115 persons. According to the State Department, North Korea is not conclusively linked to any terrorist acts since 1987. A North Korean spokesman in 1993 condemned all forms of terrorism, and said his country resolutely opposed the encouragement and support of terrorism. A similar statement was made in November 1995. Nevertheless, North Korea continues to provide political sanctuary to members of a group that hijacked a Japan Airlines flight in 1970 and may be linked to the murder of a South Korean diplomat in Vladivostoc in 1996.

An Informal Watchlist?

Some suggest that there is utility in drawing to Congress' attention countries that do not currently qualify for inclusion in the terrorism list but where added scrutiny may be warranted. Such a list would be similar to the Attorney General's National Security Threat List which includes sponsors of international terrorism, the activities of which warrant monitoring by the FBI within the United States. Although informal, it would no doubt be controversial and speculative. Nevertheless, it would reflect legitimate concerns of those in the intelligence and policy community and might serve as an informal warning mechanism to countries that their activities are being scrutinized. For example, the State Department warned Pakistan in January 1993 that it was under "active continuing review" to determine whether it should be placed on the terrorism list. When the list came out in April, 1993, Pakistan was not on it. (See CRS Issue Brief IB94041, *Pakistan-U.S. Relations*.) Sudan was also warned that it was being subjected to special review prior to its being placed on the terrorism list in August 1993.

Currently, some informally discussed candidates for such a list include (1) **Afghanistan** — concerns are that Islamic fundamentalist terrorists continue to train and operating out of the country and/or enter or exit with impunity, and more specifically that the Taliban continues to offer sanctuary to Osama bin Laden and his associated terror networks (2) **Pakistan** — concerns are that support may be provided: (a) to militant separatists in Kashmir and Punjab some of whom have reportedly vowed revenge for comrades killed in U.S. missile attacks on terrorist training camps in Afghanistan, and (b) to those who have tried to use Pakistani territory for bases and training.   (3) **Yugoslavia** — concerns exist over potential use of terrorism in reaction to NATO military operations. Another concern is that militant Iranian elements remaining in the territory of the former Yugoslavia may resort to terrorist violence against European nations and the United States.

Legislative Initiatives

The FY1999 Omnibus Consolidated and Emergency Supplemental Appropriations Act (**P.L. 105-277**), adopted by Congress on October 21, 1998, included appropriationsfor a number of measures to counter terrorism. Under Foreign Operations (Sec.101), some $200 million were provided for anti-terrorism and anti-proliferation efforts. The Act provided over $2.4 billion in emergency supplementals for anti-terrorism and embassy security. It established a Counterterrorism Fund of $145 million to reimburse the Department of Justice costs for preparing for and dealing with terrorist threats, especially involving weapons of mass destruction. Under Foreign Affairs Restructuring and Reform, the Act establishes within the Department of State, the position of Coordinator for Counterterrorism to supervise international counterterrorism activities. The Omnibus Act establishes a 10-member National Commission on Terrorism, to be appointed by the House and Senate, including experts on terrorism, to review policies on prevention and punishment of terrorist acts. The Commission is to issue a final report within 6 months of its first meeting.

Foreign Policy of the United States
Volume 1

ELECTION MONITORING: THE ROLE OF INTERNATIONAL OBSERVERS AND GENERAL GUIDELINES FOR OBSERVATION

Mark P. Sullivan

SUMMARY

This report examines two topics, the role of international election observers and some general guidelines for monitoring elections abroad. It draws from the proceedings of a Congressional Research Service (CRS) workshop on Monitoring Foreign Elections held on April 11, 1994.[1] The workshop's principal speaker was Richard Soudriette, Director of the International Foundation for Electoral Systems (IFES). In addition, several CRS analysts who have served as election observers shared their experiences at the workshop.

International observers serve the following four functions: to help confer legitimacy on elections; to help discourage fraud; to provide moral support for the democratic process; and to provide an opportunity for electoral officials to learn from and share information and practices with electoral officials from other countries. Guidelines for international observation include responsibilities in three areas: advanced preparation, the observation process itself, and the evaluation process. Advanced preparation prior to election day, including knowledge of a country's electoral law, is a common denominator for an effective observer mission. With regard to the observation process, important duties include the responsibilities to maintain strict impartiality and not to interfere in the electoral process. Regarding the evaluation process, elections cannot be evaluated solely on the success of voting day activities, but rather, additional aspects of the electoral process should be examined in order to assess its overall success.

INTRODUCTION

While a variety of international observer groups have been involved in monitoring the fairness of elections worldwide since the late 1940s, election monitoring has increased considerably since the end of the Cold War. The high-profile 1986 elections in the Philippines -- where President Ferdinand Marcos was ousted after widespread electoral fraud -- also spurred the development of election observation activities. In

---

[1] Highlights of the workshop proceedings are available from CRS on tape. See: CRS Audio Brief 50300, *Monitoring Foreign Elections,* by the Foreign Affairs and National Defense Division.

recent years, the United Nations has increased its involvement in monitoring foreign elections, including Nicaragua and Haiti in 1990, Angola in 1992, Cambodia in 1993, and most recently El Salvador and South Africa in 1994.[2]   Other international organizations such as the Organization of American States and the Conference on Security and Cooperation in Europe have increased their monitoring activities in recent years.

The United States increasingly has supported the monitoring of foreign elections as part of its support for the development of electoral processes in developing countries and/or formerly nondemocratic regimes.[3]   The U.S. Agency for International Development and the National Endowment for Democracy have financed the monitoring of foreign elections by such groups as the National Democratic Institute for International Affairs, the International Republican Institute, the International Foundation for Electoral Systems, and the Carter Center at Emory University.

ROLE OF INTERNATIONAL OBSERVERS

IFES Director Richard Soudriette identified four main reasons for having international observers: to help confer legitimacy on elections; help discourage fraud; provide moral support for the democratic process; and provide an opportunity for electoral officials to learn from and share information and practices with electoral officials from other countries.

In terms of conferring legitimacy, many countries judge that observers help send a message out to the world that they have just held free and fair elections. The Council of Europe notes that the term "free and fair elections" has become a hallowed phrase worldwide.   Indeed, many international agreements incorporate the concept of democratic elections. According to Article 25 (c) of the International Covenant on Civil and Political Rights, "every citizen shall have the right and the opportunity...to vote and to be elected at genuine periodic elections which shall be by universal and equal suffrage and shall be held by secret ballot, guaranteeing the free expression of the will of the electors."

The presence of observers can discourage people from becoming involved in practices that could be considered fraudulent. Mr. Soudriette cautioned, however, that electoral observers should not make "snap decisions" on whether there is or is not fraud, based on being in a country for just one or two days. He commented that an observer must prepare before the election by reviewing and reading material about the election process, including information on the electoral list and the system for controlling multiple voting. Mr. Soudriette noted, "only amateurs steal elections on election day" so it is imperative to prepare and have a thorough knowledge of the electoral process.

---

[2] For further information see: Stoelting, David. The Challenge of UN-Monitored Elections in Independent Nations. *Stanford Journal of International Law*. V. 28, Spring 1992. pp. 371-424. LRS 92-11507.

[3] For further information, see CRS Report 94-349 F, *Foreign Election Monitoring by the United States: A Brief Survey*, by Ellen C. Collier. April 21, 1994. 6 p.

A third reason for the presence of observers is that they provide moral support for the democratic process, with the effect of encouraging people to get out and vote. The presence of observers can have a calming effect on the political environment, even in cases when there have been reports circulating about potential violence. As an example, Mr. Soudriette pointed to the case of the May 1993 elections in Cambodia where the presence of observers was a significant factor in giving people the courage to come out on election day despite reports that the Khmer Rouge was going to attack voters.

A fourth, and often downplayed, reason for having international election observers is the opportunity for electoral officials to learn and share experiences with their counterparts from other countries. Often international observer teams include current or past election officials, people with substantial expertise that will be able to make significant contributions to the observation process. Mr. Soudriette cited the example of the 1994 elections in El Salvador where after the first electoral round in March, observers who served as election officials in their own countries were able to make helpful suggestions to the Supreme Election Tribunal in El Salvador, which agreed to implement the suggestions for the second electoral round in April. The opportunity to learn and share can be a significant aspect of election observation.

GENERAL GUIDELINES FOR OBSERVATION

The following discussion examines general guidelines for monitoring elections in foreign countries that were either raised in the April 1994 CRS workshop or addressed in literature on election monitoring. These guidelines can be divided into three categories: preparation, observation, and evaluation.

Preparation. A common denominator for an effective observer mission is advanced preparation prior to election day. The organization sponsoring the observer group is responsible for preparing the *terms of reference* for the electoral mission. These terms of reference should include an explanation of the objectives of the mission and provide guidance to the observers on the specific election and election environment. Observers should be familiar with the basic electoral law of the country. In many countries, election handbooks or other instruction material that is developed for elections officials or pollworkers prove to be invaluable to election observers in understanding the mechanics of the voting process in the particular country. Observer missions might include individuals who are familiar with the politics and culture of the country being observed as well as individuals who have worked in electoral administration in their own countries.

The sponsoring organization of the electoral mission should provide observers with background information on the countries to be visited, including information on the country's history, current political developments, and electoral processes, as well as advice about climate and living conditions in the country. Ideally, observers should be conversant in the language of the country being observed, but if not, arrangements should be made by the sponsoring organization for translators. The sponsoring organization also generally sets up briefings for the observers prior to election day in the country being observed, including meetings with government officials, political party leaders and candidates, electoral officials, and representatives of organizations such as labor unions and human rights organizations. An observer at the 1986 Philippines elections stressed the importance of observers learning about the local social and political conditions of areas where they will be assigned. In many cases, observers may be assigned to areas of the host country where conditions vary considerably from conditions in the capital city. U.S. press coverage of foreign countries often focuses on conditions in the capital. This may be misleading to observers who are deployed to outlying regions where conditions might be quite different.

Observation. A basic responsibility for observers of foreign elections is to obtain official *credentials* from the host country. In most cases, the country's electoral body is the institution which provides these credentials, often in the form of official identifications such as badges or arm bands. On election day, when observers are visiting polling sites, it is necessary for observers to identify themselves to polling officials before beginning to take notes or ask questions of voters or other acts of observation. This is essentially an act of common courtesy and an action that should prevent misunderstandings that could arise.

In some host countries, the government or the electoral body supervising the elections will prepare a *code of conduct* for the behavior of observers. For example, in the 1994 South African elections, the government prepared a code of conduct which set forth the responsibilities of the international observers. These obligations, which are similar to requirements for observers in many countries, included: maintaining strict impartiality; prominently displaying identification as an observer; refraining from wearing clothing or carrying material that might denote support for or opposition to any political party; attending special briefings, training workshops, and other meetings for observers; and refraining from giving direct or indirect assistance to any party or person in connection with the elections.

One of the most important obligations of electoral observers is the responsibility not to interfere in the electoral process or to dictate to electoral officials or voters in any way what they should be doing. The Council of Europe maintains that observers, while questioning and commenting, should not criticize or hinder the electoral process. There should be complete impartiality on the part of the observer so as not to give the impression of interference. This neutrality, along with an amiable (or at least non-judgmental) and cooperative demeanor, will help the observer gain the confidence of electoral officials and the public.

Another responsibility for the observer is making sure not to bring any cultural biases that might shade his or her view of the election process. According to the National Democratic Institute for International Affairs, while there are broad international standards for free and fair elections, "at the same time, each electoral process must be evaluated in the context of a country's history, politics and culture."[4] An observer at El Salvador's 1984 elections noted that some observers were dismayed when they first saw that the Salvadorans were using clear plastic ballot boxes. After talking to voters, however, the observers realized that Salvadorans were enthusiastic

---

[4] Stoddard, Michael D. Evaluating Elections: Basic Principle and Issues and Selected Case Studies. National Democratic Institute for International Affairs. March 1994. p. 1.

tnat it could be seen that the boxes were indeed empty when polling places first opened.

The organization sponsoring the observer group usually provides some type of form or checklist to observers to be filled out for each polling site visited on election day. The purpose is to be able to construct an accurate and consistent form of reporting so that the observer group as a whole will be able to evaluate information from polling sites around the country.

Information that might be included on such a checklist includes: the region or town of the polling site; the name of the polling station; the time visited; the number of registered voters at the polling station and the number who have already voted; whether the polling station was laid out to ensure secrecy for the voter; whether election materials and equipment (such as ballots, ballot boxes, indelible ink, stamps and stamp pads, etc.) were present and sufficient; whether the atmosphere at the polling station was orderly and peaceful; whether electoral officials were present and well trained; whether there was representation of all political parties at the polling stations; whether there was any campaigning inside the polling station; whether ballot boxes were adequately protected against tampering; whether police or security forces were present at the polling station; or whether there were any problems with people not being able to vote because of either not being on the voting list or not having proper voting credentials.

An observer should also be present at the counting process once the polling station is closed. Details to be observed during the counting process include the following: whether there was a sufficient number of election officials to conduct the count and were they well trained; whether the number of ballots in the ballots boxes matched the overall number of electors who voted at that polling station; the process of how ballots are deemed to be invalid or spoiled; the security of the ballots during all stages of the vote count; and the procedure in which the result of the count is announced and transmitted to the appropriate electoral authorities.

Evaluation. According to a handbook published by the Council of Europe,[5] observers are responsible for evaluating whether the election meets the following ten requirements: 1) the administration of the election was fair and impartial; 2) citizens who wanted to participate in the election process, either as a candidate or a voter, were not improperly restricted; 3) freedom of movement, assembly, association and expression were respected during the election campaign; 4) freedom for political parties to conduct peaceful political activity was respected during the campaign period; 5) all political parties conducted their political activities within the law; 6) political parties and other groups taking part in the election had unbiased access to the press, radio, and television to advertise and express their views; 7) political parties had equal security during the campaign; 8) voters were able to cast their ballots freely and without fear or undue influence; 9) the secrecy of the ballot was maintained; and 10) arrangements for voting and counting the vote followed satisfactory standards to avoid fraud and to secure a free and fair election.

---

[5] Council of Europe. Handbook for Observers of Elections. Strasbourg, France. 1992. p. 7.

As suggested by this list, elections cannot be evaluated solely on the success of voting day activities. There are several components of an election that should be examined in order to assess the overall electoral process. These consist of: the election framework (including the electoral system and election law that should ensure the concept of fairness); voter registration and eligibility; candidate registration and eligibility; the campaign period, including resources, administration and enforcement of election rules, equal access to the media, and voter education; election day, including both voting and counting; and the review process or the mechanism for filing complaints and appeals.

Some election monitoring groups choose to focus solely on the mechanics of the vote and vote count process rather than the overall electoral environment. This approach may be warranted if other monitoring groups or organizations already have made assessments of the pre-election period and environment. However, if such assessments have not been made, the observer group focussing exclusively on election day activities runs the risk of not being to appraise accurately the degree to which the overall election process was fair.

The final responsibility of an observer group is to issue a statement or report on its findings. According to the International Human Rights Law Group, a public statement should be issued promptly in cases where it "may deter attempts by the authorities to manipulate the electoral process" or in cases where it "may inhibit ill-founded challenges to valid election results."[6] Before issuing a statement, however, it is important that there is a consensus among the members of the observer group. Consultation among the members of the observation group should help distinguish between isolated instances of irregularities that observers might have witnessed and any systemic irregularities or attempt at fraud. Consultation should also help avoid making any inaccurate snap judgements of the electoral process.

---

[6] Garber, Larry. Guidelines for International Election Observing. The International Human Rights Law Group. Washington D.C. 1984 (3rd printing 1990). p. 19.

Foreign Policy of the United States
Volume 1

ECONOMIC SANCTIONS TO ACHIEVE U.S. FOREIGN POLICY GOALS: DISCUSSION AND GUIDE TO CURRENT LAW

Dianne E. Rennack

Robert D. Shuey

ABSTRACT

This report provides background on foreign policy sanctions. It addresses the following questions: Why do we apply sanctions? What objectives does the U.S. government seek to achieve when it imposes sanctions? Who imposes sanctions? What tools are available? How likely is it that sanctions will achieve the stated goal? What secondary consequences might sanctions have? What change is required for the sanctions to be lifted? Would multilateral sanctions be more desirable and achievable? The report also provides an uncomplicated map of where sanctions policies and options currently may be found in U.S. law. This report will be updated as events warrant.

Summary

As the close of the 106ᵗʰ Congress, 1ˢᵗ session, nears, there are last-minute efforts to place one or more sanctions measures into a bill that has its own momentum. H.R. 434, the African Growth and Opportunity Act, is under consideration to carry a variety of trade-related amendments. It has been mentioned in the press as a possible vehicle for S. 757, the Sanctions Policy Reform Act. It is also possible that H.R. 434 could advance "Food and Medicine for the World Act." The Senate agreed to food and medicine exemption language earlier in the session; that language was excised from the agriculture appropriations bill in conference. A new version of the bill has been introduced as S. 1771 in the Senate and as H.R. 3140 in the House.

The 106ᵗʰ Congress has under consideration more than 100 bills or joint resolutions to impose new sanctions, ease current regimes, or overhaul the entire process that the legislative and executive branches employ when considering the use of sanctions. Of these, enactment of the "Enhancement of Trade, Security, and Human Rights Through Sanctions Reform Act," H.R. 1244, or its counterpart, the "Sanctions Policy Reform Act," S. 757, could most change the way the United States uses sanctions as a foreign policy tool. The bills seek to clarify the use of unilateral sanctions in U.S. foreign. The bills revise procedures both branches follow before enacting or imposing sanctions, and require extensive reporting on expected costs and benefits of sanctions. The Administration and many Members of Congress have spoken in favor of some sort of overhaul; there are serious points of disagreement, however, between the two branches, particularly when new proposals seek to reduce the President's flexibility in using sanctions as a foreign policy tool.

Some suggest that there is a post-Cold War trend toward sanctions becoming the method of first resort in foreign policy. Others contend that sanctions, unilateral or otherwise, are a peacetime means to improving international behavior in important areas such as human rights or weapons proliferation, and should not be avoided solely for trade concerns. Particular attention is paid to the domestic impact of sanctions. A frequently cited report issued by the Institute for International Economic (April 1997) concludes that U.S. unilateral sanctions may have cost U.S. businesses some $15-19 billion in 1995. The Congressional Budget Office, on the other hand, has found that sanctions have had a negligible effect on the overall U.S. economy, with a loss of perhaps $1 billion in 1997, compared to U.S. national income of $6.6 trillion.

This report addresses how and why sanctions are applied, who has the authority, under what terms that authority is exercised, what objectives the U.S. government seeks to achieve or advance when imposing (or lifting) sanctions, the secondary consequences of imposing sanctions, and the option of multilateral sanctions. The report also offers a list of current U.S. laws that require or authorize the imposition of sanctions.

Contents

Defining Economic Sanctions
Issues Related to Economic Sanctions
    Why do we apply sanctions?
    What objectives does the U.S. government seek to achieve
        when it imposes sanctions?
    Who imposes sanctions?
    What tools are available?
    How likely is it that sanctions will achieve the stated goal?
    What secondary consequences might sanctions have?
    What change is required for the sanctions to be lifted?
    Would multilateral sanctions be more desirable and achievable?
Current Law
    General U.S. national security or foreign policy objectives
    U.S. trade policy legislation sometimes used for
        foreign policy objectives
    Extradition
    Proliferation, generally
    Missile proliferation
    Nuclear proliferation
    Chemical/Biological weapons proliferation
    Communism (Marxist-Leninist countries)
    Coercive family planning programs (including abortion and
        involuntary sterilization)
    Human rights
    Religious freedom
    Worker rights
    Use of forced/prison/convict labor
    Environmental degradation
    Military coups d'état
    Debt arrearages, default
    Terrorism
    United Nations or other international organization participation
    Emigration
    Diplomatic relations (including action taken when severed)
    Drugs (international narcotics control)
    Missing in action
    Armed conflict (engaging against U.S. Armed Forces)
    World economy disruption, vital commodities disruption
    Parking fines
    Humanitarian assistance disruption
    Expropriation, confiscation, nationalization, mob action, or
        other seizure of or threat to property
    Crime Control
    Palestine Liberation Organization (PLO); Palestinian Authority
Current Law Related to Specific Countries
    Afghanistan
    Angola
    Azerbaijan

Bosnia-Hercegovina
Burma (Myanmar)
Cambodia
Chile
Colombia
Congo (former Zaire)
Croatia
Cuba
Guatemala
Haiti
Honduras
Indonesia
Iran
Iraq
Liberia
Libya
Mauritania
Nicaragua
North Korea
Pakistan
Panama
People's Republic of China
Republika Srpska
Russia (see also [Former] Soviet Union/East Bloc)
South Africa
[Former] Soviet Union/East Bloc
Sudan
Syria
Turkey
Ukraine
Vietnam (Socialist Republic of)
Yugoslavia (Serbia and Montenegro)

Both the Congress and the President in recent years have increasingly relied on economic sanctions as a means to establish and promote their foreign policy objectives, and yet the efficacy of economic sanctions is considered controversial. Most recently the President announced that the United States would begin to ease some of the sanctions the United States has held against North Korea since 1950. The change in policy, which allows for freer trade, investment, financial transactions, and travel between the two countries, was arrived at after U.S. coordinator for North Korea policy (and former U.S. Secretary of Defense serving President Bush) William Perry recommended taking a number of steps to improve relations. North Korea agreed to refrain from testing its long-range Taepo Dong-2 missile in exchange for a move toward normalization — including the lifting of some sanctions — and continued negotiations between the two countries. Chairmen of the Senate Committee on Foreign Relations and House Committee on International Relations each had immediate adverse reactions to the President's announcement. Representative Gilman described the new U.S.-North Korea relationship as one based on "extortion," with "...no assurances that North Korea has halted missile development or its program for weapons of mass destruction."[1] Sanctions remain in place that were imposed against North Korea for its support of international terrorism. Sanctions triggered by North Korean entities' involvement with proliferation of weapons of mass destruction also remain active, as required by law.

Congress and the executive branch have also been at odds in recent days over the use of sanctions, or lack of use, against Indonesia, Russia, and China, and throughout the 106th Congress over sanctions imposed against Cuba, India, Pakistan, Iraq, Iran, and Yugoslavia.

Over the last several years the use of sanctions has come under substantial scrutiny for a variety of reasons. Troubling reports of the lack of food and medical supplies available to the civilian population in Iraq, for example, led the United Nations to implement an oil-for-food program in December 1996, a step some have

---

[1] "Clinton Eases North Korea Sanctions," *Associated Press,* Terence Hunt, September 17, 1999; "White House Announces Decision to Ease Some North Korea Sanctions," *White House Press Release,* 17 September 1999; "Press Briefing on U.S. Relations with North Korea," Secretary of State Albright and Dr. William Perry, September 17, 1999 [http://secretary.state.gov/www/statements/1999/990917a.html].

argued undermines benefits the sanctions might provide.[2] India and Pakistan each tested nuclear explosive devices in May 1998, despite the sanctions certain to come from the international community.[3] The U.S. government responded with broad economic sanctions, only to discover that the economic prohibitions would take a devastating toll on U.S. wheat growers. Congress quickly moved to amend the law, with the President's support and signature, that prohibited Department of Agriculture subsidization of U.S. commercial wheat sales to Pakistan. The result was lifting, in a matter of weeks, sanctions that had been imposed for what some argued was one of the most serious and dangerous of offenses, nuclear proliferation. Others, however, contended that the longer-term consequences of denying Pakistan U.S. agricultural commodities would have destabilized all of South Asia, and perhaps resulted in Pakistan failing as a state.[4]

Selling wheat to Pakistan, in turn, invigorated a larger discussion on the use of food and medicine in foreign policy. Excluding food and medicine from sanctions regimes was taken up but unfinished in the 105th Congress; the 106th Congress has before it some 15 legislative proposals that would make it more difficult for the executive branch to prohibit commercial sales of agricultural commodities and medicines.[5] Indeed, on April 28, the President announced that the United States would exempt commercial sales of agricultural commodities and medicine from future

---

[2] For further discussion, see *Iraq: Humanitarian Needs, Impact of Sanctions, and the "Oil for Food" Program*, by Lois McHugh, CRS Report 98-680 F, August 13, 1998.

[3] *India-Pakistan Nuclear Tests and U.S. Response*, by Barbara L. LePoer, *et al.*, CRS Report 98-570 F, updated November 24, 1998; *Nuclear Sanctions: Section 102(b) of the Arms Export Control Act and Its Application to India and Pakistan*, by Jeanne Grimmett, CRS Report 98-486 A, updated September 21, 1999.

[4] Language that would authorize the President to waive the sanctions applied against India and Pakistan for an indefinite period, including the sanctions against Pakistan referred to as the "Pressler amendment" sanctions, is incorporated into the Department of Defense Appropriations Act, 2000 (H.R. 2561) at title IX. The bill was signed by the President on October 25, 1999, as P.L. 106-79 (113 Stat. 1212). On October 27, 1999, the President issued a determination (Presidential Determination No. 2000-4) that basically continued the policy adopted toward India and Pakistan in 1998. The President waived restrictions on USDA agricultural commodities financial support to the two countries. In issuing the determination, the President also allowed programs of the Export-Import Bank, Overseas Private Investment Corporation, Trade and Development Agency, and International Military Education and Training programs to operate in India. In light of Pakistan's military *coup d'etat*, Representative Pallone introduced H.R. 3095 on October 18, 1999, to amend P.L. 106-79 to keep the Pressler amendment in current law and applied against Pakistan. Language in the annual foreign operations appropriations measure that limits foreign assistance to countries the governments of which have attained power by overthrowing a democratically elected regime pertains to Pakistan as well.

[5] The Senate Committee on Foreign Relations and Senate Committee on Agriculture, Nutrition, and Forestry, each held hearings on May 11 to consider and collect public opinion on sanctions that have an impact on agricultural commodities. While these hearings were oversight in nature, particular attention was given to S. 425, the Food and Medicine for the World Act (introduced by Senator Ashcroft) and S. 566, the Agricultural Trade Freedom Act (introduced by Senator Lugar), respectively. See *Economic Sanctions and U.S. Agricultural Exports*, by Remy Jurenas, CRS Report RL30108.

unilateral sanctions imposed by the executive branch. The President directed the Secretary of the Treasury to issue new regulations that would allow commercial food and medical exports to Libya, Iran, and Sudan, three states previously restricted from such transactions by dint of their being on the State Department's list of countries that support acts of international terrorism. Only two days later the President announced new sanctions against Yugoslavia (Serbia and Montenegro), expressly directing the Secretary of the Treasury to "authorize commercial sales of agricultural commodities and products, medicine, and medical equipment for civilian end use...under appropriate safeguards to prevent diversion to military, paramilitary, or political use by the Government of the Federal Republic of Yugoslavia..."[6]

Of all the sanctions reform proposals, that with the most bipartisan support would exempt food, agricultural commodities, medicine, and medical supplies from economic sanctions. A version of the "Food and Medicine for the World Act," a bill first introduced as S. 425, was passed by the Senate in the FY2000 agriculture appropriations measure (H.R. 1906/S. 1233), only to be excised in conference. Similar language was introduced as S. 1771 in the Senate on October 22, 1999, by Senator Ashcroft. S. 1771 was sent directly to the Senate legislative calendar and read the first time. Similar language was introduced in the House by Rep. Nethercutt as H.R. 3140 on October 25, 1999, and referred to the Committees on International Relations, Rules, and Agriculture. S. 1712, the Export Administration Act of 1999, also exempts the application of sanctions toward agricultural commodities and medicines (Title IV). That measure was reported out of committee on October 8, 1999 (S.Rept. 106-180), and placed on the Senate Legislative Calendar.

By mid-October, Members of the 106th Congress had already introduced more than 100 bills or joint resolutions to impose new sanctions, ease current regimes, or overhaul the entire process that the legislative and executive branches employ when considering the use of sanctions. Of these, enactment of the "Enhancement of Trade, Security, and Human Rights Through Sanctions Reform Act," H.R. 1244, or its counterpart, the "Sanctions Policy Reform Act," S. 757, could most change the way the United States uses sanctions as a foreign policy tool. The bills seek to clarify the use of unilateral sanctions in U.S. foreign policy imposed at the initiative of either the Administration or Congress. The bills would revise procedures both branches follow before enacting or imposing sanctions, and would require extensive reporting as to the expected costs and benefits of imposing sanctions.[7]

---

[6] *Humanitarian Exemptions from Sanctions,* Statement by the Press Secretary, the White House, April 28, 1999; *Economic Sanctions,* Press Briefing by Stuart E. Eizenstat, Under Secretary of State for Economic, business, and Agricultural Affairs, and Richard Newcomb, Director of the Office of Foreign Assets Control, Treasury Department; and Secretary Eizenstat's testimony before the Senate Committee on Agriculture, Nutrition, and Forestry, May 11, 1999; Department of the Treasury, Office of Foreign Assets Control, 31 CFR Parts 538, 550, and 560, 64 FR 41784, August 2, 1999 (effective date July 27, 1999). Regarding Yugoslavia: Executive Order 13088, as amended by Executive Order 13121 of April 30, 1999, 64 F.R. 24021.

[7] Other bills might have substantial impact on the use of sanctions in foreign policy; the annual foreign operations appropriations bill, for example, often includes sanctions language

(continued...)

As the close of the 106th Congress, 1st session, approaches, there are last-minute efforts to place one or more sanctions measures into a bill that has its own momentum. H.R. 434, the African Growth and Opportunity Act, is under consideration to carry a variety of trade-related amendments. It has been mentioned in the press as a possible vehicle for S. 757, the Sanctions Policy Reform Act. It is also possible that H.R. 434 could advance "Food and Medicine for the World Act." The Senate agreed to food and medicine exemption language earlier in the session; that language was excised from the agriculture appropriations bill in conference. A new version of the bill has been introduced as S. 1771 in the Senate and as H.R. 3140 in the House.

This report provides background on the range of actions that might be termed sanctions, and a set of criteria that legislators might consider when proposing them, to help legislators judge when sanctions might be appropriate and the approach that might be most effective. Provided as well is an uncomplicated "map" of where sanctions policies and options currently may be found in U.S. law.

Defining Economic Sanctions

Generally, economic sanctions might be defined as "coercive economic measures taken against one or more countries to force a change in policies, or at least to demonstrate a country's opinion about the other's policies."[8] The most-often quoted study on sanctions defines the term as "...the deliberate, government-inspired withdrawal, or threat of withdrawal, of customary trade or financial relations."[9] Economic sanctions typically include measures such as trade embargoes; restrictions on particular exports or imports; denial of foreign assistance,[10] loans, and investments; or control of foreign assets and economic transactions that involve U.S. citizens or businesses. These definitions of economic sanctions would exclude diplomatic

---

[7] (...continued)
(H.R. 2606 was vetoed on October 18, 1999, for reasons unrelated to sanctions; it is likely to be incorporated into an omnibus appropriations bill). S. 1712, the Export Administration Act of 1999, was reported out by the Senate Committee on Banking, Housing, and Urban Affairs, on October 8, 1999 (S. Rep.t. 106-180), should enliven the sanctions debate with its numerous references to sanctions imposed for reasons of national security, foreign policy, proliferation of weapons of mass destruction, and export controls, to name a few. See *Export Administration Act of 1979 Reauthorization*, Helit Barel *et al.*, CRS Report RL30169.

[8] Carter, Barry E., *International Economic Sanctions: Improving the Haphazard U.S. Legal Regime*. Cambridge: Cambridge University Press, 1988. P. 4.

[9] Hufbauer, Gary Clyde, Jeffrey J. Schott and Kimberly Ann Elliott, *Economic Sanctions Reconsidered: History and Current Policy*. Washington, DC: Institute for International Economics, 1990 (second edition). p. 2.

[10] Some contend that the denial of foreign assistance should not be considered a sanction. Their position is that foreign assistance is not an entitlement; no country should expect its availability. The denial of foreign assistance is included in this discussion because it fits the definition used, that is, denial of foreign assistance to force a targeted country to change its behavior is in keeping with "coercive economic measures taken against one or more countries to force a change in policies, or at least to demonstrate a country's opinion about the other's policies."

démarches, reductions in embassy staff or closing of embassies, mobilizing armed forces or going to war — tools clearly intended to change another country's behavior through other than economic means. The use of "carrots" (e.g., granting most-favored-nation status for another year or offering economic or military assistance to a country if it conforms to certain standards) would not qualify as a sanction.

Issues Related to Economic Sanctions

In any sanctions debate, one might consider the following questions to assess the benefits and/or costs of imposing sanctions against a country, company, or individual:

Why do we apply sanctions? Economic sanctions are used when one country (or alliance of countries) wants to condemn or coerce change in the behavior of another country — its government, individuals, or businesses — that violates important international standards or threatens U.S. national interests. The U.S. government might impose sanctions when other efforts to change behavior have failed, such as diplomacy, public suasion, cultural and scientific exchanges, state visits, targeted technical assistance, military training and education, or other friendly means. Sanctions might be positioned at the middle of a continuum, between the extremes of complete cooperation and agreement at one end, and to the other end open hostility, use of force, or all-out war. The United States has aimed sanctions at governments that consistently violate internationally recognized human rights; at governments that sponsor international terrorism or harbor terrorists from elsewhere; at governments, individuals or corporations that engage in the proliferation of weapons of mass destruction; at individuals or governments that traffic narcotics; at governments that conduct aggression against their neighbors, threaten regional stability, or threaten U.S. security or foreign policy interests.

What objectives does the U.S. government seek to achieve when it imposes sanctions? United States policymakers do not always state the goals or objectives they hope to accomplish through the imposition of economic sanctions. Sanctions might be imposed when taking no action seems not enough of a response, but at the same time policymakers might resist committing to stronger measures. Generally, however, the U.S. government may choose to impose sanctions to:

- express its condemnation of a particular practice such as military aggression; human rights violations; militarization that destabilizes a country, its neighbors or the region; proliferation of nuclear, biological, or chemical weapons or missiles; political, economic, or military intimidation; terrorism; drug trafficking; or extreme national political policies contrary to basic interests of values of the United States (e.g., apartheid, communism);

- punish those engaged in objectionable behavior and deter its repetition;

- make it more expensive, difficult, or time-consuming to engage in objectionable behavior;

- block the flow of economic support that could be used by the targeted entity against the United States or U.S. interests;

- dissuade others from engaging in objectionable behavior;

- isolate a targeted country (or company or individual);

- force a change or termination of objectionable behavior; or

- coerce a change in the leadership or form of government in a targeted country.

Who imposes sanctions?   The President has broad authority to impose sanctions, either pursuant to declaring a national emergency and then invoking powers vested in his office in the International Emergency Economic Powers Act, or by exercising authority stated in various public laws (some of which are described at the end of this report).   In other instances, Congress might take the lead, either by conferring new Presidential authority to impose sanctions, or by requiring sanctions to be imposed unless the President determines and certifies that certain conditions have been met.   Some sanctions are mandatory and are triggered automatically when certain conditions exist.   Congress, for example, has required the imposition of sanctions when duly elected governments are overthrown by military *coup d'etat*, or when any non-nuclear weapon state explodes a nuclear device.   Some behavior that would trigger the imposition of sanctions, such as proliferation or support of international terrorism, requires that the President or Secretary of State determine and certify that a violation of a standard has occurred.   In most instances, the Administration has considerable flexibility in making such determinations and also has the authority to waive sanctions when imposed.

What tools are available? All of the following economic policy tools have been used at one time or another, triggered by a variety of repugnant behaviors.[11]

- Foreign assistance, all or some programs, could be terminated, suspended, limited, conditioned, or prohibited.   Foreign assistance to particular organizations that operate in the targeted country could be curtailed.   U.S. government arms sales and transfers, military assistance, and International Military Education and Training (IMET) funding could be similarly restricted. Scientific and technological cooperation, assistance,. and exchanges could be reduced or halted.

- Both public and private sector financial transactions could be restricted; assets in U.S. jurisdictions could be seized or frozen, or transactions related to travel or other forms of exchange could be limited or prohibited.

- Importation and exportation of some or all commodities could be curtailed by denying licenses, closing off shipping terminuses, or limiting related transactions.

- Government procurement contracts could be canceled or denied.

---

[11] Government leaders also have a range of diplomatic, political, cultural, and military tools at their disposal to use instead of or in conjunction with economic sanctions.

- Negative votes on loans, credits, or grants in international financial institutions could be cast, or the United States could abstain in voting.

- Trade agreements or other bilateral accords could be abrogated, made conditional, or not renewed. Beneficial trade status could be denied, withdrawn, or made conditional. Trade and import quotas for particular commodities could be lessened or eliminated altogether. The U.S. tax code could be amended to discourage commerce with a sanctioned state.

- Funding for investment, through the Overseas Private Investment Corporation, Trade and Development Agency, or Export-Import Bank, could be curtailed.

- Aviation, maritime, and surface access to the United States could be canceled or denied.

- Certain acts associated with sanctionable behavior could be made a criminal offense — making the targeted individual subject to fines or imprisonment. Additionally, sanctions could be applied against those individuals, businesses, or countries that continue to trade with or support targeted individuals, businesses, or countries.

How likely is it that sanctions will achieve the stated goal? Effectiveness is the most difficult aspect of sanctions policy to evaluate. The impact, cost and benefit of sanctions cannot be considered in a vacuum. A recent study considers geographic proximity, common language, volume of trade, a country's relative wealth, and membership in a common trading bloc all factors that might determine the success or failure of a unilaterally imposed sanctions regime.[12] One should also consider the United States' relative importance — in terms of trade, culture, scientific and intellectual exchanges, and history — to the targeted country. How important to the targeted country is our economic cooperation? Is the United States a significant trading partner, or only marginally engaged? Consider, for example, that at the time that sanctions were imposed against the former Yugoslavia, the United States took in only about 5 percent of that country's exports. The support of more substantial trading partners in Europe was needed to have any hope of having an impact.

United States businesses frequently argue that U.S. sanctions that hinder their exports or imports in turn benefit their foreign competitors. Some contend that staying engaged as trading partners or investors in a problem country will have better long-term effect. The United States seeks to isolate Cuba, for example, while Cuba's European trading partners contend that full trade relations afford them opportunities to discuss human rights concerns with the island nation.

Of course, relatively modest goals that do not challenge the vital interests of the targeted country or person are more likely to be achieved than are far-reaching goals, such as a change in the form of government, change in its leadership, or relinquishing

---

[12] Hufbauer, Gary Clyde and Kimberly Ann Elliott, Tess Cyrus, and Elizabeth Winston. *U.S. Economic Sanctions: Their Impact on Trade, Jobs, and Wages.* Washington, DC: Institute for International Economics, 1997. 17 p. and tables.

territory. The smaller the goal, the more likely it can be achieved. Similarly, the lesser the cost of imposing sanctions, the more sellable and manageable the policy will be to the implementing country or alliance of countries.

What secondary consequences might sanctions have? Whether or not successful in achieving their central purpose, sanctions sometimes have undesirable — perhaps unexpected — fallout. Sanctions against former Yugoslavia, for example, were particularly hard on the economies of Serbia's neighboring states. At the same time, some analysts argue, sanctions against Serbia and Montenegro actually bolstered nationalist political movements there. In another instance, long-standing sanctions against South Africa in the 1980s, some speculate, led that nation to develop weapons manufacturing capabilities — conventional and nuclear — that remain cause for concern today. Most recently, when the United States campaigned for European friends to join in sanctions against Iran by blocking investment in Iran's oil fields in 1995, for example, nearly all of Europe declined, pointing out that they were running out of fuel sources that were not under some sanctions regime. A short while later, trading partners of Nigeria found themselves wanting to punish that country for human rights issues but were unable to restrict trade with yet another oil producer.

Other secondary — and unintended — consequences arise in nearly all cases where sanctions are applied for some duration. Analysts express concern for the impact on the non-governmental population, particularly if food, medicine, or other basic human needs are affected. A recent study of the impact of U.S. sanctions policy on health and nutrition in Cuba concluded that U.S. restrictions on that country's ability to import food and medicine has "dramatically harmed the health and nutrition of large numbers of ordinary Cuban citizens."[13] The State Department has countered these charges, incidentally, with documentation of increased humanitarian shipments of medicine and other health-related supplies to Cuba from the United States in recent years, and with statistics that indict the Cuban government for misuse of their own treasury and inattention to its own people. Indeed, the State Department reports that the United States, since 1992, has become the largest donor of humanitarian assistance to Cuba.[14] Similar reports abound regarding Iraq and the impact of U.N.-sponsored multilateral sanctions, with those supporting sanctions and those favoring lifting the sanctions for humanitarian reasons arguing equally passionately.[15]

Nearer to home, loss of trade, the impact on U.S. jobs, potential loss of procurement contracts or other trade relations, loss of confidence in the reliability of American suppliers subject to unilateral economic prohibitions, all need to be factored in. Two Senate committees held hearings on agricultural commodities sanctions in May 1999, where witnesses representing the agricultural sector spoke about the impact of denying American farmers access to markets in terrorist states. Herb Karst, President of the National Barley Growers Association, testified that U.S. policy

---

[13] *Denial of Food and Medicine: The Impact of the U.S. Embargo on Health & Nutrition in Cuba*, American Association for World Health. March 1997.

[14] "The U.S. Embargo and Health Care in Cuba: Myth Versus Reality," U.S. Department of State, Press Statement, May 14, 1997.

[15] *Iran: Humanitarian Needs...*, op cit.

removed U.S. grain exporters from 3.5% of the global market. For barley growers, he estimated that U.S. sanctions against Libya and Iran in 1997-98 blocked U.S. growers from more than 9% of the world barley market, or more than twice what U.S. barley growers otherwise exported for that time period.[16]

The Congressional Budget Office (CBO), on the other hand, has found that sanctions on foreign commerce have had a negligible effect on the overall U.S. economy.   In a report prepared at the request of the House Committee on International Relations, CBO found that many sanctions do not add to restrictions on commerce and that, when they do, the cost is often small because commerce with the targeted state is small (as it might be with developing countries), that loss to the U.S. economy overall is offset by funds saved (by forgoing foreign aid or trade promotion funding), or that domestic business finds other markets (for both import and export).[17] Earlier research by CBO put the domestic cost of sanctions at less than $1 billion in lost national income per year (compared with a total national income of $6.6 trillion for 1997, the year on which CBO based its analysis). Even this cost was thought likely to be only short-term, that exporters would find replacement markets and recover. At the same time, CBO did note that sanctions could "result in sharp disruption to and dislocation of specific U.S. firms and workers."[18]

One might consider, then, how the potential secondary costs of imposing sanctions, incurred by surrounding states, civilian populations in the targeted states, or even by domestic interests, compare to the benefit of achieving the stated goal. For what duration will the secondary costs have to be borne; what long-term damage might the secondary costs inflict? And what is the cost, if any, of doing nothing?

What change is required for the sanctions to be lifted? When sanctions are imposed via enactment of public law, what is required to terminate the restrictions is usually clearly stated. If a policy is unevenly applied, however, the standard might be less clear. China, for example, as a nonmarket economy, is denied permanent most-favored nation status on the basis of laws relating to trade, nonmarket economies, and emigration. The annual debate to renew China's MFN status, however, rarely has much to do with freedom of emigration of China's population. If sanctions are applied for a lengthy period, other problems arise, or the circumstances that triggered the sanctions at the outset might evolve. The sought after change in behavior could be redefined over time, or multilateral or domestic support for the sanctions could deteriorate. In some instances, sanctions are imposed to achieve a goal that is unclear, ever-changing, or perhaps unattainable.   In such circumstances, if the sanctions are lifted or waived, it may effectively signal a friendly change of policy. If the U.S. government terminates sanctions when it appears that the targeted country has not budged at all from its sanctionable behavior, however, future attempts to

---

[16] Prepared testimony of Herb Karst, President of the National Barley Growers Association, before the Senate Committee on Agriculture, Nutrition, and Forestry, May 11, 1999.

[17] *The Domestic Costs of Sanctions on Foreign Commerce,* by Congressional Budget Office, March 1999, 52 p.

[18] Prepared testimony of Jan Paul Acton, Assistant Director of the Natural Resources and Commerce Division, Congressional Budget Office, before the House Committee on International Relations. June 3. 1998.

achieve a standard of behavior through sanctions may be compromised. The constantly changing political landscape of the former Yugoslavia over the last seven years provides numerous incidents to demonstrate the dilemma of sending confusing signals to allies as well as the sanctioned state.

Would multilateral sanctions be more desirable and achievable? It is generally agreed that sanctions imposed by all or most of the nations on which a targeted country relies for trade and support (such as through the United Nations or other multinational organization) stand a much better chance of having an impact than unilateral restrictions or prohibitions. Consensus is difficult to reach among countries considering another country's behavior, however, and as a result multilateral sanctions are imposed infrequently. Comprehensive multilateral sanctions are even more rare. Attempts that fail to solidify international opinion against one country's objectionable behavior can actually give support to those committing the behavior (for example, every year the United States is condemned by the U.N. General Assembly for its unilateral sanctions regime against Cuba).

Current Law

Each sanction has its own duration, severity, and comprehensiveness or selectivity. Each section of law has its own terms for triggering the imposition, as well as reporting on, easing or tightening, waiving, and terminating the sanction. Some laws make sanctions mandatory; others provide discretionary authority to the President or his delegate to impose sanctions. Nearly all laws include some sort of waiver authority that allows the President to not impose the sanction even if an incident warrants it. Only a few laws specifically spell out what recourse Congress might take when it finds itself in disagreement with the executive branch on the imposition, waiving, or termination of a sanction.

Some laws generally authorize the executive branch to make and carry out foreign policy and would not be considered sanctions legislation at first glance. Such authority is often cited when the President changes policy to the detriment of a targeted country. Using legislative authority to cut foreign assistance, for example, might be an administrative decision, or it might be a step taken to punish a country in violation of any number of international standards. Disallowing participation in various trade-supporting programs (such as the Overseas Private Investment Corporation or the Export-Import Bank) might be a change in policy to recognize a country's graduation from such needs, or it might be considered a punitive step taken to change the recipient country's behavior.

The following list is intended to serve only as a guide to where the authority to impose sanctions stands in the law. Careful reading of the public law text is required to determine the intent of the sanctions, what triggers their imposition, the extent of the sanction, and what is required to have the restrictions lifted. The list groups laws into broad foreign policy categories. A brief note of what form the sanction might take is included parenthetically. Many of the restrictions of foreign assistance will be found in the FY1999 foreign operations appropriations act; such a law is enacted anew each fiscal year (or, in absence of an appropriations act, a continuing resolution may extend the terms of a previous year's appropriations act). For specific countries, any law written specifically to address conditions in, or relations with, that country would apply, but other laws of general effect written to address an issue might apply to that country as well. This list should not be considered comprehensive but is an index of basic sanctions legislation.

General U.S. national security or foreign policy objectives.

§ 621, Foreign Assistance Act of 1961 (Public Law 87-195; 22 USC 2381) (authorizes President to administer foreign assistance programs and policy; authorizes the President to prohibit foreign assistance because of illegal activities, such as fraud or corruption)

§ 633A, Foreign Assistance Act of 1961 (Public Law 87-195; 22 USC 2393a) (prohibits foreign assistance when certain informational requests are not met by recipient)

§ 3, Arms Export Control Act (Public Law 90-629; 22 USC 2753) (authorizes President to administer U.S. government arms sales and transfers with conditions and exceptions)

§ 38, Arms Export Control Act (Public Law 90-629; 22 USC 2778) (authorizes the President to limit sales and transfers in interest of world peace and security of United States. Violation of terms of section or related regulations may result in $1 million fine, 10-year imprisonment, or both)

§ 42, Arms Export Control Act (Public Law 90-629; 22 USC 2791) (authorizes the President to cancel arms sales, credits, or contracts on national security grounds)

§ 5(b), Trading with the Enemy Act (Public Law 65-91; 50 USC App. 5(b))[19] (authorizes the President to investigate, regulate, or prohibit transactions, or to freeze assets)

Title II, National Emergencies Act (Public Law 94-412; 50 USC 1621, 1622) (authorizes declaration and administration of national emergencies — required to administer authority under International Emergency Economic Powers Act)

§ 203, International Emergency Economic Powers Act (Public Law 95-223; 50 USC 1701) (authorizes control or prohibition of most financial transactions)

§ 1237, Strom Thurmond National Defense Authorization Act for Fiscal Year 1999 (public Law 105-261; 50 USC 1701 note) (authorizes the use of sec. 203 of the International Emergency Economic Powers Act where an action involves "persons operating directly or indirectly in the United States...that are Communist Chinese military companies")

§ 2(b)(5)(B), Export-Import Bank Act of 1945 (Public Law 79-173; 12 USC 635(b)(5)(B)) (restricts Export-Import Bank services with country engaged in armed conflict against U.S. armed forces)

§ 5, Export Administration Act of 1979 (Public Law 96-72; 50 USC App. 2404) (imposes national security export controls)

§ 6, Export Administration Act of 1979 (Public Law 96-72; 50 USC App. 2405) (imposes foreign policy export controls)

---

[19] The Trading with the Enemy Act continues to apply only to Cuba and North Korea. Presidential authority to impose similar national emergency-related sanctions may be found in the National Emergencies Act and the International Emergency Economic Powers Act.

§ 11, Export Administration Act of 1979 (Public Law 96-72; 50 USC App. 2410) (imposes penalties for violations of Act, generally)

§ 11A, Export Administration Act of 1979 (Public Law 96-72; 50 USC App. 2410a) (prohibits contracts, importation for regulations violators)

§ 233, Trade Expansion Act of 1962 (Public Law 87-794; 19 USC 1864) (authorizes President to sanction importation for violations of sec. 5 Export Administration Act national security controls)

U.S. trade policy legislation sometimes used for foreign policy objectives.

§ 125, Trade Act of 1974 (Public Law 93-618; 19 USC 2135) (authorizes President to terminate or withdraw from trade agreements)

§ 126, Trade Act of 1974 (Public Law 93-618; 19 USC 2136) (authorizes President to terminate or withdraw from trade agreements where reciprocal nondiscriminatory treatment has not been upheld)

§ 604, Trade Act of 1974 (Public Law 93-618; 19 USC 2483) (authorizes President to change the Harmonized Tariff Schedules)

§ 212(b)(4), (5), Caribbean Basin Economic Recovery Act (Public Law 98-67; 19 USC 2702(b)(4), (5)) (denies beneficiary country status)

§ 232, Trade Expansion Act of 1962 (Public Law 87-794; 19 USC 1862) (authorizes President to set duties or import restrictions based on national security issues)

§ 620(d), Foreign Assistance Act of 1961 (Public Law 87-195; 22 USC 2370(d)) (prohibits foreign assistance loans)

§8038, Department of Defense Appropriations Act, 1999 (Public Law 105-262; 41 USC 10b-2) (requires the Secretary of Defense to rescind waiver of Buy American Act when a country violates defense procurement agreements in discriminating against American products)

Extradition.

§ 212(b)(6) Caribbean Basin Economic Recovery Act (Public Law 98-67; 19 USC 2702(b)(6)) (denies beneficiary country status)

Proliferation, generally.

§ 620(s), Foreign Assistance Act of 1961 (Public Law 87-195; 22 USC 2370(s)) (conditions foreign assistance and loans)

§ 3(f), Arms Export Control Act (Public Law 90-629; 22 USC 2753(f)) (prohibits sales or leases to nuclear explosive device proliferators)

§ 38, Arms Export Control Act (Public Law 90-629; 22 USC 2778) (establishes penalty for violating U.S. import/export terms for defense articles and services)

§ 6(k), Export Administration Act of 1979 (Public Law 96-72; 50 USC App. 2405(k)) (restricts exportation)

§ 1211, National Defense Authorization Act for Fiscal Year 1998 (Public Law 105-85) (restricts exportation of high performance computers)

Missile proliferation.

§§ 72, 73, Arms Export Control Act (Public Law 90-629; 22 USC 2797a, 2797b) (restricts contracts, denies, export licenses, may deny importation)

§ 6(l), Export Administration Act of 1979 (Public Law 96-72; 50 USC App. 2405(l)) (restricts exportation)

§ 11B, Export Administration Act of 1979 (Public Law 96-72; 50 USC App. 2410b) (restricts contracts, denies export licenses, may deny importation)

Nuclear proliferation.

§ 307, Foreign Assistance Act of 1961 (Public Law 87-195; 22 USC 2227) (prohibits use of U.S. foreign assistance paid in as U.S. proportionate share to international organizations when those organizations run programs in Burma, Iraq, North Korea, Syria, Libya, Iran, Cuba, or with the Palestine Liberation Organization. Further prohibits funding for International Atomic Energy Agency participation in certain projects in Cuba.)

§§ 101, 102, Arms Export Control Act (Public Law 90-629; 22 USC 2799aa, 2799aa-1) (prohibits foreign or military assistance)[20]

§ 701(b), International Financial Institutions Act (Public Law 95-118; 22 USC 262d(b)) (opposes international financial institution support)

§ 2(b)(1)(B), Export-Import Bank Act of 1945 (Public Law 79-173; 12 USC 635(b)(1)(B)) (denies Bank support where President determines in U.S. national interests related to terrorism, nuclear proliferation, environmental protection, human rights)

§ 2(b)(4), 2(b)(5)(C) Export-Import Bank Act of 1945 (Public Law 79-173; 12 USC 635(b)(4)) (prohibits Export-Import Bank support)

§ 5(b), Export Administration Act of 1979 (Public Law 96-72; 50 USC App. 2404) (restricts exports for national security reasons)

Export-Import Bank of the United States, title I, Foreign Operations, Export Financing, and Related Programs Appropriations Act, 1999 (sec. 101(d) of division A of Public Law 105-277; 112 Stat. 2681-150) (prohibits Export-Import Bank funding to other than non-nuclear weapon state, if that state detonates a nuclear explosive after enactment of this Act (October 21, 1998))

§ 129, Atomic Energy Act of 1954 (Public Law 83-703; 42 USC 2158) (prohibits transfer of nuclear materials, equipment, related technology)

§ 304(b), Nuclear Non-Proliferation Act of 1978 (Public Law 95-242; 42 USC 2155a) (authorizes Department of Commerce to regulate exports significant to nuclear explosion purposes)

§ 402, Nuclear Non-Proliferation Act of 1978 (Public Law 95-242; 42 USC 2153a) (prohibits exports related to nuclear enrichment)

§ 821, Nuclear Proliferation Prevention Act of 1994 (Public Law 103-236; 22 USC 3201 note) (prohibits contracts with individuals)

---

[20] See also the India-Pakistan Relief Act of 1998, title IX of the Agriculture, Rural Development, Food and Drug Administration, and Related Agencies Appropriations Act, 1999 (sec. 101(a) of division A of Public Law 105-277; 22 USC 2799aa-1 note), which waived the applicability of these sections for India and Pakistan for one year upon enactment. The Act also waived §2(b)(4) of the Export-Import Bank Act of 1945 and §620E(e) of the Foreign Assistance Act of 1961.

§ 823, Nuclear Proliferation Prevention Act of 1994 (Public Law 103-236; 22 USC 3201 note) (opposes international financial institution support)

§ 824, Nuclear Proliferation Prevention Act of 1994 (Public Law 103-236; 22 USC 3201 note) (prohibits financial institutions from financing certain transactions)

§ 620G, Foreign Assistance Act of 1961 (Public Law 87-195; 22 USC 2378a) (prohibits foreign assistance for most sales of antitank shells containing depleted uranium penetrating component)

Chemical/Biological weapons proliferation.

§ 81, Arms Export Control Act (Public Law 90-629; 22 USC 2798) (requires import and U.S. government procurement sanctions against CW/BW proliferators)

§ 6(m), Export Administration Act of 1979 (Public Law 96-72; 50 USC App. 2405(m)) (restricts exportation)

§ 11C, Export Administration Act of 1979 (Public Law 96-72; 50 USC App. 2410c) (requires import and U.S. government procurement sanctions against CW/BW proliferators)

§ 307, Chemical and Biological Weapons Control and Warfare Elimination Act of 1991 (Public Law 102-182; 22 USC 5605) (terminates most foreign assistance, arms sales, certain exports; may restrict international financial institution support, U.S. bank support, exports, imports, diplomatic relations, aviation access to United States)

Chapter 11B, 18 USC (added by § 201, Chemical Weapons Convention Implementation Act of 1998) (states penalties for those who "develop, produce, or otherwise acquire, transfer directly or indirectly, receive, stockpile, retain, own, possess, or use or threaten to use, any chemical weapon...")

§ 2332c, 18 USC (added by § 521, Antiterrorism and Effective Death Penalty Act of 1996) (makes use of chemical weapon in certain instances a criminal offense)

§103, Chemical Weapons Convention Implementation Act of 1998 (division I of Public Law 105-277; 22 USC 6713) (establishes civil liability for violating the Chemical Weapons Convention, states terms of sanctions against foreign persons, foreign governments for such violations)

Communism (Marxist-Leninist countries).

§ 620(f), (h), Foreign Assistance Act of 1961 (Public Law 87-195; 22 USC 2370(f), (h)) (prohibits foreign assistance)

§ 2(b)(2), Export-Import Bank Act of 1945 (Public Law 79-173; 12 USC 635(b)(2)) (prohibits Export-Import Bank transactions with Marxist-Leninist state)

§ 502(b)(1), Trade Act of 1974 (Public Law 93-618; 19 USC 2462) (denies beneficiary developing country status)

§ 5(b), Export Administration Act of 1979 (Public Law 96-72; 50 USC App. 2404) (authorizes the President to restrict exportation to Communist states, to states with policies "adverse to the national security interests of the United States")

§ 43, Bretton Woods Agreements Act (Public Law 79-171; 22 USC 286aa) (opposes international financial institution support)

§ 212(b)(1), Caribbean Basin Economic Recovery Act (Public Law 98-67; 19 USC 2702(b)(1)) (denies beneficiary country status)

Coercive family planning programs (including abortion and involuntary sterilization).
§ 104(f), Foreign Assistance Act of 1961 (prohibits development assistance from being made available for coercive family planning programs)

Development Assistance, title II, Foreign Operations, Export Financing, and Related Programs Appropriations Act, 1999 (sec. 101(d) of division A of Public Law 105-277; 112 Stat. 2681-153) (prohibits development assistance from being made available for coercive family planning programs)

§ 518, Foreign Operations, Export Financing, and Related Programs Appropriations Act, 1999 (sec. 101(d) of division A of Public Law 105-277, 112 Stat. 2681-176) (prohibits development assistance from being made available for coercive family planning programs or for lobbying for or against abortion)

Human rights.
§ 116, Foreign Assistance Act of 1961 (Public Law 87-195; 22 USC 2151n) (prohibits most U.S. foreign economic assistance to any country the government of which engages in a "consistent pattern of gross violations of internationally recognized human rights")[21]

§ 502B, Foreign Assistance Act of 1961 (Public Law 87-195; 22 USC 2304) (prohibits most U.S. security assistance to any country the government of which engages in a "consistent pattern of gross violations of internationally recognized human rights")

§ 239(i), Foreign Assistance Act of 1961 (Public Law 87-195; 22 USC 2199(i)) (requires Overseas Private Investment Corporation to consider human rights when conducting programs)

§ 660, Foreign Assistance Act of 1961 (Public Law 87-195; 22 USC 2420) (prohibits funds for police training)

§ 701(a), (b), (f) International Financial Institutions Act (Public Law 95-118; 22 USC 262d) (opposes bank loans)

§ 568, Foreign Operations, Export Financing, and Related Programs Appropriations Act, 1999 (sec. 101(d) of division A of Public Law 105-277; 112 Stat. 2681-194) ("Leahy amendment;" prohibits foreign assistance to security forces of any foreign country if Secretary of state "has credible evidence that such unit has committed gross violations of human rights")

§ 579, Foreign Operations, Export Financing, and Related Programs Appropriations Act, 1997 (§ 101(c) of title I of Public Law 104-208; 22 USC 262k-2) (opposes most international financial institution transactions for any country with a custom of female genital mutilation that has not taken steps to improve education to prevent such practices)

---

[21] Section 2216 of the Foreign Relations Authorization Act, Fiscal Years 1998 and 1999 (title XX of subdivision B of division G of Public Law 105-277; 112 Stat. 2681-815), added the status of child labor practices in a country to reporting requirements under this section.

§ 2(b)(1)(B), Export-Import Bank Act of 1945 (Public Law 79-173; 12 USC 635(b)(1)(B)) (denies Bank support where President determines in U.S. national interests related to terrorism, nuclear proliferation, environmental protection, human rights, child labor)

§ 8130, Department of Defense Appropriations Act, 1999 (Public Law 105-262; 112 Stat. 2335) (prohibits funding to support any training of a foreign country's security forces if a member of that security force unit "has committed a gross violation of human rights, unless all necessary corrective steps have been taken")

Religious freedom.
Title IV, International Religious Freedom Act of 1998 (Public Law 105-292; 22 USC 6441 *et seq.*) (§405, in particular, authorizes the President to use a wide range of diplomatic and economic restrictions)

Worker rights.
§ 231A, Foreign Assistance Act of 1961 (Public Law 87-195; 22 USC 2191a) (limits Overseas Private Investment Corporation activities)

§§ 502(b)(7), (c)(7), 504, Trade Act of 1974 (Public Law 93-618; 19 USC 2462, 2464) (authorizes the President to take into account country's worker rights record when considering beneficiary developing country status)

§ 212(b)(7) Caribbean Basin Economic Recovery Act (Public Law 98-67; 19 USC 2702(b)(7)) (denies beneficiary country status)

§ 538, Foreign Operations, Export Financing, and Related Programs Appropriations Act, 1999 (sec. 101(d) of division A of Public Law 105-277; 112 Stat. 2681-182) (prohibits foreign assistance to projects that contribute to the violation of internationally recognized worker rights as defined in § 502(a)(4) of the Trade Act of 1974)

Use of forced/prison/convict labor.
§ 307, Tariff Act of 1930 (Public Law 71-361; 19 USC 1307) (prohibits importation of goods produced or manufactured with prison labor)[22]

Environmental degradation.
§ 118, Foreign Assistance Act of 1961 (Public Law 87-195; 22 USC 2151p-1) (denies foreign assistance related to deforestation)

§ 2(b)(1)(B), Export-Import Bank Act of 1945 (Public Law 79-173; 12 USC 635(b)(1)(B)) (denies Export-Import Bank support where President determines in U.S. national interests related to terrorism, nuclear proliferation, environmental protection, human rights)

§ 533, Foreign Operations, Export Financing, and Related Programs Appropriations Act, 1991 (Public Law 101-513; 22 USC 262*l*) (requires

---

[22] See also title XXXVII of the Strom Thurmond National Defense Authorization Act for Fiscal Year 1999 (Public Law 105-261; 112 Stat. 2274), which authorized the hiring of additional U.S. Customs Service personnel in order to monitor the importation of products made with forced labor (§3701). The title also requires the Commissioner of Customs to report to Congress on the situation (§3702), and states the sense of the Congress that the President should scrutinize memoranda of understanding relating to reciprocal trade that the United States has with other countries regarding the use of forced labor.

U.S. Executive Directors of multilateral development banks to promote global climate change programs — includes voting against or abstaining on loans)

§ 609(b), Sea Turtle Conservation provisions (Public Law 101-162; 16 USC 1537 note) (bans importation of shrimp and shrimp products the harvest of which adversely affects sea turtle populations, unless President determines that government of harvester documents regulatory programs and sea turtle population security)

§ 901, Dolphin Protection Consumer Information Act (Public Law 101-627; 16 USC 1835) (authorizes punitive measure against those found to have mislabeled tuna products for distribution in the United States)

§ 7, Rhinoceros and Tiger Conservation Act of 1997 (Public Law 103-391; 16 USC 5305a) (prohibits sale, importation, exportation of rhinoceros or tiger products; imposes criminal and civil penalties)

Military coups d'état.

§ 508, Foreign Operations, Export Financing, and Related Programs Appropriations Act, 1999 (sec. 101(d) of division A of Public Law 105-277; 112 Stat. 2681-171) (prohibits foreign assistance)

Debt arrearages, default.

§ 620(c), (q) Foreign Assistance Act of 1961 (Public Law 87-195; 22 USC 2370) (prohibits or suspends foreign assistance; for FY1999, not applicable for Nicaragua, Brazil, and Liberia, and for narcotics-related assistance for FY1999, not applicable for Colombia, Bolivia, and Peru)

§ 512, Foreign Operations, Export Financing, and Related Programs Appropriations Act, 1999 (sec. 101(d) of division A of Public Law 105-277; 112 Stat. 2681-172) (prohibits foreign assistance; for FY1999, not applicable for Nicaragua , Brazil, and Liberia, and for narcotics-related assistance for FY1999, not applicable for Colombia, Bolivia, and Peru)

Terrorism.

§ 620A, Foreign Assistance Act of 1961 (Public Law 87-195; 22 USC 2371) (prohibits foreign assistance)

§ 620G, Foreign Assistance Act of 1961 (Public Law 87-195; 22 USC 2377) (prohibits foreign assistance)

§ 620H, Foreign Assistance Act of 1961 (Public Law 87-195; 22 USC 2378) (prohibits foreign assistance)

§ 40, Arms Export Control Act (Public Law 90-629; 22 USC 2780) (prohibits sale, transfer, lease, loan, grant, credit, foreign assistance associated with munitions items to terrorist states)

§ 40A, Arms Export Control Act (Public Law 90-629; 22 USC 2781) (prohibits sale or license for export of defense articles or defense services to country determined by President, in a fiscal year, to be not cooperating with U.S. antiterrorism efforts)

§ 505, International Security and Development Cooperation Act of 1985 (Public Law 99-83; 22 USC 2349aa-9) (authorizes the President to ban importation of goods and services from state found to support international terrorism)

§ 701(a)(2), (f), International Financial Institutions Act (Public Law 95-118; 22 USC 262d(a)(2), (f)) (opposes international financial institution loans to those offering refuge to skyjackers)

§ 1621, International Financial Institutions Act (Public Law 95-118; 22 USC 262p-4q) (opposes International financial institution loans to terrorist states)

§ 6, Bretton Woods Agreements Act Amendments, 1978 (Public Law 95-435; 22 USC 286e-11) (requires opposition to International Monetary Fund assistance)

§ 502(b)(2)(F), Trade Act of 1974 (Public Law 93-618; 19 USC 2462) (withholding of beneficiary developing country designation)

§ 6(j), Export Administration Act of 1979 (Public Law 96-72; 50 USC App. 2405(j)) ("Fenwick amendment," requires export licenses)

§ 528, Foreign Operations, Export Financing, and Related Programs Appropriations Act, 1999 ((sec. 101(d) of division A of Public Law 105-277; 112 Stat. 2681-178) (prohibits bilateral foreign assistance)

§ 551, Foreign Operations, Export Financing, and Related Programs Appropriations Act, 1999 (sec. 101(d) of division A of Public Law 105-277; 112 Stat. 2681-187) (prohibits foreign assistance to any country providing lethal military equipment to a terrorist state)

§ 2332b, 18 USC (added by §702, Antiterrorism and Effective Death Penalty Act of 1996) (makes terrorist acts that transcend national boundaries a criminal offense)

§ 2332d, 18 USC (added by § 321, Antiterrorism and Effective Death Penalty Act of 1996) (makes financial transactions with a terrorist state a criminal offense)

§ 2339A, 18 USC (added by § 323, Antiterrorism and Effective Death Penalty Act of 1996) (makes providing material support to a terrorist or terrorist state a criminal offense)

§ 2339B, 18 USC (added by § 303, Antiterrorism and Effective Death Penalty Act of 1996) (makes providing material support or resources to designated foreign terrorist organizations a criminal offense)

§ 2(b)(1)(B), Export-Import Bank Act of 1945 (Public Law 79-173; 12 USC 635(b)(1)(B)) (denies Bank support where President determines in U.S. national interests related to terrorism, nuclear proliferation, environmental protection, human rights)

United Nations or other international organization participation.

§ 307, Foreign Assistance Act of 1961 (Public Law 87-195; 22 USC 2227) (prohibits use of U.S. foreign assistance paid in as U.S. proportionate share to international organizations when those organizations run programs in Burma, Iraq, North Korea, Syria, Libya, Iran, Cuba, or with the Palestine Liberation Organization, "or, at the discretion of the President, Communist countries listed at sec. 620(f) of this Act". Further prohibits funding for International Atomic Energy Agency participation in certain projects in Cuba.)

§ 620(u), Foreign Assistance Act of 1961 (Public Law 87-195; 22 USC 2370(u)) (conditions foreign assistance on arrearage of UN dues)

§ 5, United Nations Participation Act of 1945 (Public Law 79-264; 22 USC 287c) (restricts economic and communications relations)

Title IV, International Organizations and Programs, Foreign Operations, Export Financing, and Related Programs Appropriations Act, 1999 (sec. 101(d) of division A of Public Law 105-277; 112 Stat. 2681-169) (prohibits IO&P foreign assistance for United Nations Population Fund (UNFPA), Korean Peninsula energy Development Organization (KEDO), and the International Atomic Energy Agency (IAEA).

§ 535, Foreign Operations, Export Financing, and Related Programs Appropriations Act, 1999 (sec. 101(d) of division A of Public Law 105-277; 112 Stat. 2681-181) (prohibits foreign assistance and transactions under the Arms Export Control Act to any country not in compliance with U.N. sanctions against Iraq)

§ 574, Foreign Operations, Export Financing, and Related Programs Appropriations Act, 1999 (sec. 101(d) of division A of Public Law 105-277; 112 Stat. 2681-198) (reduces foreign assistance to any country not in compliance with U.N. sanctions imposed against Libya)

Emigration.
§ 402, Trade Act of 1974 (Public Law 93-618; 19 USC 2432) ("Jackson-Vanik amendment," restricts commercial agreements, denies most-favored-nation status)

Diplomatic relations (including action taken when severed).
§ 620(t), Foreign Assistance Act of 1961 (Public Law 87-195; 22 USC 2370(u)) (prohibits foreign assistance and assistance under Agricultural Trade Development and Assistance Act of 1954)

Drugs (international narcotics control).
§ 486, 487, 490, Foreign Assistance Act of 1961 (Public Law 87-195; 22 USC 2291e, 2291f, 2291j) (restricts foreign assistance, narcotics control assistance)

§ 13, International Development Association Act (Public Law 86-565; 22 USC 284k) (opposes international financial institution support)

§ 802, Narcotics Control Trade Act (title VIII of Public Law 93-618; 19 USC 2492) (denies preferential tariff treatment, imposes importation duty, curtails air traffic between country and United States, reduces U.S. customs staff)

§ 803, Narcotics Control Trade Act (title VIII of Public Law 93-618; 19 USC 2493) (restricts sugar quota)

Missing in action.
§ 701(b)(4), International Financial Institutions Act (Public Law 95-118; 22 USC 262d(b)(4)) (requires U.S. executive directors to international financial institutions to consider MIA issue when voting on international financial institution loans to Vietnam, Laos, Russia, independent states of former Soviet Union, and Cambodia)

§ 403, Trade Act of 1974 (Public Law 93-618; 19 USC 2433). (authorizes the President to deny nondiscriminatory trade treatment, trade-related credits and investment guarantees, or commercial agreements to countries not cooperating with U.S. efforts to account fully for MIA in Southeast Asia)

Armed conflict (engaging against U.S. Armed Forces).
   § 2(b)(5), Export-Import Bank Act of 1945 (Public Law 79-173; 12 USC
      635(b)(5)) (prohibits Export-Import Bank credits)

World economy disruption, vital commodities disruption.
   § 502(b)(2), (b)(3), (e)(2), Trade Act of 1974 (Public Law 93-618; 19 USC
      2462) (para. (2) in part, is specifically directed at Organization of
      Petroleum Exporting Countries (OPEC))
   § 502(b)(5), Trade Act of 1974 (Public Law 93-618; 19 USC 2462) (conditions
      beneficiary developing country designation)
   § 7, Export Administration Act of 1979 (Public Law 96-72; 50 USC App. 2406)
      (restricts exports relating to short supply)
   § 8, Export Administration Act of 1979 (Public Law 96-72; 50 USC App. 2407)
      (prohibits cooperating with foreign boycotts)
   § 513, Foreign Operations, Export Financing, and Related Programs
      Appropriations Act, 1999 (sec. 101(d) of division A of Public Law 105-
      277; 112 Stat. 2681-172) (prohibits direct assistance, Export-Import Bank
      support, Overseas Private Investment Corporation funding, where
      commodity might disrupt world market)
   § 514, Foreign Operations, Export Financing, and Related Programs
      Appropriations Act, 1999 (sec. 101(d) of division A of Public Law 105-
      277; 112 Stat. 2681-173) (requires the Secretary of the Treasury to advise
      U.S. Executive Directors of international financial institutions to oppose
      loans where funds would be used for production or extraction of any
      commodity or mineral for export where commodity or mineral is in world
      surplus supply and its production would cause substantial injury to U.S.
      producers)

Parking fines.
   § 552, Foreign Operations, Export Financing, and Related Programs
      Appropriations Act, 1999 (sec. 101(d) of division A of Public Law 105-
      277; 112 Stat. 2681-187) (withholds portion of foreign assistance from
      nations whose agents or representatives in the United States are cited as
      parking scofflaws)

Humanitarian assistance disruption.
   § 620I, Foreign Assistance Act of 1961 (Public Law 87-195; 22 USC 2379)
      (prohibits foreign assistance)

**Expropriation, confiscation, nationalization, mob action, or other seizure
of or threat to property.**
   § 620(a), (g), (j), (l), (o), Foreign Assistance Act of 1961 (Public Law 87-195;
      22 USC 2370) (prohibits foreign assistance)
   § 620(e), Foreign Assistance Act of 1961 (Public Law 87-195; 22 USC 2370(e))
      (suspends foreign assistance)
   § 12, International Development Association Act (Public Law 86-565; 22 USC
      284j) (opposes international financial institution support)
   § 502(b)(4), Trade Act of 1974 (Public Law 93-618; 19 USC 2462) (denies
      beneficiary developing country designation)

§ 212(b)(2), (3), Caribbean Basin Economic Recovery Act (Public Law 98-67;
19 USC 2702(b)(2), (3)) (denies beneficiary country designation)

§ 2225, Foreign Relations Authorization Act, Fiscal Years 1998 and 1999 (title
XX of subdivision B of division G of Public Law 105-277; 8 USC 1182d)
(authorizes the Secretary of State to deny issuance of a visa to an alien
trafficking in property confiscated or expropriated from any U.S. national)

Crime Control.

§ 6(n), Export Administration Act of 1979 (Public Law 96-72; 50 USC App.
2405(n)) (restricts exports)

Palestine Liberation Organization (PLO); Palestinian Authority.

§ 307, Foreign Assistance Act of 1961 (Public Law 87-195; 22 USC 2227)
(prohibits use of U.S. foreign assistance paid in as U.S. proportionate share
to international organizations when those organizations run programs in
Burma, Iraq, North Korea, Syria, Libya, Iran, Cuba, or with the Palestine
Liberation Organization)

§ 553, Foreign Operations, Export Financing and Related Programs
Appropriations Act, 1999 (sec. 101(d) of division A of Public Law 105-
277; 112 Stat. 2681-187) (prohibits foreign assistance to the PLO for the
West Bank and Gaza unless the President invokes authority pursuant to §
604(a) of the Middle East Peace Facilitation Act of 1995)

§ 566, Foreign Operations, Export Financing and Related Programs
Appropriations Act, 1999 (sec. 101(d) of division A of Public Law 105-
277; 112 Stat. 2681-194) (prohibits Economic Support Funds for the
Palestinian Authority)

§ 114(a), State Department Authorization Act, FY1984-1985 (Public Law 98-
164; 22 USC 287e note) (prohibits U.S. funds to United Nations from
being used to support certain Palestinian entities (similar language in
subsequent foreign relations authorization measures)

§ 414, Foreign Relations Authorization Act, FY1990-1991 (Public Law 101-
246; 22 USC 287e note) (prohibits U.S. funds to United Nations if it
accords the PLO status equal to that of its member states)

§ 37, Bretton Woods Agreements Act (Public Law 79-171; 22 USC 286w)
(states that granting of member or observer status to PLO by the
International Monetary Fund would "result in a serious diminution of
United States support")

§ 1003, Anti-Terrorism Act of 1987 (Public Law 100-204; 22 USC 5202)
(prohibits to receive anything of value from, expend funds from, or
establish an office for, the PLO)

Current Law Related to Specific Countries

Afghanistan.

§ 620D, Foreign Assistance Act of 1961 (Public Law 87-195; 22 USC 2374)
(prohibits foreign assistance)

Angola.

§ 2(b)(11), Export-Import Bank Act of 1945 (Public Law 79-173; 12 USC
635(b)(11)) (prohibits Export-Import Bank credits)

§ 316, National Defense Authorization Act for Fiscal Year 1987 (Public Law 99-661; 10 USC 2304 note) (prohibits Department of Defense contracts)

Azerbaijan.
§ 907, FREEDOM Support Act (Public Law 102-511; 22 USC 5812 note) (restricts foreign assistance to Azerbaijan) (waived, in part, for FY1999 by paragraph titled "Assistance for the New Independent States of the Former Soviet Union", subsec. (f), in title II of sec. 101(d) of division A of Public Law 105-277; 112 Stat. 2681-160)

Bosnia-Hercegovina.
Assistance for Eastern Europe and the Baltic States, title II, Foreign Operations, Export Financing, and Related Programs Appropriations Act, 1999 (sec. 101(d) of division A of Public Law 105-277; 112 Stat. 2681-159) (authorizes President to withhold economic revitalization funds for Bosnia-Hercegovina if he finds noncompliance with Dayton Agreement concerning the withdrawal of foreign forces and cessation of cooperation between Iranian and Bosnian intelligence communities)
§ 570, Foreign Operations, Export Financing, and Related Programs Appropriations Act, 1999 (sec. 101(d) of division A of Public Law 105-277; 112 Stat. 2681-195) (prohibits foreign assistance (excluding humanitarian, democratization, or border protection assistance, U.S. Armed Forces in Bosnia-requested project support, funds to implement the Brcko Arbital Decision, Dayton Agreement-related monetary or fiscal policy support, direct lending to a non-sanctioned entity, or assistance to the International Police Task Force for training a civilian police force), transactions under the Arms Export Control Act, and U.S. support of international financial institution funding to any country, entity or canton where the Secretary of State has found and determined that authorities of that entity have failed to take necessary and significant steps to apprehend and transfer to the International Criminal Tribunal for the former Yugoslavia any indicted person)

Burma (Myanmar).
§ 138, Customs and Trade Act of 1990 (Public Law 101-382) (authorizes President to impose such economic sanctions as he determines to be appropriate)
§ 307, Foreign Assistance Act of 1961 (Public Law 87-195; 22 USC 2227) (prohibits use of U.S. foreign assistance paid in as U.S. proportionate share to international organizations when those organizations run programs in Burma, Iraq, North Korea, Syria, Libya, Iran, Cuba, or with the Palestine Liberation Organization)
§ 570, Foreign Operations, Export Financing, and Related Programs Appropriations Act, 1997 (§ 101(c) of title I of Public Law 104-208) (prohibits most foreign assistance; requires "no" votes in international financial institutions; authorizes President to restrict visas and impose investment sanctions, until such time that the President determines and certifies that Burma has made measurable and substantial progress in improving human rights and implementing democratic government)

Cambodia.

§ 906, International Security and Development Cooperation Act of 1985 (Public Law 99-83) (prohibits certain aid to Khmer Rouge)

Cambodia, title II, Foreign Operations, Export Financing, and Related Programs Appropriations Act, 1999 (sec. 101(d) of division A of Public Law 105-277; 112 Stat. 2681-156) (prohibits   most foreign assistance to Government of Cambodia (excluding demining or activities administered by nongovernmental organizations))

§ 578, Foreign Operations, Export Financing, and Related Programs Appropriations Act, 1999 (sec. 101(d) of division A of Public Law 105-277; 112 Stat. 2681-200) (requires the Secretary of the Treasury to instruct U.S. executive directors of international financial institutions to oppose loans to Government of Cambodia, except loans supporting basic human needs)

Chile.

§ 726, International Security and Development Cooperation Act of 1981 (Public Law 97-113) (prohibits most security and military assistance to Chile until the President certifies on certain conditions in human rights, terrorism, extraterritorial assassination) (such a certification was made in Department of State Public Notice 1333 of September 30, 1990)

Colombia.

§ 520, Foreign Operations, Export Financing, and Related Programs Appropriations Act, 1999 (sec. 101(d) of division A of Public Law 105-277; 112 Stat. 2681-176) (prohibits foreign assistance unless provided through Committee on Appropriations notification procedures)

Congo (former Zaire).

§ 520, Foreign Operations, Export Financing, and Related Programs Appropriations Act, 1999 (sec. 101(d) of division A of Public Law 105-277; 112 Stat. 2681-176) (prohibits foreign assistance unless provided through Committee on Appropriations notification procedures)

§ 575, Foreign Operations, Export Financing, and Related Programs Appropriations Act, 1999 (sec. 101(d) of division A of Public Law 105-277; 112 Stat. 2681-199) (prohibits some foreign assistance to the central Government of the Democratic Republic of Congo until President determines and certifies that government is investigating and prosecuting human rights violations, and is implementing a credible democratic transition program)

Croatia.

§ 570, Foreign Operations, Export Financing, and Related Programs Appropriations Act, 1999 (sec. 101(d) of division A of Public Law 105-277; 112 Stat. 2681-195) (prohibits foreign assistance (excluding humanitarian, democratization, or border protection assistance, U.S. Armed Forces in Bosnia-requested project support, funds to implement the Brcko Arbital Decision, Dayton Agreement-related monetary or fiscal policy support, direct lending to a non-sanctioned entity, or assistance to the International Police Task Force for training a civilian police force), transactions under the Arms Export Control Act, and U.S. support of international financial institution funding to any country, entity or canton where the Secretary of State has found and determined that authorities of that entity have failed to take necessary and significant steps to apprehend and transfer to the International Criminal Tribunal for the former Yugoslavia any indicted person)

Cuba.

§ 307, Foreign Assistance Act of 1961 (Public Law 87-195; 22 USC 2227) (prohibits use of U.S. foreign assistance paid in as U.S. proportionate share to international organizations when those organizations run programs in Burma, Iraq, North Korea, Syria, Libya, Iran, Cuba, or with the Palestine Liberation Organization. Further prohibits funding for International Atomic Energy Agency participation in certain projects in Cuba.)

§ 620(a), Foreign Assistance Act of 1961 (Public Law 87-195; 22 USC 2370(a)) (prohibits foreign assistance; authorizes total embargo)

§620(y), Foreign Assistance Act of 1961 (Public Law 87-195; 22 USC 2370(y)) (reduces foreign assistance to any country found to be assisting Cuba's nuclear power development)

§ 902(c), Food Security Act of 1985 (Public Law 99-198; 7 USC 1446 note) (prohibits sugar import quota to any country found to be importing for reexport to the United States sugar produced in Cuba)

§ 507, Foreign Operations, Export Financing, and Related Programs Appropriations Act, 1999 (sec. 101(d) of division A of Public Law 105-277; 112 Stat. 2681-170) (prohibits direct foreign assistance)

§ 523, Foreign Operations, Export Financing, and Related Programs Appropriations Act, 1999 (sec. 101(d) of division A of Public Law 105-277; 112 Stat. 2681-177) (prohibits indirect foreign assistance)

§ 1704(b), Cuban Democracy Act of 1992 (Public Law 102-484; 22 USC 6003(b)) (authorizes the prohibition of foreign assistance, arms export assistance, and debt forgiveness to any country conducting trade with Cuba)

§ 1705, Cuban Democracy Act of 1992 (Public Law 102-484; 22 USC 6004) (limits terms for donations and exportation of food and medicine to Cuba)

§ 1706, Cuban Democracy Act of 1992 (Public Law 102-484; 22 USC 6005) (prohibits licenses for exportation to Cuba; restricts port access to ships that have docked in Cuba; restricts remittances)

§ 102(h), Cuban Liberty and Democratic Solidarity (LIBERTAD) Act of 1996 (Public Law 104-114;22 USC 6032) (codifies 31 CFR part 515 (Cuban Assets Control Regulations) in permanent law)

§ 103, Cuban Liberty and Democratic Solidarity (LIBERTAD) Act of 1996 (Public Law 104-114;22 USC 6033) (prohibits indirect financing of any transaction involving confiscated property the claim to which is owned by a U.S. national)

§ 104, Cuban Liberty and Democratic Solidarity (LIBERTAD) Act of 1996 (Public Law 104-114;22 USC 6034) (authorizes opposition in international financial institutions to admission of Cuba; reduces U.S. contribution to any international financial institution that completes most transactions with Cuba)

§ 105, Cuban Liberty and Democratic Solidarity (LIBERTAD) Act of 1996 (Public Law 104-114;22 USC 6035) (requires continued effort to maintain suspension of Government of Cuba from Organization of American States participation)

§ 111(b), Cuban Liberty and Democratic Solidarity (LIBERTAD) Act of 1996 (Public Law 104-114;22 USC 6041(b)) (withholds assistance from any country found to be supporting the completion of Cuba's nuclear facility at Juragua, Cuba)

§ 302, Cuban Liberty and Democratic Solidarity (LIBERTAD) Act of 1996 (Public Law 104-114;22 USC 6082) (makes liable for civil claims anyone trafficking in confiscated property, to which a U.S. citizen has made a claim, in Cuba)

§ 401, Cuban Liberty and Democratic Solidarity (LIBERTAD) Act of 1996 (Public Law 104-114;22 USC 6091) (authorizes the Secretary of State to deny a visa to any alien who has trafficked in confiscated property in Cuba)

Guatemala.

International Military Education and Training, title III, Foreign Operations, Export Financing, and Related Programs Appropriations Act, 1999 (sec. 101(d) of division A of Public Law 105-277; 112 Stat. 2681-164) (restricts International Military Education and Training funding)

Foreign Military Financing Program, title III, Foreign Operations, Export Financing, and Related Programs Appropriations Act, 1999 (sec. 101(d) of division A of Public Law 105-277; 112 Stat. 2681-166) (prohibits Foreign Military Finance funding)

Haiti.

§ 520, Foreign Operations, Export Financing, and Related Programs Appropriations Act, 1999 (sec. 101(d) of division A of Public Law 105-277; 112 Stat. 2681-176) (prohibits foreign assistance unless provided through Committee on Appropriations notification procedures)

§ 561, Foreign Operations, Export Financing, and Related Programs Appropriations Act, 1999 (sec. 101(d) of division A of Public Law 105-277; 112 Stat. 2681-191) (requires Presidential certification on narcotics control, human rights, privatization, and emigration, issues before foreign assistance is made available)

§ 616, Department of State Appropriations Act, FY1999 (sec. 101(b) of division A of Public Law 105-277; 112 Stat. 2681-114) (prohibits State Department funding for visa issuance to certain Haitians involved in extrajudicial and political killings, or to certain members of the Haitian High Command during 1991-1994)

Honduras.

§ 520, Foreign Operations, Export Financing, and Related Programs Appropriations Act, 1999 (sec. 101(d) of division A of Public Law 105-277; 112 Stat. 2681-176) (prohibits foreign assistance unless provided through Committee on Appropriations notification procedures)

Indonesia.

International Military Education and Training, title III, Foreign Operations, Export Financing, and Related Programs Appropriations Act, 1999 (Public Law 105-277; 112 Stat. 2681-164) (restricts International Military Education and Training funding)

§ 569, Foreign Operations, Export Financing, and Related Programs Appropriations Act, 1999 (sec. 101(d) of division A of Public Law 105-277; 112 Stat. 2681-195) (requires any agreement for sale, transfer, or licensing of lethal equipment or helicopter for Indonesia entered into by United States to state that the United States expects that the items will not be used in East Timor)

Iran.

§ 307, Foreign Assistance Act of 1961 (Public Law 87-195; 22 USC 2227) (prohibits use of U.S. foreign assistance paid in as U.S. proportionate share to international organizations when those organizations run programs in Burma, Iraq, North Korea, Syria, Libya, Iran, Cuba, or with the Palestine Liberation Organization)

§ 507, Foreign Operations, Export Financing, and Related Programs Appropriations Act, 1999 (sec. 101(d) of division A of Public Law 105-277; 112 Stat. 2681-170) (prohibits direct foreign assistance)

§ 523, Foreign Operations, Export Financing, and Related Programs Appropriations Act, 1999 (sec. 101(d) of division A of Public Law 105-277; 112 Stat. 2681-177) (prohibits indirect foreign assistance)

§ Iraq Sanctions Act of 1990 (§ 586 through 586J of Public Law 101-513) (made applicable to Iran pursuant to § 1603, Public Law 102-484; see discussion under "Iraq")

§ 1604, Iran-Iraq Arms Nonproliferation Act of 1992 (Public Law 102-484; 50 USC 1701 note) (sanctions individuals for contributing to Iraq's or Iran's efforts to acquire chemical, biological, nuclear, or destabilizing numbers and types of advanced conventional weapons)

§ 1605, Iran-Iraq Arms Nonproliferation Act of 1992 (Public Law 102-484; 50 USC 1701 note) (sanctions foreign countries for contributing to Iraq's or Iran's efforts to acquire chemical, biological, nuclear, or destabilizing numbers and types of advanced conventional weapons)

§§ 5, 6, Iran and Libya Sanctions Act of 1996 (Public Law 104-172; 50 USC 1701 note) (authorizes the President to impose two or more of following sanctions on person if found to have engaged in investment in Iran: prohibit Export-Import Bank assistance, deny export licenses, prohibit U.S. financial institutions from making loans to sanctioned person, further restrict financial institutions from certain transactions, prohibit procurement contracts, restrict importation)

Iraq.

§ 586C, 586F, 586G, Iraq Sanctions Act (in title V of the Foreign Operations, Export Financing, and Related Programs Appropriations Act, 1991; Public Law 101-513) (continues President's imposition of trade embargo; prohibits arms sales, foreign military financing programs, export licenses for U.S. Munitions List items, items controlled for national security or foreign policy reasons, and nuclear equipment, materials, and technology. Requires U.S.

vote against international financial institution funding, prohibited Export-Import bank funding, Commodity Credit Corporation assistance, and most U.S. foreign assistance)

§ 307, Foreign Assistance Act of 1961 (Public Law 87-195; 22 USC 2227) (prohibits use of U.S. foreign assistance paid in as U.S. proportionate share to international organizations when those organizations run programs in Burma, Iraq, North Korea, Syria, Libya, Iran, Cuba, or with the Palestine Liberation Organization)

§ 507, Foreign Operations, Export Financing, and Related Programs Appropriations Act, 1999 (sec. 101(d) of division A of Public Law 105-277; 112 Stat. 2681-170) (prohibits direct foreign assistance)

§ 523, Foreign Operations, Export Financing, and Related Programs Appropriations Act, 1999 (sec. 101(d) of division A of Public Law 105-277; 112 Stat. 2681-177) (prohibits indirect foreign assistance)

§ 535, Foreign Operations, Export Financing, and Related Programs Appropriations Act, 1999 (sec. 101(d) of division A of Public Law 105-277; 112 Stat. 2681-181) (prohibits foreign assistance and transactions under the Arms Export Control Act to any country not in compliance with U.N. sanctions against Iraq)

§ 1604, Iran-Iraq Arms Nonproliferation Act of 1992 (Public Law 102-484; 50 USC 1701 note) (sanctions individuals for contributing to Iraq's or Iran's efforts to acquire chemical, biological, nuclear, or destabilizing numbers and types of advanced conventional weapons)

§ 1605, Iran-Iraq Arms Nonproliferation Act of 1992 (Public Law 102-484; 50 USC 1701 note) (sanctions foreign countries for contributing to Iraq's or Iran's efforts to acquire chemical, biological, nuclear, or destabilizing numbers and types of advanced conventional weapons)

Liberia.

Foreign Military Financing Program, title III, Foreign Operations, Export Financing, and Related Programs Appropriations Act, 1999 (sec. 101(d) of division A of Public Law 105-277; 112 Stat. 2681-165) (prohibits Foreign Military Financing funding)

§520, Foreign Operations, Export Financing, and Related Programs Appropriations Act, 1999 (sec. 101(d) of division A of Public Law 105-277; 112 Stat. 2681-176) (prohibits foreign assistance unless provided through Committee on Appropriations notification procedures)

Libya.

§ 307, Foreign Assistance Act of 1961 (Public Law 87-195; 22 USC 2227) (prohibits use of U.S. foreign assistance paid in as U.S. proportionate share to international organizations when those organizations run programs in Burma, Iraq, North Korea, Syria, Libya, Iran, Cuba, or with the Palestine Liberation Organization)

§ 504, International Security and Development Cooperation Act of 1985 (Public Law 99-83) (authorizes the President to prohibit importation and exportation of goods and services from/to Libya)

§ 507, Foreign Operations, Export Financing, and Related Programs Appropriations Act, 1999 (sec. 101(d) of division A of Public Law 105-277; 112 Stat. 2681-170) (prohibits direct foreign assistance)

§ 523, Foreign Operations, Export Financing, and Related Programs
Appropriations Act, 1999 (sec. 101(d) of division A of Public Law 105-
277; 112 Stat. 2681-177) (prohibits indirect foreign assistance)

§§ 5, 6, Iran and Libya Sanctions Act of 1996 (Public Law 104-172; 50 USC
1701 note) (authorizes the President to impose two or more of following
sanctions on person if found to have engaged in investment in Libya:
prohibit Export-Import Bank assistance, deny export licenses, prohibit U.S.
financial institutions from making loans to sanctioned person, further
restrict financial institutions from certain transactions, prohibit procurement
contracts, restrict importation)

§ 5, Iran and Libya Sanctions Act of 1996 (Public Law 104-172; 50 USC 1701
note) (further requires mandatory sanctions as described above if person is
found to have contributed to Libya's ability to acquire chemical, biological,
or nuclear weapons or destabilizing numbers and types of advanced
conventional weapons, or enhanced Libya's military or paramilitary
capabilities; contributed to Libya's petroleum resource development;
contributed to Libya's ability to maintain its aviation capabilities)

Mauritania.
§ 202, Human Rights, Refugee, and Other Foreign Relations Provisions Act of
1996 (Public Law 104-319; 22 USC 2151 note) (states the President
should prohibit economic and military assistance and arms transfers to
Government of Mauritania for human rights reasons)

Nicaragua.
§ 722, International Security and Development Cooperation Act of 1985 (Public
Law 99-83) (prohibits foreign assistance and arms sales to paramilitary
organizations and insurgent groups in Nicaragua)

North Korea.
§ 307, Foreign Assistance Act of 1961 (Public Law 87-195; 22 USC 2227)
(prohibits use of U.S. foreign assistance paid in as U.S. proportionate share
to international organizations when those organizations run programs in
Burma, Iraq, North Korea, Syria, Libya, Iran, Cuba, or with the Palestine
Liberation Organization)

International Organizations and Programs, title IV, Foreign Operations, Export
Financing, and Related Programs Appropriations Act, 1999 (sec. 101(d) of
division A of Public Law 105-277; 112 Stat. 2681-169) (prohibits IO & P
funding from being made available for Korean Peninsula Energy
Development Organization (KEDO) programs)

§ 507, Foreign Operations, Export Financing, and Related Programs
Appropriations Act, 1999 (sec. 101(d) of division A of Public Law 105-
277; 112 Stat. 2481-170) (prohibits direct foreign assistance)

§ 523, Foreign Operations, Export Financing, and Related Programs
Appropriations Act, 1999 (sec. 101(d) of division A of Public Law 105-
277; 112 Stat. 2681-177) (prohibits indirect foreign assistance)

§ 8060, Department of Defense Appropriations Act, 1999 (Public Law 105-262;
112 Stat. 2311) (prohibits DOD appropriations assistance)

Pakistan.
§ 620E(e), Foreign Assistance Act of 1961 (Public Law 87-195; 22 USC 2375(e)) (prohibits military assistance and military sales) (waived for one year, through October 1999, pursuant to sec. 902 of the India-Pakistan Relief Act of 1998 (title IX of sec. 101(a) of division A of Public Law 105-277; 112 Stat. 2681-40; see footnote 8)

§ 520, Foreign Operations, Export Financing, and Related Programs Appropriations Act, 1999 (sec. 101(d) of division A of Public Law 105-277; 112 Stat. 2681-176) (prohibits foreign assistance unless provided through Committee on Appropriations notification procedures)

Panama.
§ 1302, National Defense Authorization Act, Fiscal Year 1989 (Public Law 100-456; 22 USC 2151 note) (prohibits U.S. funding for Panamanian Defense Force)

People's Republic of China.
§ 103, International Development and Finance Act of 1989 (Public Law 101-240; 12 USC 635 note) (prohibits finance of trade with, or credits, loan, credit guarantees, insurance or reinsurance to China; waived on day it was signed into law)

§ 902, Foreign Relations Authorization Act, Fiscal Years 1990 and 1991 (Public Law 101-246; 22 USC 2151 note) (continues: suspension of Overseas Private Investment Corporation insurance, reinsurance, financing or guarantees; suspension of new projects by the Trade and Development Agency; suspension of exports of most defense articles on the U.S. Munitions List (USML); and nuclear trade and cooperation. Prohibits: export licenses for crime control and detection equipment; Suspends: U.S. satellite exports and liberalization of multilateral export controls)[23]

§ 610, Departments of Commerce, Justice, and State, the Judiciary, and Related Agencies Appropriations Act, 1990 (Public Law 101-162). (prohibits State Department appropriations to be used for approving export licenses to China for launch of U.S.-built satellites; waived on case-by-case basis)

§ 523, Foreign Operations, Export Financing, and Related Programs Appropriations Act, 1999 (sec. 101(d) of division A of Public Law 105-277; 112 Stat. 2681-177) (prohibits indirect foreign assistance)

§ 2826, National Defense Authorization Act for Fiscal Year 1998 (Public Law 105-85) (prohibits conveyance of Long Beach Naval Station property to the China Ocean Shipping Company — COSCO)

§ 8120, National Defense Authorization Act for Fiscal Year 1999 (Public Law 105-262; 112 Stat. 2332) (prohibits and U.S. DOD funds for procurement or research, development, test, and evaluation (RDTE) from being used to "enter into or renew a contract with any company owned, or partially owned, by the People's Republic of China or the People's Liberation Army of the People's Republic of China)

---

[23] Section 1515 of the Strom Thurmond National Defense Authorization Act for Fiscal Year 1999 (Public Law 105-261; 22 USC 2778 note) added new reporting requirements to any report issued pursuant to §902(b) to allow for satellite exports to China.

Republika Srpska.

§ 570, Foreign Operations, Export Financing, and Related Programs Appropriations Act, 1999 (sec. 101(d) of division A of Public Law 105-277; 112 Stat. 2681-195) (prohibits foreign assistance (excluding humanitarian, democratization, or border protection assistance, U.S. Armed Forces in Bosnia-requested project support, funds to implement the Brcko Arbital Decision, Dayton Agreement-related monetary or fiscal policy support, direct lending to a non-sanctioned entity, or assistance to the International Police Task Force for training a civilian police force), transactions under the Arms Export Control Act, and U.S. support of international financial institution funding to any country, entity or canton where the Secretary of State has found and determined that authorities of that entity have failed to take necessary and significant steps to apprehend and transfer to the International Criminal Tribunal for the former Yugoslavia any indicted person)

Russia (see also [Former] Soviet Union/East Bloc).

§ 498A(b), Foreign Assistance Act of 1961 (Public Law 87-195;22 USC 2295A(b)) (states ineligibility for foreign assistance to governments of the independent states)

§ 498A(d), Foreign Assistance Act of 1961 (Public Law 87-195;22 USC 2295A(d)) (reduces foreign assistance when Russia is found to be assisting Cuba with intelligence facilities)

Assistance for the New Independent States of the Former Soviet Union, title II, Foreign Operations, Export Financing, and Related Programs Appropriations Act, 1999 (sec. 101(d) of division A of Public Law 105-277; 112 Stat. 2681-159) (Subsec. (c) withholds 50 percent of funding under this paragraph until the President determines and certifies that Russia has terminated arrangements with Iran to provide that country nuclear technical expertise, training, technology, or equipment)

§ 517, Foreign Operations, Export Financing, and Related Programs Appropriations Act, 1999 (sec. 101(d) of division A of Public Law 105-277; 112 Stat. 2681-174) (prohibits foreign assistance without agreement with Russia that such assistance will not be subject to certain customs duties)

§ 572, Foreign Operations, Export Financing, and Related Programs Appropriations Act, 1999 (sec. 101(d) of division A of Public Law 105-277; 112 Stat. 2681-198) (prohibits foreign assistance to Government of the Russian Federation unless President determines and certifies that the Government of the Russian Federation "has implemented no statute, executive order, regulation or similar government action that would discriminate, or would have as its principal effect discrimination, against religious groups or religious communities...")

§ 2(b)(12), Export-Import Bank Act of 1945 (12 USC 635(b)(12)) (prohibits Export-Import Bank guarantees, insurance, credits, or other participation in connection with transactions of the Russian military if the military or government transfer or deliver an SS-N-22 missile system to China)

§ 1304, Strom Thurmond National Defense Authorization Act for Fiscal Year 1999 (Public Law 105-261; 22 USC 5952 note) (restricts Cooperative Threat Reduction funds to Russia for chemical weapons destruction until

President certifies on implementation of Bilateral Destruction Agreement and general national security issues)
§ 1305, Strom Thurmond National Defense Authorization Act for Fiscal Year 1999 (Public Law 105-261; 22 USC 5952 note) (prohibits Cooperative Threat Reduction (CTR) funds to Russia for biological weapons destruction until Secretary of Defense reports on Russia's use of CTR funds to develop new strains of anthrax)

South Africa.
Development Assistance, title II, Foreign Operations, Export Financing, and Related Programs Appropriations Act, 1999 (sec. 101(d) of division A of Public Law 105-277; 112 Stat. 2681-155) (prohibits development assistance funds to Central Government until Secretary of State certifies that U.S. is working with Government of South Africa toward the repeal, suspension, or termination of Medicines and Related Substances Control Amendment Act No. 90 of 1997)

[Former] Soviet Union/East Bloc.
§ 498A(b), Foreign Assistance Act of 1961 (Public Law 87-195;22 USC 2295A(b)) (states ineligibility for foreign assistance to governments of the independent states)
§ 11A, Export Administration Act of 1979 (Public Law 96-72; 50 USC App. 2410a) (prohibits exports)
Assistance for the New Independent States (NIS) of the Former Soviet Union, title II, Foreign Operations, Export Financing, and Related Programs Appropriations Act, 1998 (Public Law 105-118; 111 Stat. 2395) (subsec. (c) prohibits most foreign assistance to any NIS violating another NIS's sovereignty (excludes humanitarian and refugee relief assistance. Subsec. (d) prohibits funding under this paragraph to be used for enhancing military capacity (excluding demilitarization, demining, or nonproliferation programs))
§ 517, Foreign Operations, Export Financing, and Related Programs Appropriations Act, 1999 (sec. 101(d) of division A of Public Law 105-277; 112 Stat. 2681-174) (prohibits foreign aid if a new independent state fails to make progress in implementing economic reforms; its government uses such aid to expropriate or seize assets; or it violates the territorial integrity or national sovereignty of another new independent state. Nor may funds may not be used to enhance military capability.)

Sudan.
Foreign Military Financing Program, title III, Foreign Operations, Export Financing, and Related Programs Appropriations Act, 1999 (sec. 101(d) of division A of Public Law 105-277; 112 Stat. 2681-166) (prohibits Foreign Military Financing funding)
§ 507, Foreign Operations, Export Financing, and Related Programs Appropriations Act, 1999 (sec. 101(d) of division A of Public Law 105-277; 112 2681-170) (prohibits direct foreign assistance)
§ 520, Foreign Operations, Export Financing, and Related Programs Appropriations Act, 1999 (sec. 101(d) of division A of Public Law 105-

277; 112 Stat. 2681-176) (prohibits foreign assistance unless provided through Committee on Appropriations notification procedures)

Syria.

§ 307, Foreign Assistance Act of 1961 (Public Law 87-195; 22 USC 2227) (prohibits use of U.S. foreign assistance paid in as U.S. proportionate share to international organizations when those organizations run programs in Burma, Iraq, North Korea, Syria, Libya, Iran, Cuba, or with the Palestine Liberation Organization)

§ 507, Foreign Operations, Export Financing, and Related Programs Appropriations Act, 1999 (sec. 101(d) of division A of Public Law 105-277; 112 Stat. 2681-170) (prohibits direct foreign assistance)

§ 523, Foreign Operations, Export Financing, and Related Programs Appropriations Act, 1999 (sec. 101(d) of division A of Public Law 105-277; 112 Stat. 2681-177) (prohibits indirect foreign assistance)

Turkey.

§ 620(x), Foreign Assistance Act of 1961 (Public Law 87-195; 22 USC 2370(x)) (suspends military assistance and transactions)

Ukraine.

Assistance for the New Independent States of the Former Soviet Union, title II, Foreign Operations, Export Financing, and Related Programs Appropriations Act, 1999 (sec. 101(d) of division A of Public Law 105-277; 112 Stat. 2681-161) (subsec. (g) withholds 50 percent of funding made available to Ukraine under this paragraph, with certain exceptions, until the Secretary of State reports to the Committees on Appropriations that Ukraine has undertaken significant economic reforms)

Vietnam (Socialist Republic of).

§ 609, State Department Appropriations Act, FY1999 (sec. 101(b) of division A of Public Law 105-277; 112 Stat. 2681-112) (prohibits State Department funding for diplomatic or consular post until certain conditions are met)

Yugoslavia (Serbia and Montenegro).

§ 1511, National Defense Authorization Act for Fiscal Year 1994 (Public Law 103-160; 50 USC 1701 note) (prohibits broad range of relations, freezes assets, travel, assistance, international financial institution support)

§ 520, Foreign Operations, Export Financing, and Related Programs Appropriations Act, 1999 (sec. 101(d) of division A of Public Law 105-277; 112 Stat. 2681-176) (prohibits foreign assistance unless provided through Committee on Appropriations notification procedures)

§ 539, Foreign Operations, Export Financing, and Related Programs Appropriations Act, 1999 (sec. 101(d) of division A of Public Law 105-277; 112 Stat. 2681-182) (prohibits use of any funds to lift sanctions until President certifies on certain conditions in Kosovo, and on Serbia's compliance with the Dayton peace agreement and cooperation with the International Criminal Tribunal)

§ 570, Foreign Operations, Export Financing, and Related Programs Appropriations Act, 1999 (sec. 101(d) of division A of Public Law 105-

277; 112 Stat. 2681-195) (prohibits foreign assistance (excluding humanitarian, democratization, or border protection assistance, U.S. Armed Forces in Bosnia-requested project support, funds to implement the Brcko Arbital Decision, Dayton Agreement-related monetary or fiscal policy support, direct lending to a non-sanctioned entity, or assistance to the International Police Task Force for training a civilian police force), transactions under the Arms Export Control Act, and U.S. support of international financial institution funding to any country, entity or canton where the Secretary of State has found and determined that authorities of that entity have failed to take necessary and significant steps to apprehend and transfer to the International Criminal Tribunal for the former Yugoslavia any indicted person)

Foreign Policy of the United States
Volume 1

FOREIGN POLICY ROLES OF THE PRESIDENT AND CONGRESS

Richard F. Grimmett

SUMMARY

In the post-Cold War world, Presidents have continued to commit U.S. Armed Forces to potential hostilities without specific authorization from Congress, and the War Powers Resolution has come under new scrutiny. On January 4, 1995, Senate Majority Leader Robert Dole introduced S. 5, legislation aimed at placing greater restrictions on the use of American armed forces in peacekeeping operations of the United Nations, and a measure that would repeal most of the War Powers Resolution, except for its reporting requirements. The House, through various measures, including H.R. 7, which passed that body on February 16, 1995, sought to require congressional approval for U.S. participation in multinational peacekeeping missions. On June 7, the House defeated, by a vote of 217-201, an amendment to repeal the central features of the War Powers Resolution that have been deemed unconstitutional by every President since the law's enactment in 1973.

The War Powers Resolution (Public Law 93-148) was passed over the veto of President Nixon on November 7, 1973, to assure that both Congress and the President participated in decisions to send U.S. Armed Forces into hostilities. Section 4(a)(1) requires the President to report to Congress any introduction of U.S. forces into hostilities or imminent hostilities. When such a report is submitted, or is required to be submitted, section 5(b) requires that the use of forces must be terminated within 60 to 90 days unless Congress authorizes such use or extends the time period. Section 3 requires that the "President in every possible instance shall consult with Congress before introducing" U.S. Armed Forces into hostilities or imminent hostilities.

Since 1973 Presidents have submitted over fifty reports under the War Powers Resolution, but only one, on the *Mayaguez* seizure, cited section 4(a)(1) which triggers the time limit. President Ford submitted four reports, President Carter one, President Reagan fourteen, and President Bush six reports. President Clinton by December 1995 had submitted 25 reports. In several instances U.S. Armed Forces have been used in hostile situations without formal reports to Congress.

Congress determined that the requirements of section 4(a)(1) became operative on August 29, 1983, in the Multinational Force in Lebanon Resolution, and authorized continued U.S. participation in the Multinational Force for 18 months. Congress also authorized the deployment of military personnel to the Sinai to participate in the Multinational Force and Observers in 1981, and the use of military force against Iraq in 1991.

In several instances neither the President, Congress, nor the courts proved willing to trigger the War Powers Resolution mechanism. Some Members of Congress contend that the Resolution has proved ineffective and should be amended. Some suggest it should be repealed. Other Members contend that the Resolution has been effective by increasing legislative-executive communication and congressional leverage.

TABLE OF CONTENTS

THE WAR POWERS RESOLUTION: TWENTY-TWO YEARS OF EXPERIENCE

INTRODUCTION

Under the Constitution, the war powers are divided between Congress and the President. Among other relevant grants, Congress has the power to declare war and raise and support the armed forces (Article I, section 8), while the President is Commander in Chief (Article II, section 2). It is generally agreed that the Commander in Chief role gives the President power to utilize the armed forces to repel attacks against the United States, but there has long been controversy over whether he is constitutionally authorized to send forces into hostile situations abroad without a declaration of war or other congressional authorization.

Congressional concern about Presidential use of armed forces without congressional authorization intensified after the Korean conflict. During the Vietnam war, Congress searched for a way to assert authority to decide when the United States should become involved in a war or the armed forces utilized in circumstances that might lead to hostilities. On November 7, 1973, it passed the War Powers Resolution (P.L. 93-148) over the veto of President Nixon. The main purpose of the Resolution was to assure that both branches share in decisions that might get the United States involved in war. The drafters sought to circumscribe the President's authority to use armed forces abroad in hostilities or potential hostilities without a declaration of war or other congressional authorization, yet provide enough flexibility to permit him to respond to attack or other emergencies.

The record of the War Powers Resolution since its enactment has been mixed, and after more than 22 years it remains controversial. Some Members of Congress believe the Resolution has on some occasions served as a restraint on the use of armed forces by Presidents, provided a mode of communication, and given Congress a vehicle for asserting its war powers. Others have sought to amend the Resolution because they believe it has failed to assure a congressional voice in committing U.S. troops to potential conflicts abroad. Others in Congress, along with executive branch officials, contend that the President needs more flexibility in the conduct of foreign policy and that the time limitation in the War Powers Resolution is unconstitutional and impractical. Some have argued for its repeal.

This report examines the provisions of the War Powers Resolution, the experience with it since 1973, and proposed amendments. Appendix 1 lists instances which Presidents have reported to Congress under the War Powers Resolution, and Appendix 2 lists instances of the use of U.S. armed forces that were not reported.

PROVISIONS OF THE WAR POWERS RESOLUTION (P.L. 93-148)

TITLE

Section 1 establishes the title, "The War Powers Resolution." The law is frequently referred to as the "War Powers Act," the title of the measure passed by the Senate. Although the latter is not technically correct, it does serve to emphasize that the War Powers Resolution, embodied in a joint resolution which complies with constitutional requirements for lawmaking, is a law.

PURPOSE AND POLICY

Section 2 states the Resolution's purpose and policy, with Section 2(a) citing as the primary purpose to "insure that the collective judgment of both the Congress and the President will apply to the introduction of United States Armed Forces into hostilities, or into situations where imminent involvement in hostilities is clearly indicated by the circumstances, and to the continued use of such forces in hostilities or in such situations."

Section 2(b) points to the Necessary and Proper Clause of the Constitution as the basis for legislation on the war powers. It provides that "Under Article I, section 8, of the Constitution it is specifically provided that Congress shall have the power to make all laws necessary and proper for carrying into execution, not only its own powers but also all other powers vested by the Constitution in the Government of the United States...."

Section 2(c) states the policy that the powers of the President as Commander in Chief to introduce U.S. armed forces into situations of hostilities or imminent hostilities "are exercised only pursuant to --

(1)   a declaration of war,
(2)   specific statutory authorization, or
(3)   a national emergency created by attack upon the United States, its territories or possessions, or its armed forces."

CONSULTATION REQUIREMENT

Section 3 of the War Powers Resolution requires the President "in every possible instance" to consult with Congress before introducing U.S. Armed Forces into situations of hostilities and imminent hostilities, and to continue consultations as long as the armed forces remain in such situations. The House report elaborated:

A considerable amount of attention was given to the definition of **consultation**. Rejected was the notion that consultation should be synonymous with merely being informed. Rather, consultation in this provision means that a decision is pending on a problem and that Members of Congress are being asked by the President for their advice and opinions and, in appropriate circumstances, their approval of action contemplated. Furthermore, for consultation to be meaningful, the President himself must participate and all information relevant to the situation must be made available.[1]

The House version specifically called for consultation between the President and the leadership and appropriate committees. This was changed to less specific wording in conference, however, in order to provide more flexibility.

REPORTING REQUIREMENTS

Section 4 requires the President to report to Congress whenever he introduces U.S. armed forces abroad in certain situations. Of key importance is section 4(a)(1) because it triggers the time limit in section 5(b). Section 4(a)(1) requires reporting within 48 hours, in the absence of a declaration of war or congressional authorization, the introduction of U.S. armed forces "into hostilities or into situations where imminent involvement in hostilities is clearly indicated by the circumstances."

Some indication of the meaning of hostilities and imminent hostilities is given in the House report on its War Powers bill:

> The word **hostilities** was substituted for the phrase **armed conflict** during the subcommittee drafting process because it was considered to be somewhat broader in scope. In addition to a situation in which fighting actually has begun, **hostilities** also encompasses a state of confrontation in which no shots have been fired but where there is a clear and present danger of armed conflict. "**Imminent hostilities**" denotes a situation in which there is a clear potential either for such a state of confrontation or for actual armed conflict.[2]

Section 4(a)(2) requires the reporting of the introduction of troops "into the territory, airspace or waters of a foreign nation, while equipped for combat, except for deployments which relate solely to supply, replacement, repair, or training of such forces." According to the House report this was to cover

> the initial commitment of troops in situations in which there is no actual fighting but some risk, however small, of the forces being involved in hostilities. A report would be required any time combat military forces were sent to another nation to alter or preserve the

---

[1] U.S. Congress. House Report 93-287, p. 6.

[2] U.S. Congress. House Report 93-287, p. 7.

existing political status quo or to make the U.S. presence felt. Thus, for example, the dispatch of Marines to Thailand in 1962 and the quarantine of Cuba in the same year would have required Presidential reports. Reports would not be required for routine port supply calls, emergency aid measures, normal training exercises, and other noncombat military activities.[3]

Section 4(a)(3) requires the reporting of the introduction of troops "in numbers which substantially enlarge United States Armed Forces equipped for combat already located in a foreign nation." The House report elaborated:

While the word "substantially" designates a flexible criterion, it is possible to arrive at a common-sense understanding of the numbers involved. A 100% increase in numbers of Marine guards at an embassy -- say from 5 to 10 -- clearly would not be an occasion for a report. A thousand additional men sent to Europe under present circumstances does not significantly enlarge the total U.S. troop strength of about 300,000 already there. However, the dispatch of 1,000 men to Guantanamo Bay, Cuba, which now has a complement of 4,000 would mean an increase of 25%, which is substantial. Under this circumstance, President Kennedy would have been required to report to Congress in 1962 when he raised the number of U.S. military advisers in Vietnam from 700 to 16,000.[4]

All of the reports under Section 4(a), which are to be submitted to the Speaker of the House and the President pro tempore of the Senate, are to set forth:

(A) the circumstances necessitating the introduction of United States Armed Forces;

(B) the constitutional and legislative authority under which such introduction took place; and

(C) the estimated scope and duration of the hostilities or involvement.

Section 4(b) requires the President to furnish such other information as Congress may request to fulfill its responsibilities relating to committing the nation to war.

Section 4(c) requires the President to report to Congress periodically, and at least every six months, whenever U.S. forces are introduced into hostilities or any other situation in section 4(a).

---

[3] U.S. Congress. H. Rept. 93-287, p. 7.

[4] U.S. Congress. H. Rept. 93-287, p. 8.

The objectives of these provisions, the conference report stated, was to "ensure that the Congress by right and as a matter of law will be provided with all the information it requires to carry out its constitutional responsibilities with respect to committing the Nation to war and to the use of United States Armed Forces abroad."[5]

CONGRESSIONAL ACTION

Section 5(a) deals with congressional procedures for receipt of a report under section 4(a)(1). It provides that if a report is transmitted during a congressional adjournment, the Speaker of the House and the President pro tempore of the Senate, when they deem it advisable or if petitioned by at least 30% of the Members of their respective Houses, shall jointly request the President to convene Congress in order to consider the report and take appropriate action.

Section 5(b) was intended to provide teeth for the War Powers Resolution. After a report "is submitted or is required to be submitted pursuant to section 4(a)(1), whichever is earlier", section 5(b) requires the President to terminate the use of U.S. Armed Forces after 60 days unless Congress (1) has declared war or authorized the action; (2) has extended the period by law; or (3) is physically unable to meet as a result of an armed attack on the United States. The 60 days can be extended for 30 days by the President if he certifies that "unavoidable military necessity respecting the safety of United States Armed Forces" requires their continued use in the course of bringing about their removal.

Section 5(c) requires the President to remove the forces at any time if Congress so directs by concurrent resolution; the effectiveness of this subsection is uncertain because of the 1983 Supreme Court decision on the legislative veto. It is discussed in Part II of this report.

PRIORITY PROCEDURES

Section 6 establishes expedited procedures for congressional consideration of a joint resolution or bill introduced to authorize the use of armed forces under section 5 (b). They provide for:

(a) A referral to the House Foreign Affairs or Senate Foreign Relations Committee, the committee to report one measure not later than 24 calendar days before the expiration of the 60 day period, unless the relevant House determines otherwise by a vote;

(b) The reported measure to become the pending business of the relevant House and be voted on within three calendar days, unless that House

---

[5] U.S. Congress. H. Rept. 93-547, p. 8.

determines otherwise by vote; in the Senate the debate is to be equally divided between proponents and opponents;

(c) A measure passed by one House to be referred to the relevant committee of the other House and reported out not later than 14 calendar days before the expiration of the 60 day period, the reported bill to become the pending business of that House and be voted on within 3 calendar days unless determined otherwise by a vote;

(d) Conferees to file a report not later than four calendar days before the expiration of the 60 day period. If they cannot agree within 48 hours, the conferees are to report back in disagreement, and such report is to be acted on by both Houses not later than the expiration of the 60 day period.

Section 7 establishes similar priority procedures for a concurrent resolution to withdraw forces under section 5(c). For a recent use of these procedures see the section on the legislative veto, below.

INTERPRETIVE PROVISIONS

Section 8 sets forth certain interpretations relating to the Resolution. Section 8(a) states that authority to introduce armed forces is not to be inferred from any provision of law or treaty unless it specifically authorizes the introduction of armed forces into hostilities or potential hostilities and states that it is "intended to constitute specific statutory authorization within the meaning of this joint resolution." This language was derived from a Senate measure and was intended to prevent a security treaty or military appropriations act from being used to authorize the introduction of troops. It was also aimed against using a broad resolution like the Tonkin Gulf Resolution [6] to justify hostilities abroad. This resolution had stated that the United States was prepared to take all necessary steps, including use of armed force, to assist certain nations, and it was cited by Presidents and many Members as congressional authorization for the Vietnam war.

Section 8(b) states that further specific statutory authorization is not required

to permit members of United States Armed Forces to participate jointly with members of the armed forces of one or more foreign countries in the headquarters operations of high-level military commands which were established prior to the date of enactment of this joint resolution and pursuant to the United Nations Charter or any treaty ratified by the United States prior to such date.

---

[6] P.L. 88-408, approved Aug. 10, 1964; repealed in 1971 by P.L. 91-672.

This section was added by the Senate to make clear that the resolution did not prevent U.S. forces from participating in certain joint military exercises with allied or friendly organizations or countries. The conference report stated that the "high-level" military commands meant the North Atlantic Treaty Organization, (NATO), the North American Air Defense Command (NORAD) and the United Nations command in Korea.

Section 8(c) defines the introduction of armed forces to include the assignment of armed forces to accompany regular or irregular military forces of other countries when engaged, or potentially engaged, in hostilities. The conference report on the War Powers Resolution explained that this was language modified from a Senate provision requiring specific statutory authorization for assigning members of the Armed Forces for such purposes. The report of the Senate Foreign Relations Committee on its bill said:

> The purpose of this provision is to prevent secret, unauthorized military support activities and to prevent a repetition of many of the most controversial and regrettable actions in Indochina. The ever deepening ground combat involvement of the United States in South Vietnam began with the assignment of U.S. "advisers" to accompany South Vietnamese units on combat patrols; and in Laos, secretly and without congressional authorization, U.S. "advisers" were deeply engaged in the war in northern Laos.[7]

Section 8(d) states that nothing in the Resolution is intended to alter the constitutional authority of either the Congress or the President. It also specifies that nothing is to be construed as granting any authority to introduce troops that would not exist in the absence of the Resolution. The House report said that this provision was to help insure the constitutionality of the Resolution by making it clear that nothing in it could be interpreted as changing the powers delegated by the Constitution.

Section 9 is a separability clause, stating that if any provision or its application is found invalid, the remainder of the Resolution is not to be affected.

CONSTITUTIONAL QUESTIONS RAISED

From its inception, the War Powers Resolution was controversial because it operated on the national war powers, powers divided by the Constitution in no definitive fashion between the President and Congress. Congress adopted the resolution in response to the perception that Presidents had assumed more authority to send forces into hostilities than the framers of the Constitution had intended for the Commander in Chief. President Nixon in his veto message challenged the constitutionality of the essence of the War Powers Resolution,

---

[7] U.S. Congress. Senate Report 93-220, p. 24.

and particularly two provisions.[8] He argued that the legislative veto provision, permitting Congress to direct the withdrawal of troops by concurrent resolution, was unconstitutional. He also argued that the provision requiring withdrawal of troops after 60-90 days unless Congress passed legislation authorizing such use was unconstitutional because it checked Presidential powers without affirmative congressional action.

WAR POWERS OF PRESIDENT AND CONGRESS

The heart of the challenge to the constitutionality of the War Powers Resolution rests on differing interpretations by the two branches of the respective war powers of the President and Congress. These differing interpretations, especially the assertions of Presidential authority to send forces into hostile situations without a declaration of war or other authorization by Congress, were the reason for the enactment of the Resolution.

The congressional view was that the framers of the Constitution gave Congress the power to declare war, meaning the ultimate decision whether or not to enter a war. Most Members of Congress agreed that the President as Commander in Chief had power to lead the U.S. forces once the decision to wage war had been made, to defend the nation against an attack, and perhaps in some instances to take other action such as rescuing American citizens. But, in this view, he did not have the power to commit armed forces to war. By the early 1970s, the congressional majority view was that the constitutional balance of war powers had swung too far toward the President and needed to be corrected. Opponents argued that Congress always held the power to forbid or terminate U.S. military action by statute or refusal of appropriations, and that without the clear will to act the War Powers Resolution would be ineffective.

In his veto message, President Nixon said the Resolution would impose restrictions upon the authority of the President which would be dangerous to the safety of the Nation and "attempt to take away, by a mere legislative act, authorities which the President has properly exercised under the Constitution for almost 200 years."

The War Powers Resolution in section 2(c) recognized the constitutional powers of the President as Commander-in-Chief to introduce forces into hostilities or imminent hostilities as "exercised only pursuant to (1) a declaration of war, (2) specific statutory authorization, or (3) a national emergency created by attack upon the United States, its territories or possessions, or its armed forces." The executive branch has contended that the President has much broader authority to use forces, including for such purposes as to rescue American citizens abroad, rescue foreign nationals where such action facilitates the rescue of U.S. citizens, protect U.S. Embassies and legations, suppress civil

---

[8] United States. President (Nixon). Message vetoing House Joint Resolution 542, A Joint Resolution Concerning the War Powers of Congress and the President. October 24, 1973. House Document No. 93-171.

insurrection, implement the terms of an armistice or cease-fire involving the United States, and carry out the terms of security commitments contained in treaties.[9]

LEGISLATIVE VETO

On June 23, 1983, the Supreme Court in *INS* v. *Chadha*, ruled unconstitutional the legislative veto provision in section 244(c)(2) of the Immigration and Nationality Act.[10] Although the case involved the use of a one-House legislative veto, the decision cast doubt on the validity of any legislative veto device that was not presented to the President for signature. The Court held that to accomplish what the House attempted to do in the *Chadha* case "requires action in conformity with the express procedures of the Constitution's prescription for legislative action: passage by a majority of both Houses and presentment to the President." On July 6, 1983, the Supreme Court affirmed a lower court's decision striking down a provision in another law[11] that permitted Congress to disapprove by concurrent (two-House) resolution.[12]

Since section 5(c) requires forces to be removed by the President if Congress so directs by a concurrent resolution, it is constitutionally suspect under the reasoning applied by the Court.[13] A concurrent resolution is adopted by both chambers, but it does not require presentment to the President for signature or veto. Some legal analysts contend, nevertheless, that the War Powers Resolution is in a unique category which differs from statutes containing a legislative veto over delegated authorities.[14] Perhaps more important, some observers contend, if a majority of both Houses ever voted to withdraw U.S.

---

[9] U.S. Congress. House. Committee on International Relations. War Powers: A Test of Compliance relative to the Danang Sealift, the Evacuation of Phnom Penh, the Evacuation of Saigon, and the Mayaguez Incident. Hearings, May 7 and June 4, 1975. Washington, U.S. Govt. Printing Off., 1975. p. 69.

[10] 462 U.S. 919 (1983).

[11] Federal Trade Commission Improvements Act of 1980.

[12] *Process Gas Consumers Group* v. *Consumer Energy Council*, 463 U.S. 1216 (1983).

[13] Celada, Raymond. J. *Effect of the Legislative Veto Decision on the Two-House Disapproval Mechanism to Terminate U.S. Involvement in Hostilities Pursuant to Unilateral Presidential Action.* CRS Report, August 24, 1983.

[14] Gressman, Prof. Eugene. In U.S. Congress. House. Committee on Foreign Affairs. The U.S. Supreme Court Decision Concerning the Legislative Veto. Hearings, July 19, 20, and 21, 1983. 98th Congress, 1st sess. Washington, U.S. GPO, 1983, p. 155-157. Buchanan, G. Sidney. In Defense of the War Powers Resolution: *Chadha* Does Not Apply. *Houston Law Review*, Vol. 22, p. 1155; Ely, John Hart. Suppose Congress Wanted a War Powers Act that Worked. *Columbia Law Review*, Vol. 88, p. 1379 (see p. 1395-1398).

forces, the President would be unlikely to continue the action for long, and Congress could withhold appropriations to finance further action. Because the War Powers Resolution contains a separability clause in section 9, most analysts take the view that the remainder of the joint resolution would not be affected even if section 5(c) were found unconstitutional.[15]

Congress has taken action to fill the gap left by the possible invalidity of the concurrent resolution mechanism for the withdrawal of troops. On October 20, 1983, the Senate voted to amend the War Powers Resolution by substituting a joint resolution, which requires presentment to the President, for the concurrent resolution in section 5(c), and providing that it would be handled under the expedited procedures in section 7. The House and Senate conferees agreed not to amend the War Powers Resolution itself, but to adopt a free standing measure relating to the withdrawal of troops. The measure, which became law, provided that any joint resolution or bill to require the removal of U.S. armed forces engaged in hostilities outside the United States without a declaration of war or specific statutory authorization would be considered in accordance with the expedited procedures of section 601(b) of the International Security and Arms Export Control Act of 1976,[16] except that it would be amendable and debate on a veto limited to 20 hours.[17] The priority procedures embraced by this provision applied in the Senate only. Handling of such a joint resolution by the House was left to that Chamber's discretion.

House Members attempted to use section 5(c) to obtain a withdrawal of forces from Somalia. On October 22, 1993, Representative Benjamin Gilman introduced H.Con.Res. 170, pursuant to section 5(c) of the War Powers Resolution, directing the President to remove U.S. Armed Forces from Somalia by January 31, 1994. Using the expedited procedures called for in section 5(c), the Foreign Affairs Committee amended the date of withdrawal to March 31, 1994, (the date the President had already agreed to withdraw the forces), and the House adopted H.Con.Res. 170. The Foreign Affairs Committee reported:[18]

> Despite such genuine constitutionality questions, the committee acted in accordance with the expedited procedures in section 7. The committee action was premised on a determination that neither individual Members of Congress nor Committees of Congress should make unilateral judgments about the constitutionality of provisions of law.

---

[15] U.S. Congress. House. Committee on Foreign Affairs. U.S. Supreme Court Decision Concerning the Legislative Veto, Hearings, p. 52.

[16] Public Law 94-329, signed June 30, 1976.

[17] Senate amendment to S. 1324. Section 1013, State Department Authorization Act for FY 1984, Public Law 98-164, approved Nov. 22, 1983.

[18] H. Rept. 103-329, November 5, 1993, p. 2. See below for further discussion of the Somalia case.

Despite the use of the phrase "directs the President", the sponsor of the resolution and Speaker of the House Thomas Foley expressed the view that because of the *Chadha* decision, the resolution would be non-binding.

AUTOMATIC WITHDRAWAL PROVISION

The automatic withdrawal provision has become perhaps the most controversial provision of the War Powers Resolution. Section 5(b) requires the President to withdraw U.S. forces from hostilities within 60-90 days after a report is submitted or required to be submitted under section 4(a)(1). The triggering of the time limit has been a major factor in the reluctance of Presidents to report, or Congress to insist upon a report, under section 4(a)(1).

Drafters of the War Powers Resolution included a time limit to provide some teeth for Congress, in the event a President assumed a power to act from provisions of resolutions, treaties, or the Constitution which did not constitute an explicit authorization. The Senate report called the time limit "the heart and core" of the bill that "represents, in an historic sense, a restoration of the constitutional balance which has been distorted by practice in our history and, climatically, in recent decades."[19] The House report emphasized that the Resolution did not grant the President any new authority or any freedom of action during the time limits that he did not already have.

Administration officials have objected that the provision would require the withdrawal of U.S. forces simply because of congressional inaction during an arbitrary period. Since the resolution recognizes that the President has independent authority to use armed forces in certain circumstances, they state, "on what basis can Congress seek to terminate such independent authority by the mere passage of time?"[20] In addition, they argue, the imposition of a deadline interferes with successful action, signals a divided nation and lack of resolve, gives the enemy a basis for hoping that the President will be forced by domestic opponents to stop an action, and increases risk to U.S. forces in the field. The issue has not been dealt with by the courts.

MAJOR CASES AND ISSUES PRIOR TO THE PERSIAN GULF WAR

Perceptions of the War Powers Resolution tended to be set during the Cold War. During the 1970s the issues revolved largely around the adequacy of

---

[19] The Senate bill had a time limit of 30 days. U.S. Congress. Senate. Committee on Foreign Relations. War Powers. Report to accompany S. 440. Senate Report 220, 93d Congress, 1st Session. p. 28.

[20] Sofaer, Abraham D. Prepared statement in: U.S. Congress. Senate. Committee on Foreign Relations. The War Power After 200 Years: Congress and the President at a Constitutional Impasse. Hearings before the Special Subcommittee on War Powers. July 13-September 29, 1988. S. Hrg. 100-1012. p. 1059.

consultation. The 1980s raised more serious issues of Presidential compliance and congressional willingness to use the War Powers Resolution to restrain Presidential action. In regard to Lebanon in 1983, Congress found it could invoke the War Powers Resolution, but in the 1987-1988 Persian Gulf tanker war Congress proved reluctant to do so. Following is a summary of major U.S. military actions and the issues they raised relating to the War Powers Resolution from its enactment in 1973 to August 1990.[21]

VIETNAM EVACUATIONS AND MAYAGUEZ: WHAT IS CONSULTATION?

As the Vietnam war ended, on three occasions, in April 1975, President Ford used U.S. forces to help evacuate American citizens and foreign nationals. In addition, in May 1975 President Ford ordered the retaking of a U.S. merchant vessel, the *SS Mayaguez* which had been seized by Cambodian naval patrol vessels. All four actions were reported to Congress citing the War Powers Resolution. The report on the Mayaguez recapture was the only War Powers report to date to specifically cite section 4(a)(1), but the question of the time limit was moot because the action was over by the time the report was filed.

Among the problems revealed by these first four cases were differences of opinion between the two branches on the meaning of consultation. The Ford Administration held that it had met the consultation requirement because the President had directed that congressional leaders be notified prior to the actual commencement of the introduction of armed forces. The prevailing congressional view was that consultation meant that the President seek congressional opinion, and take it into account, prior to making a decision to commit armed forces.[22]

IRAN HOSTAGE RESCUE ATTEMPT: WHEN IS CONSULTATION NECESSARY AND POSSIBLE?

After an unsuccessful attempt on April 24, 1980, to rescue American hostages being held in Iran, President Carter submitted a report to Congress to meet the requirements of the War Powers Resolution, but he did not consult in advance. The Administration took the position that consultation was not required because the mission was a rescue attempt, not an act of force or aggression against Iran. In addition, the Administration contended that

---

[21] Appendix 1 lists in chronological order all instances reported under the Resolution. Appendix 2 lists other instances of the deployment to or use of armed forces in potentially hostile situations which were not reported.

[22] U.S. Congress. House. Committee on International Relations. War Powers: A Test of Compliance Relative to the Danang Sealift, the Evacuation of Phnom Penh, the Evacuation of Saigon, and the Mayaguez Incident. Hearings, May 7 and June 4, 1975. Washington, U.S. GPO, 1975. p. 3.

consultation was not possible or required because the mission depended upon total surprise.

Some Members of Congress complained about the lack of consultation, especially because legislative-executive meetings had been going on since the Iranian crisis had begun the previous year. Just before the rescue attempt, the Senate Foreign Relations Committee had sent a letter to Secretary of State Cyrus Vance requesting formal consultations under the War Powers Resolution. Moreover, shortly before the rescue attempt, the President outlined plans for a rescue attempt to Senate Majority Leader Robert Byrd but did not say it had begun. Senate Foreign Relations Committee Chairman Frank Church stressed as guidelines for the future: (1) consultation required giving Congress an opportunity to participate in the decision making process, not just informing Congress that an operation was underway; and (2) the judgment could not be made unilaterally but should be made by the President and Congress.[23]

EL SALVADOR: WHEN ARE MILITARY ADVISERS IN IMMINENT HOSTILITIES?

One of the first cases to generate substantial controversy because it was never reported under the War Powers Resolution was the dispatch of U.S. military advisers to El Salvador. At the end of February 1981, the Department of State announced the dispatch of 20 additional military advisers to El Salvador to aid its government against guerilla warfare. There were already 19 military advisers in El Salvador sent by the Carter Administration. The Reagan Administration said the insurgents were organized and armed by Soviet bloc countries, particularly Cuba. By March 14, the Administration had authorized a total of 54 advisers, including experts in combat training.

The President did not report the situation under the War Powers Resolution. A State Department memorandum said a report was not required because the U.S. personnel were not being introduced into hostilities or situations of imminent hostilities. The memorandum asserted that if a change in circumstances occurred that raised the prospect of imminent hostilities, the Resolution would be complied with. A justification for not reporting under section 4(a)(2) was that the military personnel being introduced were not equipped for combat.[24] They would, it was maintained, carry only personal sidearms which they were authorized to use only in their own defense or the defense of other Americans.

The State Department held that section 8(c) of the War Powers Resolution was not intended to require a report when U.S. military personnel might be

---

[23] U.S. Congress. Senate. Committee on Foreign Relations. The situation in Iran. Hearing, 96th Congress, 2nd session. May 8, 1980. Washington, U.S. Govt. Print. Off., 1980. p. iii.

[24] Congressional Record, March 5, 1981, V. 127, p. 3743.

involved in training foreign military personnel, if there were no imminent involvement of U.S. personnel in hostilities. In the case of El Salvador, the memorandum said, U.S. military personnel "will not act as combat advisors, and will not accompany Salvadoran forces in combat, on operational patrols, or in any other situation where combat is likely."

On May 1, 1981, eleven Members of Congress challenged the President's action by filing suit on grounds that he had violated the Constitution and the War Powers Resolution by sending the advisers to El Salvador. Eventually there were 29 co-plaintiffs, but by June 18, 1981, an equal number of Members (13 Senators and 16 Representatives) filed a motion to intervene in the suit, contending that a number of legislative measures were then pending before Congress and that Congress had ample opportunity to vote to end military assistance to El Salvador if it wished.

On October 4, 1982, U.S. District Court Judge Joyce Hens Green dismissed the suit. She ruled that Congress, not the court, must resolve the question of whether the U.S. forces in El Salvador were involved in a hostile or potentially hostile situation. While there might be situations in which a court could conclude that U.S. forces were involved in hostilities, she ruled, the "subtleties of fact-finding in this situation should be left to the political branches." She noted that Congress had taken no action to show it believed the President's decision was subject to the War Powers Resolution.[25] On November 18, 1983, a Federal circuit court affirmed the dismissal and on June 8, 1984, the Supreme Court declined consideration of an appeal of that decision.[26]

As the involvement continued and casualties occurred among the U.S. military advisers, various legislative proposals relating to the War Powers Resolution and El Salvador were introduced. Some proposals required a specific authorization prior to the introduction of U.S. forces into hostilities or combat in El Salvador.[27] Other proposals declared that the commitment of U.S. Armed Forces in El Salvador necessitated compliance with section 4(a) of the War Powers Resolution, requiring the President to submit a report.[28]

---

[25] *Crockett* v. *Reagan*, 558 F. Supp. 893 (D.D.C. 1982).

[26] 720 F. 2d 1355 (D.C.Cir. 1983), *cert. den.*, 467 U.S. 1251 (1984).

[27] On March 8, 1982, Senator Robert Byrd introduced the War Powers Resolution Amendment of 1982 (S. 2179) specifically providing that U.S. armed forces shall not be introduced into El Salvador for combat unless (1) the Congress has declared war or specifically authorized such use; or (2) such introduction was necessary to meet a clear and present danger of attack on the United States or to provide immediate evacuation of U.S. citizens. Similar bills were introduced in the House, e.g. H. R. 1619 and H. R. 1777 in the 98th Congress.

[28] H. Con. Res. 87, 97th Congress.

Neither approach was adopted in legislation, but the Senate Foreign Relations Committee reported that the President had "a clear obligation under the War Powers Resolution to consult with Congress prior to any future decision to commit combat forces to El Salvador."[29]   On July 26, 1983, the House rejected an amendment to the Defense Authorization bill (H.R. 2969) to limit the number of active duty military advisers in El Salvador to 55, unless the President reported them under section 4(a)(1) of the War Powers Resolution.[30] Nevertheless, the Administration in practice kept the number of trainers at 55.

HONDURAS: WHEN ARE MILITARY EXERCISES MORE THAN TRAINING?

Military exercises in Honduras in 1983 and subsequent years raised the question of when military exercises should be reported under the War Powers Resolution.   Section 4(a)(2) requires the reporting of introduction of troops equipped for combat, but exempts deployments which relate solely to training.

On July 27, 1983, President Reagan announced "joint training exercises" planned for Central America and the Caribbean. The first contingent of U.S. troops landed in Honduras on August 8, 1983, and the series of ground and ocean exercises continued for several years, involving thousands of ground troops plus warships and fighter planes.

The President did not report the exercises under the War Powers Resolution. He characterized the maneuvers as routine and said the United States had been regularly conducting joint exercises with Latin American countries since 1965. Some Members of Congress, on the other hand, contended that the exercises were part of a policy to support the rebels or "contras" fighting the Sandinista Government of Nicaragua, threatening that government, and increased the possibility of U.S. military involvement in hostilities in Central America.

Several Members of Congress called for reporting the actions under the War Powers Resolution, but some sought other vehicles for congressional control. In 1982, the Boland amendment to the Defense Appropriations Act had already prohibited use of funds to overthrow the Government of Nicaragua or provoke a military exchange between Nicaragua or Honduras.[31] Variations of this amendment followed in subsequent years. After press reports in 1985 that the option of invading Nicaragua was being discussed, the Defense Authorization Act for Fiscal Year 1986 stated the sense of Congress that U.S.

---

[29] Report on S.J.Res. 158, Sec. III, S. Rept. 97-470, June 9, 1982.

[30] Congressional Record, July 26, 1983, p. H5623.

[31] The initial statutory restriction was contained in the Continuing Appropriations Resolution for 1983, P.L. 97-377. This was followed by a $24 million ceiling on intelligence agency support in fiscal year 1984.

armed forces should not be introduced into or over Nicaragua for combat.[32] In 1986, after U.S. helicopters ferried Honduran troops to the Nicaraguan border area, Congress prohibited U.S. personnel from participating in assistance within land areas of Honduras and Costa Rica within 120 miles of the Nicaraguan border, or from entering Nicaragua to provide military advice or support to paramilitary groups operating in that country.[33] Gradually the issue died with peace agreements in the region and the electoral defeat of the Sandinista regime in Nicaragua in 1990.

LEBANON: HOW CAN CONGRESS INVOKE THE WAR POWERS RESOLUTION?

The War Powers Resolution faced a major test when Marines sent to participate in a Multinational Force in Lebanon in 1982 became the targets of hostile fire in August 1983. During this period President Reagan filed 3 reports under the War Powers Resolution, but he did not report under section 4(a)(1) that the forces were being introduced into hostilities or imminent hostilities, thus triggering the 60-90 day time limit.

On September 29, 1983, Congress passed the Multinational Force in Lebanon Resolution determining that the requirements of section 4(a)(1) of the War Powers Resolution became operative on August 29, 1983.[34] In the same resolution, Congress authorized the continued participation of the Marines in the Multinational Force for 18 months. The resolution was a compromise between Congress and the President. Congress obtained the President's signature on legislation invoking the War Powers Resolution for the first time, but the price for this concession was a congressional authorization for the U.S. troops to remain in Lebanon for 18 months.

The events began on July 6, 1982, when President Reagan announced he would send a small contingent of U.S. troops to a multinational force for temporary peacekeeping in Lebanon. Chairman of the House Foreign Affairs Committee Clement Zablocki wrote President Reagan that if such a force were sent, the United States would be introducing forces into imminent hostilities and a report under section 4(a)(1) would be required. When the forces began to land on August 25, President Reagan reported but did not cite section 4(a)(1) and said the agreement with Lebanon ruled out any combat responsibilities. After overseeing the departure of the Palestine Liberation Organization force,

---

[32]   Sec. 1451 of P.L.99-145, approved Nov. 8, 1985. A similar provision was contained in the defense authorization for 1988-1989, sec.1405 of P.L.100-180, approved Dec. 4, 1987.

[33] Continuing Appropriations Resolution, P. L. 99-591, approved Oct. 30, 1986. Continued in P.L. 100-202, approved Dec. 22, 1987.

[34] P.L. 98-119, approved Oct. 12, 1983.

the Marines in the first Multinational Force left Lebanon on September 10, 1982.

The second dispatch of Marines to Lebanon began on September 20, 1982. President Reagan announced that the United States, France, and Italy had agreed to form a new multinational force to return to Lebanon for a limited period of time to help maintain order until the lawful authorities in Lebanon could discharge those duties. The action followed three events that took place after the withdrawal of the first group of Marines: the assassination of Lebanon President-elect Bashir Gemayel, the entry of Israeli forces into West Beirut, and the massacre of Palestinian civilians by Lebanese Christian militiamen.

On September 29, 1982, President Reagan submitted a report that 1,200 Marines had begun to arrive in Beirut, but again he did not cite section 4(a)(1), saying instead that the American force would not engage in combat. As a result of incidents in which Marines were killed or wounded, there was again controversy in Congress on whether the President's report should have been filed under section 4(a)(1). In mid-1983 Congress passed the Lebanon Emergency Assistance Act of 1983 requiring statutory authorization for any substantial expansion in the number or role of U.S. Armed Forces in Lebanon. It also included Section 4(b) that stated:

> Nothing in this section is intended to modify, limit, or suspend any of the standards and procedures prescribed by the War Powers Resolution of 1983.[35]

President Reagan reported on the Lebanon situation for the third time on August 30, 1983, still not citing section 4(a)(1), after fighting broke out between various factions in Lebanon and two Marines were killed.

The level of fighting heightened, and as the Marine casualties increased and the action enlarged, there were more calls in Congress for invocation of the War Powers Resolution. Several Members of Congress said the situation had changed since the President's first report and introduced legislation that took various approaches. Senator Charles Mathias introduced S.J. Res. 159 stating that the time limit specified in the War Powers Resolution had begun on August 31, 1983, and authorizing the forces to remain in Lebanon for a period of 120 days after the expiration of the 60-day period. Representative Thomas Downey introduced H. J. Res. 348 directing the President to report under section 4(a)(1) of the War Powers Resolution. Senator Robert Byrd introduced S.J. Res. 163 finding that section 4(a)(1) of the war powers resolution applied to the present circumstances in Lebanon. The House Appropriations Committee approved an amendment to the continuing resolution for fiscal year 1984 (H.J. Res. 367), sponsored by Representative Clarence Long, providing that after 60 days, funds could not be "obligated or expended for peacekeeping activities in Lebanon by United States Armed Forces," unless the President had submitted a report under section 4(a)(1) of the War Powers Resolution. A similar amendment was later

---

[35] P.L. 98-43, approved June 27, 1983.

rejected by the full body, but it reminded the Administration of possible congressional actions.

On September 20, congressional leaders and President Reagan agreed on a compromise resolution invoking section 4(a)(1) and authorizing the Marines to remain for 18 months. The resolution became the first legislation to be handled under the expedited procedures of the War Powers Resolution. On September 28, the House passed H.J. Res. 364 by a vote of 270 to 161. After three days of debate, on September 29, the Senate passed S.J. Res. 159 by a vote of 54 to 46. The House accepted the Senate bill by a vote of 253 to 156. As passed, the resolution contained four occurrences that would terminate the authorization before eighteen months: (1) the withdrawal of all foreign forces from Lebanon, unless the President certified continued U.S. participation was required to accomplish specified purposes; (2) the assumption by the United Nations or the Government of Lebanon of the responsibilities of the Multinational Force; (3) the implementation of other effective security arrangements; or (4) the withdrawal of all other countries from participation in the Multinational Force.[36]

Shortly afterward, on October 23, 1983, 241 U.S. Marines in Lebanon were killed by a suicide truck bombing, bringing new questions in Congress and U.S. public opinion about U.S. participation. On February 7, 1984, President Reagan announced the Marines would be redeployed and on, March 30, 1984, reported to Congress that U.S. participation in the Multinational Force in Lebanon had ended.

GRENADA: DO THE EXPEDITED PROCEDURES WORK?

On October 25, 1983, President Reagan reported to Congress "consistent with" the War Powers Resolution that he had ordered a landing of approximately 1900 U.S. Army and Marine Corps personnel in Grenada. He said that the action was in response to a request from the Organization of Eastern Caribbean States which had formed a collective security force to restore order in Grenada, where anarchic conditions and serious violations of life had occurred, and to protect the lives of U.S. citizens.

Many Members of Congress contended that the President should have cited section 4(a)(1) of the War Powers Resolution, which would have triggered the 60-90 day time limitation. On November 1, 1983, the House supported this interpretation when it adopted, by a vote of 403-23, H. J. Res. 402 declaring that the requirements of section 4(a)(1) had become operative on October 25. The Senate did not act on this measure and a conference was not held. The Senate had adopted a similar measure on October 28 by a vote of 64 to 20, but on November 17 the provision was deleted in the conference report on the debt

---

[36] Public Law 98-119, signed October 12, 1983.

limit bill to which it was attached.[37] Thus both Houses had voted to invoke section 4(a)(1), but the legislation was not completed.

On November 17, White House spokesman Larry Speakes said the Administration had indicated that there was no need for action as the combat troops would be out within the 60-90 day time period. Speaker Thomas O'Neill took the position that, whether or not Congress passed specific legislation, the War Powers Resolution had become operative on October 25. By December 15, 1983, all U.S. combat troops had been removed from Grenada.

Eleven Members of Congress filed a suit challenging the constitutionality of President Reagan's invasion of Grenada. A district judge held that courts should not decide such cases unless the entire Congress used the institutional remedies available to it.[38] An appellate court held that the issue was moot because the invasion had been ended.[39]

LIBYA: SHOULD CONGRESS HELP DECIDE ON RAIDS IN RESPONSE TO INTERNATIONAL TERRORISM?

The use of U.S. forces against Libya in 1986 focused attention on the application of the War Powers Resolution to use of military force against international terrorism.

Tensions between the United States and Libya under the leadership of Col. Muammar Qadhafi had been mounting for several years, particularly after terrorist incidents at the Rome and Vienna airports on December 27, 1985. On January 7, 1986, President Reagan said that the Rome and Vienna incidents were the latest in a series of brutal terrorist acts committed with Qadhafi's backing that constituted armed aggression against the United States.

The War Powers issue was first raised on March 24, 1986, when Libyan forces fired missiles at U.S. aircraft operating in the Gulf of Sidra. In response, the United States fired missiles at Libyan vessels and at Sirte, the Libyan missile site involved. The U.S. presence in the Gulf of Sidra, an area claimed by Libya, was justified as an exercise to maintain freedom of the seas, but it was widely considered a response to terrorist activities.

Subsequently, on April 5, 1986, a terrorist bombing of a discotheque in West Berlin occurred and an American soldier was killed. On April 14 President Reagan announced there was irrefutable evidence that Libya had been

---

[37] U.S. Congress. H. Report 98-566 on H. J. Res. 308; Senate amendment numbered 3. Congressional Record November 17, 1983, p. H10189.

[38] *Conyers v. Reagan*, 578 F. Supp. 323 (D.D.C. 1984).

[39] *Conyers v. Reagan*, 765 F.2d 1124 (D.C. Cir. 1985).

responsible, and U.S. Air Force planes had conducted bombing strikes on headquarters, terrorist facilities, and military installations in Libya in response.

The President reported both cases to Congress although the report on the bombing did not cite section 4(a)(1) and the Gulf of Sidra report did not mention the War Powers Resolution at all. Since the actions were short lived, there was no issue of force withdrawal, but several Members introduced bills to amend the War Powers Resolution. One bill called for improving consultation by establishing a special consultative group in Congress.[40]   Others called for strengthening the President's hand in combatting terrorism by authorizing the President, notwithstanding any other provision of law, to use all measures he deems necessary to protect U.S. persons against terrorist threats.[41]

PERSIAN GULF, 1987: WHEN ARE HOSTILITIES IMMINENT?

The War Powers Resolution became an issue in activities in the Persian Gulf after an Iraqi aircraft fired a missile on the *USS Stark* on May 17, 1987, killing 37 U.S. sailors. The attack broached the question of whether the Iran-Iraq war had made the Persian Gulf an area of hostilities or imminent hostilities for U.S. forces. Shortly afterwards, the U.S. adoption of a policy of reflagging and providing a naval escort of Kuwaiti oil tankers through the Persian Gulf raised full force the question of whether U.S. policy was risking involvement in war without congressional authorization. During 1987 U.S. Naval forces operating in the Gulf increased to 11 major warships, 6 minesweepers, and over a dozen small patrol boats, and a battleship-led formation was sent to the Northern Arabian Sea and Indian Ocean to augment an aircraft carrier battle group already there.

For several months the President did not report any of the deployments or military incidents under the War Powers Resolution, although on May 20, 1987, after the *Stark* incident, Secretary of State Shultz submitted a report similar to previous ones consistent with War Powers provisions, but not mentioning the Resolution. No reports were submitted after the *USS Bridgeton* struck a mine on July 24, 1987, or the U.S.-chartered *Texaco-Caribbean* struck a mine on August 10 and a U.S. F-14 fighter plane fired two missiles at an Iranian aircraft perceived as threatening.

Later, however, after various military incidents on September 23, 1987, and growing congressional concern, the President began submitting reports "consistent with" the War Powers Resolution and on July 13, 1988, submitted

---

[40] S.J. Res. 340, introduced May 8, 1986. The bill was not acted upon, but the proposal was later incorporated in other proposed amendments. See below, section on amendments.

[41] S. 2335 and H.R. 4611, Anti-Terrorism Act of 1986, introduced April 17, 1986. Not acted upon.

the sixth report relating to the Persian Gulf.[42] None of the reports were submitted under section 4(a)(1) or acknowledged that U.S. forces had been introduced into hostilities or imminent hostilities. The Reagan administration contended that the military incidents in the Persian Gulf, or isolated incidents involving defensive reactions, did not add up to hostilities or imminent hostilities as envisaged in the War Powers Resolution. It held that "imminent danger" pay which was announced for military personnel in the Persian Gulf on August 27, 1987, did not trigger section 4 (a)(1). Standards for danger pay, namely, "subject to the threat of physical harm or danger on the basis of civil insurrection, civil war, terrorism, or wartime conditions," were broader than for hostilities of the War Powers Resolution, and had been drafted to be available in situations to which the War Powers Resolution did not apply. [43]

Some Members of Congress contended that if the President did not report under section 4(a)(1), Congress itself should declare such a report should have been submitted, as it had in the Multinational Force in Lebanon Resolution. Several resolutions to this effect were introduced, some authorizing the forces to remain, but none were passed.[44] The decisive votes on the subject took place in the Senate. On September 18, 1987, the Senate voted 50-41 to table an amendment to the Defense authorization bill (S. 1174) to apply the provisions of the War Powers Resolution. The Senate also sustained points of order against consideration of S.J. Res. 217, which would have invoked the War Powers Resolution, on December 4, 1987, and a similar bill the following year, S.J. Res. 305, on June 6, 1988.

The Senate opted for a different approach, which was to use legislation to assure a congressional role in the Persian Gulf policy without invoking the War Powers Resolution. Early in the situation, both Chambers passed measures requiring the Secretary of Defense to submit a report to Congress prior to the implementation of any agreement between the United States and Kuwait for U.S. military protection of Kuwaiti shipping, and such a report was submitted June 15, 1987. Later, the Senate passed a measure that called for a comprehensive report by the President within 30 days and provided expedited procedures for a joint resolution on the subject after an additional 30 days.[45] The House did not take action on the bill.

As in the case of El Salvador, some Members took the War Powers issue to court. On August 7, 1987, Representative Lowry and 110 other Members of

---

[42] For the reports, see list above under section on reporting requirements.

[43] Questions submitted to Department of State and responses thereto, March 30, 1988, in War Powers Resolution, Relevant Documents, Correspondence, Reports, p. 97-99.

[44] Bills to this effect in the House included H.J.Res. 387, introduced October 22, 1987, which also authorized the continued presence of U.S. forces in the Gulf.

[45] Byrd-Warner amendment to S.J.Res. 194, adopted by Senate Oct. 21, 1987.

Congress filed suit in the U.S. District Court for the District of Columbia, asking the court to declare that a report was required under section 4(a)(1). On December 18, 1987, the court dismissed the suit, holding it was a nonjusticiable political question, and that the plaintiffs' dispute was "primarily with fellow legislators."[46]

Compliance with the consultation requirement was also an issue. The Administration developed its plan for reflagging and offered it to Kuwait on March 7, 1987, prior to discussing the plan with Members of Congress. A June 15, 1987, report to Congress by the Secretary of Defense stated on the reflagging policy, "As soon as Kuwait indicated its acceptance of our offer, we began consultations with Congress which are still ongoing."[47] This was too late for congressional views to be weighed in on the initial decision, after which it became more difficult to alter the policy. Subsequently, however, considerable consultation developed and the President met with various congressional leaders prior to some actions such as the retaliatory actions in April 1988 against an Iranian oil platform involved in mine-laying.

With recurring military incidents, some Members of Congress took the position that the War Powers Resolution was not being complied with, unless the President reported under section 4(a)(1) or Congress itself voted to invoke the Resolution. Other Members contended the Resolution was working by serving as a restraint on the President, who was now submitting reports and consulting with Congress.[48] Still other Members suggested the Persian Gulf situation was demonstrating the need to amend the War Powers Resolution.

As a result of the Persian Gulf situation, in the summer of 1988 both the House Foreign Affairs Committee and the Senate Foreign Relations Committee, which established a Special Subcommittee on War Powers, undertook extensive assessments of the War Powers Resolution. Interest in the issue waned after a cease-fire between Iran and Iraq began on August 20, 1988, and the United States reduced its forces in the Persian Gulf area.

---

[46] *Lowry* v. *Reagan*, 676 F. Supp. 333 (D.D.C. 1987). See also Celada, Raymond J., and David M. Ackerman. *War Powers Resolution: The Controversial Act's Search for a Successful Litigation Posture.* CRS Report for Congress 93-1065 ALD, December 20, 1993.

[47] Weinberger, Caspar W. Secretary of Defense. A Report to the Congress on Security Arrangements in the Persian Gulf. June 15, 1987, p.14.

[48] When asked about abiding by the War Powers Resolution, President Reagan said "we are complying with a part of that act, although we do not call it that. But we have been consulting the Congress, reporting to them and telling them what we're doing, and in advance..." Press conference of October 22,1987. *New York Times*, October 23, 1987, p. A8.

INVASION OF PANAMA: WHY WAS THE WAR POWERS ISSUE NOT RAISED?

On December 20, 1989, President Bush ordered 14,000 U.S. military forces to Panama for combat, in addition to 13,000 already present. On December 21, he reported to Congress under the War Powers Resolution but without citing section 4(a)(1). His stated objectives were to protect the 35,000 American citizens in Panama, restore the democratic process, preserve the integrity of the Panama Canal treaties, and apprehend General Manuel Noriega, who had been accused of massive electoral fraud in the Panamanian elections and indicted on drug trafficking charges by two U.S. Federal courts. The operation proceeded swiftly and General Noriega surrendered to U.S. military authorities on January 3. President Bush said the objectives had been met, and U.S. forces were gradually withdrawn. By February 13, all combat forces deployed for the invasion had been withdrawn, leaving the strength just under the 13,597 forces stationed in Panama prior to the invasion.

The President did not consult with congressional leaders before his decision, although he did notify them a few hours in advance of the invasion. Members of Congress had been discussing the problem of General Noriega for some time. Before Congress adjourned, it had called for the President to intensify unilateral, bilateral, and multilateral measures and consult with other nations on ways to coordinate efforts to remove General Noriega from power.[49] The Senate had adopted an amendment supporting the President's use of appropriate diplomatic, economic, and military options "to restore constitutional government to Panama and to remove General Noriega from his illegal control of the Republic of Panama", but had defeated an amendment authorizing the President to use U.S. military force to secure the removal of General Noriega "notwithstanding any other provision of law."[50]

The Panama action did not raise much discussion in Congress about the War Powers Resolution. This was in part because Congress was out of session. The first session of the 101st Congress had ended on November 22, 1989, and the second session did not begin until January 23, 1990, when the operation was essentially over and it appeared likely the additional combat forces would be out of Panama within 60 days of their deployment. Moreover, the President's action in Panama was very popular in American public opinion and supported by most Members of Congress because of the actions of General Noriega. After it was over, on February 7, 1990, the House Passed H. Con. Res. 262 which stated that the President had acted "decisively and appropriately in ordering United States forces to intervene in Panama."

---

[49] P.L. 101-162, signed November 21, 1989.

[50] Amendments to National Drug Control Strategy bill, S. 1711, October 5, 1989.

MAJOR CASES AND ISSUES IN THE POST-COLD WAR WORLD:
UNITED NATIONS ACTIONS

After the end of the Cold War in 1990, the United States began to move away from unilateral military actions toward actions authorized or supported by the United Nations. Under the auspices of U.N. Security Council resolutions, U.S. forces were deployed in Kuwait and Iraq, Somalia, former Yugoslavia/Bosnia, and Haiti. This raised the new issue of whether the War Powers Resolution applied to U.S. participation in U.N. military actions. It was not a problem during the Cold War because the agreement among the five permanent members required for Security Council actions seldom existed. An exception, the Korean war, occurred before the War Powers Resolution was enacted.[51]

The more basic issue--under what circumstances congressional authorization is required for U.S. participation in U.N. military operations--is an unfinished debate remaining from 1945. Whether congressional authorization is required depends on the types of U.N. action and is governed by the U.N. Participation Act (P.L. 79-264, as amended), as well as by the War Powers Resolution and war powers under the Constitution. Appropriations action by Congress also may be determinative as a practical matter.

For armed actions under Articles 42 and 43 of the United Nations Charter, Section 6 of the U.N. Participation Act authorizes the President to negotiate special agreements with the Security Council *"which shall be subject to the approval of the Congress by appropriate Act or joint resolution"*, providing for the numbers and types of armed forces and facilities to be made available to the Security Council. Once the agreements have been concluded, further congressional authorization is not necessary, but no such agreements have been concluded.

Section 7 of the United Nations Participation Act, added in 1949 by P.L. 81-341, authorizes the detail of up to 1,000 personnel to serve in any noncombatant capacity for certain U.N. peaceful settlement activities. The United States has provided personnel to several U.N. peacekeeping missions, such as observers to the U.N. Truce Supervision Organization in Palestine since 1948, that appear to fall within the authorization in Section 7 of the Participation Act. Controversy has arisen when larger numbers of forces have been deployed or when it appears the forces might be serving as combatants.

---

[51] In that case, the Soviet Union had absented itself from the Council temporarily, and the Security Council requested members to supply the Republic of Korea with sufficient military assistance to repel the invasion of North Korea. President Truman ordered U.S. air, naval, and ground forces to Korea to repel the attack without authorization from Congress. Senator Robert Taft complained on January 5, 1951, "The President simply usurped authority in violation of the laws and the Constitution, when he sent troops to Korea to carry out the resolution of the United Nations in an undeclared war."

The War Powers Resolution neither excludes United Nations actions from its provisions nor makes any special procedures for them. Section 8(a)(2) states that authority to introduce U. S. Armed Forces into hostilities shall not be inferred from any treaty unless it is implemented by legislation specifically authorizing the introduction and stating that it is intended to constitute specific statutory authorization within the meaning of the War Powers resolution.[52] One purpose of this provision was to ensure that both Houses of Congress be affirmatively involved in any U.S. decision to engage in hostilities pursuant to a treaty, since only the Senate approved a treaty. [53]

From 1990 through 1995, Congress primarily dealt with the issue on a case by case basis, but Members also enacted some measures seeking more control over U.S. participation in future peacekeeping actions wherever they might occur. The Defense Appropriations Act for FY1994 stated the sense of Congress that funds should not be expended for U.S. Armed Forces serving under U.N. Security Council actions unless the President consults with Congress at least 15 days prior to deployment and not later than 48 hours after such deployment, except for humanitarian operations.[54] The Defense Authorization Act for FY1994 required a report to Congress by April 1, 1994, including discussion of the requirement of congressional approval for participation of U.S. Armed Forces in multinational peacekeeping missions, proposals to conclude military agreements with the U.N. Security Council under Article 43 of the U.N. Charter, and the applicability of the War Powers Resolution and the U.N. Participation Act.[55] In 1994 and 1995, Congress attempted to gain a greater role in U.N. and other peacekeeping operations through authorization and appropriation legislation. A major element of the House Republican's Contract with America, H.R. 7, would have placed notable constraints on Presidential authority to commit U.S. forces to international peacekeeping operations. Senator Dole's, S.5, The Peace Powers Act, introduced in January 1995, would have also placed greater legislative controls on such operations. General and specific funding restrictions and Presidential reporting requirements were passed for peacekeeping operations underway or in prospect. Some of these legislative

---

[52] Such a statement was made in the Authorization for Use of Military Force against Iraq Resolution, P.L. 102-1, signed January 14, 1991, and in S.J. Res. 45, authorizing the use of force in Somalia for one year, as passed by the Senate on February 4, 1993, and amended by the House on May 25, 1993; a conference was not held.

[53] U.S. Congress. Senate. Committee on Foreign Relations. War Powers; report to accompany S. 440. June 14, 1973. S. Rept. No. 220.

[54] Sec.8153, Department of Defense Appropriation Act for FY1994, H.R. 3116, P.L. 103-139, signed November 11, 1993.

[55] Sec. 1502 (11), Defense Authorization Act for FY1994, P.L. 103-160, signed November 30. 1993.

enactments led to Presidential vetoes. These legislative actions are reviewed below as they apply to given cases.[56]

PERSIAN GULF WAR, 1991: HOW DOES THE WAR POWERS RESOLUTION RELATE TO THE UNITED NATIONS AND A REAL WAR?

On August 2, 1990, Iraqi troops under the direction of President Saddam Hussein invaded Kuwait, seized its oil fields, installed a new government in Kuwait City, and moved on toward the border with Saudi Arabia. Action to repel the invasion led to the largest war in which the United States has been involved since the passage of the War Powers Resolution. Throughout the effort to repel the Iraqi invasion, President Bush worked in tandem with the United Nations, organizing and obtaining international support and authorization for multilateral military action against Iraq.

A week after the invasion, on August 9, President Bush reported to Congress "consistent with the War Powers Resolution" that he had deployed U.S. armed forces to the region prepared to take action with others to deter Iraqi aggression. He did not cite section 4(a)(1) and specifically stated, "I do not believe involvement in hostilities is imminent."

The President did not consult with congressional leaders prior to the deployment, but both houses of Congress had adopted legislation supporting efforts to end the Iraqi occupation of Kuwait, particularly using economic sanctions and multilateral efforts. On August 2, shortly before its recess, the Senate by a vote of 97-0 adopted S.Res. 318 urging the President "to act immediately, using unilateral and multilateral measures, to seek the full and unconditional withdrawal of all Iraqi forces from Kuwaiti territory" and to work for collective international sanctions against Iraq including, if economic sanctions prove inadequate, "additional multilateral actions, under Article 42 of the United Nations Charter, involving air, sea, and land forces as may be needed..." Senate Foreign Relations Committee Chairman Pell stressed, however, that the measure did not authorize unilateral U.S. military actions. Also on August 2, the House passed H.R. 5431 condemning the Iraqi invasion and calling for an economic embargo against Iraq.

The United Nations imposed economic sanctions against Iraq on August 7, and the United States and United Kingdom organized an international naval interdiction effort.[57]   Later, on August 25, the U.N. Security Council

---

[56]For background see *Multinational Peacekeeping Operations: Proposals to Enhance Congressional Oversight*, CRS Issue Brief 95006.

[57] On August 17, 1990, Acting Secretary of State Robert M. Kimmitt sent a formal letter to Congress (not mentioning the War Powers Resolution) stating, "It is not our intention or expectation that the use of force will be required to carry out these

authorized "such measures as may be necessary" to halt shipping and verify cargoes that might be going to Iraq.

Both Houses adopted measures supporting the deployment, but neither measure was enacted. On October 1, 1990, the House passed H.J.Res. 658 supporting the action and citing the War Powers Resolution without stating that Section 4(a)(1) had become operative. The resolution quoted the President's statement that involvement in hostilities was not imminent. Representative Fascell stated that H.J.Res. 658 was not to be interpreted as a Gulf of Tonkin resolution that granted the President open-ended authority, and that it made clear that "a congressional decision on the issue of war or peace would have to be made through joint consultation." The Senate did not act on H.J.Res. 658.

On October 2, 1990, the Senate by a vote of 96-3 adopted S.Con.Res. 147, stating that "Congress supports continued action by the President in accordance with the decisions of the United Nations Security Council and in accordance with United States constitutional and statutory processes, including the authorization and appropriation of funds by the Congress, to deter Iraqi aggression and to protect American lives and vital interest in the region." As in the House, Senate leaders emphasized that the resolution was not to be interpreted as an open-ended resolution similar to the Gulf of Tonkin resolution. The resolution made no mention of the War Powers Resolution. The House did not act on S.Con.Res. 147. Congress also supported the action by appropriating funds for the preparatory operation, called Operation Desert Shield, and later for the war called Operation Desert Storm.

Some Members introduced legislation to establish a special consultation group, but the Administration objected to a formally established group. On October 23, 1990, Senate Majority Leader Mitchell announced that he and Speaker Foley had designated Members of the joint bipartisan leadership and committees of jurisdiction to make themselves available as a group for consultation on developments in the Persian Gulf. By this time U.S. land, naval, and air forces numbering more than 200,000 had been deployed.

After the 101st Congress had adjourned, President Bush on November 8, 1990, ordered an estimated additional 150,000 troops to the Gulf. He incurred considerable criticism because he had not informed the consultation group of the buildup although he had met with them on October 30. On November 16, President Bush sent a second report to Congress describing the continuing and increasing deployment of forces to the region. He stated that his opinion that hostilities were not imminent had not changed. The President wrote, "The deployment will ensure that the coalition has an adequate offensive military option should that be necessary to achieve our common goals." By the end of the year, approximately 350,000 U.S. forces had been deployed to the area.

---

operations. However, if other means of enforcement fail, necessary and proportionate force will be employed to deny passage to ships that are in violation of these sanctions."

As the prospect of a war without congressional authorization increased, on November 20, 1990, Representative Dellums and 44 other Democratic Members of Congress sought a judicial order enjoining the President from offensive military operations in connection with Operation Desert Shield unless he consulted with and obtained an authorization from Congress. On November 26, 11 prominent law professors filed a brief in favor of such a judicial action, arguing that the Constitution clearly vested Congress with the authority to declare war and that Federal judges should not use the political questions doctrine to avoid ruling on the issue. The American Civil Liberties Union also filed a memorandum in favor of the plaintiffs. On December 13, Judge Harold Greene of the Federal district court in Washington denied the injunction, holding that the controversy was not ripe for judicial resolution because a majority of Congress had not sought relief and the executive branch had not shown sufficient commitment to a definitive course of action.[58] However, throughout his opinion Judge Greene rejected the administration's arguments for full Presidential war powers.

On November 29, 1990, U.N. Security Council Resolution 678 authorized member states to use "all necessary means" to implement the Council's resolutions and restore peace and security in the area, unless Iraq complied with the U.N. resolutions by January 15, 1991. As the deadline for Iraqi withdrawal from Kuwait neared, President Bush indicated that if the Iraqi forces did not withdraw from Kuwait, he was prepared to use force to implement the U.N. Security Council resolutions. Administration officials contended that the President did not need any additional congressional authorization for this purpose.[59]

Congress Authorizes the War

After the 102nd Congress convened, on January 4, 1991, House and Senate leaders announced they would debate U.S. policy beginning January 10. A week before the January 15 deadline, on January 8, 1991, President Bush requested a congressional resolution supporting the use of all necessary means to implement U.N. Security Council Resolution 678.

On January 12, 1991, both houses passed the "Authorization for Use of Military Force Against Iraq Resolution" (P.L. 102-1).[60] Section 2(a) authorized

---

[58] *Dellums* v. *Bush*, 752 F. Supp. 1141 (D.D.C. 1990).

[59] Statement by Secretary of Defense Richard Cheney. U.S. Congress. Senate. Committee on Armed Services. Crisis in the Persian Gulf Region: U.S. Policy Options and Implications. Sept. 11-December 3, 1990, S. Hrg. 101-1071, p. 701-2.

[60] The House passed H.J.Res. 77 by a vote of 250 to 183. The Senate passed S.J.Res. 2 and then considered H.J.Res. 77 as passed. The Senate vote was 52 to 47. The bill became P.L. 102-1, signed January 14, 1991. On January 12, to emphasize the congressional power to declare war, the House also adopted by a vote of 302 to 131

the President to use U.S. Armed Forces pursuant to U.N. Security Council Resolution 678 to achieve implementation of the earlier Security Council resolutions. Section 2(b) required that first the President would have to report that the United States had used all appropriate diplomatic and other peaceful means to obtain compliance by Iraq with the Security Council resolution and that those efforts had not been successful. Section 2(c) stated that it was intended to constitute specific statutory authorization within the meaning of Section 5(b) of the War Powers Resolution. Section 3 required the President to report every 60 days on efforts to obtain compliance of Iraq with the U.N. Security Council resolution.

On January 16, President Bush made the determination required by P.L. 102-1 that diplomatic means had not and would not compel Iraq to withdraw from Kuwait. On January 18, he reported to Congress "consistent with the War Powers Resolution" that he had directed U.S. forces to commence combat operations on January 16.

After the beginning of the war Members of Congress strongly supported the President as Commander in Chief in his conduct of the war. On March 19, 1991, President Bush reported to Congress that the military operations had been successful, Kuwait had been liberated, and combat operations had been suspended on February 28, 1991.

Prior to passage of P.L. 102-1, some observers questioned the effectiveness of the War Powers Resolution on grounds that the President had begun the action, deployed hundreds of thousands of troops without consultation of Congress, and was moving the Nation increasingly close to war without congressional authorization. After the passage of P.L. 102-1 and the war had begun, Chairman of the House Committee on Foreign Affairs Fascell took the position that "the War Powers Resolution is alive and well"; the President had submitted reports to Congress, and Congress, in P.L. 102-1, had provided specific statutory authorization for the use of force. In his view, the strength and wisdom of the War Powers Resolution was that it established a process by which Congress could authorize the use of force in specific settings for limited purposes, short of a total state of war.

The question is sometimes raised why Congress did not declare war against Iraq. Speaker Foley told the National Press Club on February 7, 1991, that "The reason we did not declare a formal war was not because there is any difference I think in the action that was taken and in a formal declaration of war with respect to military operations, but because there is some question about whether we wish to excite or enact some of the domestic consequences of a formal declaration of war -- seizure of property, censorship, and so forth, which the President neither sought nor desired."

H.Con.Res. 32 expressing the sense that Congress must approve any offensive military actions against Iraq; the Senate did not act on the measure.

POST-WAR IRAQ: HOW LONG DOES AN AUTHORIZATION LAST?

After the end of Operation Desert Storm, U.S. military forces were used to deal with three continuing situations in Iraq, raising the issue of how long a congressional authorization lasts for the use of force.

The first situation resulted from the Iraqi government's repression of Kurdish and Shi'ite groups. U.N. Security Council Resolution 688 of April 5, 1991, condemned the repression of the Iraqi civilian population and appealed for contributions to humanitarian relief efforts. On May 17, 1991, President Bush reported to Congress that the Iraqi repression of the Kurdish people had necessitated a limited introduction of U.S. forces into northern Iraq for emergency relief purposes. On July 16, 1991, he reported that U.S. forces had withdrawn from northern Iraq but that the U.S. remained prepared to take appropriate steps as the situation required and that, to this end, an appropriate level of forces would be maintained in the region for "as long as required."

A second situation stemmed from the cease-fire resolution, Security Council Resolution 687 of April 3, 1991, which called for Iraq to accept the destruction or removal of chemical and biological weapons and international control of its nuclear materials.   On September 16, 1991, President Bush reported to Congress that Iraq continued to deny inspection teams access to weapons facilities and that this violated the requirements of Resolution 687, and the United States if necessary would take action to ensure Iraqi compliance with the Council's decisions. He reported similar non-cooperation on January 14, 1992, and May 15, 1992.

On July 16, 1992, President Bush reported particular concern about the refusal of Iraqi authorities to grant U.N. inspectors access to the Agricultural Ministry. The President consulted congressional leaders on July 27, and in early August the United States began a series of military exercises to take 5,000 U.S. troops to Kuwait. On September 16, 1992, the President reported, "We will remain prepared to use all necessary means, in accordance with U.N. Security Council resolutions, to assist the United Nations in removing the threat posed by Iraq's chemical, biological, and nuclear weapons capability."

The third situation was related to both of the earlier ones. On August 26, 1992, the United States, Britain, and France began a "no-fly" zone, banning Iraqi fixed wing and helicopter flights south of the 32nd parallel and creating a limited security zone in the south, where Shi'ite groups were concentrated. After violations of the no-fly zones and various other actions by Iraq, on January 13, 1993, the Bush Administration announced that aircraft from the United States and coalition partners had attacked missile bases in southern Iraq and that the United States was deploying a battalion task force to Kuwait to underline the U.S. continuing commitment to Kuwait's independence. On January 19, 1993, President Bush reported to Congress that U.S. aircraft had shot down an Iraqi aircraft on December 27, 1992, and had undertaken further military actions on January 13, 17, and 18.

President Clinton said on January 21, 1993, that the United States would adhere to the policy toward Iraq set by the Bush Administration. On January 22 and 23, April 9 and 18, June 19, and August 19, 1993, U.S. aircraft fired at targets in Iraq after pilots sensed Iraqi radar or anti-aircraft fire directed at them. On September 23, 1993, President Clinton reported that since the August 19 action, the Iraqi installation fired upon had not displayed hostile intentions.

In a separate incident, on June 28, 1993, President Clinton reported to Congress "consistent with the War Powers Resolution" that on June 26 U.S. naval forces at his direction had launched a Tomahawk cruise missile strike on the Iraqi Intelligence Service's main command and control complex in Baghdad and that the military action was completed upon the impact of the missiles. He said the Iraqi Intelligence Service had planned the failed attempt to assassinate former President Bush during his visit to Kuwait in April 1993.

The question was raised as to whether the Authorization for the Use of Force in Iraq (P.L. 102-1) authorized military actions after the conclusion of the war. P.L. 102-1 authorized the President to use U.S. armed forces pursuant to U.N. Security Council Resolution 678 to achieve implementation of previous Security Council Resolutions relating to Iraq's invasion of Kuwait. The cease-fire resolution, Security Council Resolution 687, was adopted afterwards and therefore not included in Resolution 678.

Congress endorsed the view that further specific authorization was not required for U.S. military action to maintain the ceasefire agreement. Specifically, section 1095 of P.L.102-190 stated the sense of Congress that it supported the use of all necessary means to achieve the goals of Security Council Resolution 687 as being consistent with the Authorization for Use of Military Force Against Iraq Resolution. Section 1096 supported the use of all necessary means to protect Iraq's Kurdish minority, consistent with relevant U.N. resolutions and authorities contained in P.L. 102-1.

SOMALIA: WHEN DOES HUMANITARIAN ASSISTANCE REQUIRE CONGRESSIONAL AUTHORIZATION?

In Somalia, the participation of U.S. military forces in a U.N. operation to protect humanitarian assistance became increasingly controversial as fighting and casualties increased and the objectives of the operation appeared to be expanding.

On December 4, 1992, President Bush ordered thousands of U.S. military forces to Somalia to protect humanitarian relief from armed gangs. Earlier, on November 25, the President had offered U.S. forces, and on December 3, the United Nations Security Council had adopted Resolution 794 welcoming the U.S. offer and authorizing the Secretary-General and members cooperating in the U.S. offer "to use all necessary means to establish as soon as possible a secure environment for humanitarian relief operations in Somalia." The resolution also called on member states to provide military forces and authorized the Secretary-General and the states concerned to arrange for unified command and control.

On December 10, 1992, President Bush reported to Congress "consistent with the War Powers Resolution" that on December 8, U.S. armed forces entered Somalia to secure the air field and port facility of Mogadishu and that other elements of the U.S. armed forces were being introduced into Somalia to achieve the objectives of U.N. Security Council Resolution 794. He said the forces would remain only as long as necessary to establish a secure environment for humanitarian relief operations and would then turn over responsibility for maintaining this environment to a U.N. peacekeeping force. The President said that it was not intended that the U.S. armed forces become involved in hostilities, but that the forces were equipped and ready to take such measures as might be needed to accomplish their humanitarian mission and defend themselves. They would also have the support of any additional U.S. forces necessary. By mid-January, U.S. forces in Somalia numbered 25,000.

Since the President did not cite Section 4(a)(1), the 60-day time limit was not necessarily triggered. By February, however, the U.S. force strength was being reduced, and it was announced the United States expected to turn over responsibility for protecting humanitarian relief shipments in Somalia to a U.N. force that would include U.S. troops. On March 26, 1993, the Security Council adopted Resolution 814 expanding the mandate of the U.N. force and bringing about a transition from a U.S.-led force to a U.N.-led force (UNOSOM II). By the middle of May, when the change to U.N. control took place, the U.S. forces were down to approximately 4,000 troops, primarily logistics and communications support teams, but also a rapid deployment force of U.S. Marines stationed on Navy ships.

Violence within Somalia began to increase again. On June 5, 1993, attacks killed 23 Pakistani peacekeepers, and a Somali regional leader, General Aidid, was believed responsible. The next day the U.N. Security Council adopted Resolution 837 reaffirming the authority of UNOSOM II to take all necessary measures against those responsible for the armed attacks. On June 10, 1993, President Clinton reported "consistent with the War Powers Resolution" that the U.S. Quick Reaction Force had executed military strikes to assist UNOSOM II in quelling violence against it. On July 1, President Clinton submitted another report, not mentioning the War Powers Resolution, describing further air and ground military operations aimed at securing General Aidid's compound and neutralizing military capabilities that had been an obstacle to U.N. efforts to deliver humanitarian relief and promote national reconstruction.

From the beginning, a major issue for Congress was whether to authorize U.S. action in Somalia. On February 4, 1993, the Senate had passed S.J.Res. 45 that would authorize the President to use U.S. armed forces pursuant to U.N. Security Council Resolution 794. S.J.Res. 45 stated it was intended to constitute the specific statutory authorization under Section 5(b) of the War Powers Resolution. On May 25, 1993, the House amended S.J.Res. 45 to authorize U.S.

forces to remain for one year. S.J. Res. 45 was then sent to the Senate for its concurrence, but the Senate did not act on the measure.

As sporadic fighting resulted in the deaths of Somali and U.N. forces, including Americans, controversy over the operation intensified, and Congress took action through other legislative channels. In September 1993 the House and Senate adopted amendments to the Defense Authorization Act for FY1994 asking that the President consult with Congress on policy toward Somalia, and report the goals, objectives, and anticipated jurisdiction of the U.S. mission in Somalia by October 15, 1993; the amendments expressed the sense that the President by November 15, 1993, should seek and receive congressional authorization for the continued deployment of U.S. forces to Somalia. [61] On October 7, the President consulted with congressional leaders from both parties for over two hours on Somalia policy. On October 13, President Clinton sent a 33-page report to Congress on his Somalia policy and its objectives.

Meanwhile, on October 7 President Clinton said that most U.S. forces would be withdrawn from Somalia by March 31, 1994. To ensure this, the Defense Department Appropriations Act for FY1994, cut off funds for U.S. military operations in Somalia after March 31, 1994, unless the President obtained further spending authority from Congress.[62] Congress approved the use of U.S. military forces in Somalia only for the protection of American military personnel and bases and for helping maintain the flow of relief aid by giving the U.N. forces security and logistical support; it required that U.S. combat forces in Somalia remain under the command and control of U.S. commanders under the ultimate direction of the President.

Earlier, some Members suggested that the U.S. forces in Somalia were clearly in a situation of hostilities or imminent hostilities, and that if Congress did not authorize the troops to remain, the forces should be withdrawn within 60 to 90 days. After a letter from House Foreign Affairs Committee Ranking Minority Member Benjamin Gilman and Senate Foreign Relations Committee Ranking Minority Member Jesse Helms, Assistant Secretary Wendy Sherman replied on July 21, 1993, that no previous Administrations had considered that intermittent military engagements, whether constituting hostilities, would necessitate the withdrawal of forces pursuant to Section 5(b); and the War Powers Resolution, in their view, was intended to apply to sustained hostilities. The State Department did not believe congressional authorization was necessary, although congressional support would be welcome. On August 4, 1993, Representative Gilman asserted that August 4 might be remembered as the day the War Powers Resolution died because combat broke out in Somalia on June 5 and the President had not withdrawn U.S. forces and Congress had "decided to look the other way." On October 22, 1993, Representative Gilman introduced H.Con.Res. 170 directing the President pursuant to section 5(c) of the War Powers Resolution to withdraw U.S. forces from Somalia by January

---

[61] Section 1512, P.L. 103-160, signed November 30, 1993.

[62] Sec. 8151 of P.L. 103-139, signed November 11, 1993.

31, 1994. The House adopted an amended version calling for withdrawal by March 31, 1994.[63] The Senate did not act on this non-binding measure.

However, the Defense Appropriations Act for FY1995 (P.L. 103-335, signed September 30, 1994) prohibited the use of funds for the continuous presence of U.S. forces in Somalia, except for the protection of U.S. personnel, after September 30, 1994. Subsequently, on November 4, 1994, the U.N. Security Council decided to end the U.N. mission in Somalia by March 31, 1995. On March 3, 1995, U.S. forces completed their assistance to United Nations forces evacuating Somalia.

Another war powers issue was the adequacy of consultation before the dispatch of forces. On December 4, 1992, President Bush had met with a number of congressional leaders to brief them on the troop deployment. In his December 10 report, President Bush stressed that he had taken into account the views expressed in H.Con.Res. 370, S.Con.Res. 132, and P.L. 102-274 on the urgent need for action in Somalia. However, none of these resolutions explicitly authorized U.S. military action.

FORMER YUGOSLAVIA/BOSNIA: WHAT IF NO CONSENSUS EXISTS?

The issue of war powers and U.S. participation in United Nations actions was also raised by efforts to halt fighting in the territory of former Yugoslavia, particularly in Bosnia. Because some of the U.S. action has been taken within a NATO framework, action in Bosnia has also raised the issue of whether action under NATO is exempt from the requirements of the War Powers Resolution or its standard for the exercise of war powers under the Constitution. Article 11 of the North Atlantic Treaty states that its provisions are to be carried out by the parties "in accordance with their respective constitutional processes," inferring some role for Congress in the event of war. Section 8(a) of the War Powers Resolution states that authority to introduce U.S. forces into hostilities is not to be inferred from any treaty, ratified before or after 1973, unless implementing legislation specifically authorizes such introduction and says it is intended to constitute an authorization within the meaning of the War Powers Resolution. Section 8(b) states that nothing in the War Powers Resolution should be construed to require further authorization for U.S. participation in the headquarters operations of military commands established before 1973, such as NATO headquarters operations.

On August 13, 1992, the U.N. Security Council adopted Resolution 770 calling on nations to take "all measures necessary" to facilitate the delivery of humanitarian assistance to Sarajevo. Many in Congress had been advocating more assistance to the victims of the conflict. On August 11, 1992, the Senate had passed S.Res. 330 urging the President to work for a U.N. Security Council resolution such as was adopted, but saying that no U.S. military personnel should be introduced into hostilities without clearly defined objectives. On the

---

[63] For additional discussion of H.Con.Res. 170, see section on Legislative Veto, above.

same day, the House passed H.Res. 554 urging the Security Council to authorize measures, including the use of force, to ensure humanitarian relief.

During 1993 the United States participated in airlifts into Sarajevo, naval monitoring of sanctions, and aerial enforcement of a "no-fly zone." On February 10, 1993, Secretary of State Warren Christopher announced that under President Clinton, the United States would try to convince the Serbs, Muslims, and Croats to pursue a diplomatic solution and that if an agreement was reached, U.S. forces, including ground forces, would help enforce the peace. On February 28, 1993, the United States began an airdrop of relief supplies aimed at civilian populations, mainly Muslims, surrounded by fighting in Bosnia.

On March 31, 1993, the U.N. Security Council authorized member states to take all necessary measures to enforce the ban on military flights over Bosnia, the "no-fly zone". NATO planes, including U.S. planes, began patrolling over Bosnia and Hercegovina on April 12, 1993, to enforce the Security Council ban, and the next day, President Clinton reported the U.S. participation "consistent with Section 4 of the War Powers Resolution."

Conflict continued, but the situation was complicated and opinion in Congress and among U.N. and NATO members was divided. President Clinton consulted with about two dozen congressional leaders on potential further action on April 27 and received a wide range of views. On May 2, the Administration began consultation with allies to build support for additional military action to enforce a cease-fire and Bosnian Serb compliance with a peace agreement, but a consensus on action was not reached.

On June 10, 1993, Secretary of State Christopher announced the United States would send 300 U.S. troops to join 700 Scandinavians in the U.N. peacekeeping force in Macedonia.[64] The mission was established under U.N. Security Council Resolution 795 (1992), which sought to prevent the war in Bosnia from spilling over to neighboring countries. President Clinton reported this action "consistent with Section 4 of the War Powers Resolution" on July 9, 1993. He identified U.S. troops as part of a peacekeeping force, and directed in accordance with Section 7 of the U.N. Participation Act.

Planning for U.N. and NATO action to implement a prospective peace agreement included the possibility that the United States might supply 25,000 out of 50,000 NATO forces to enforce U.N. decisions. This possibility brought proposals to require congressional approval before the dispatch of further forces to Bosnia. On September 23, 1993, Senate Minority Leader Robert Dole said he intended to offer an amendment stating that no additional U.S. forces should be introduced into former Yugoslavia without advance approval from Congress. Assistant Secretary of State Stephen Oxman said on October 5 that the Clinton Administration would consult with Congress and not commit American troops

---

[64] The name of this area is in dispute. The provisional name, which is used for its designation as a member of the United Nations, is "The Former Yugoslav Republic of Macedonia." This report uses the term "Macedonia" without prejudice.

to the implementation operation for a peace agreement without congressional support, and that the Administration would act consistent with the War Powers Resolution. Congress sought to assure this in Section 8146 of P.L. 103-139, the Defense Appropriation Act for FY 1994, stating the sense of Congress that funds should not be available for U.S. forces to participate in new missions or operations to implement the peace settlement in Bosnia unless previously authorized by Congress. This provision was sponsored by the Senate by leaders Mitchell and Dole.

At the NATO summit conference in Brussels on January 11, 1994, leaders, including President Clinton, repeated an August threat to undertake air strikes on Serb positions to save Sarajevo and to consider other steps to end the conflict in Bosnia. On February 17, 1994, President Clinton reported "consistent with" the War Powers Resolution that the United States had expanded its participation in United Nations and NATO efforts to reach a peaceful solution in former Yugoslavia and that 60 U.S. aircraft were available for participation in the authorized NATO missions. On March 1, 1994, he reported that on the previous day U.S. planes patrolling the "no-fly zone" under the North Atlantic Treaty Organization (NATO) shot down 4 Serbian Galeb planes. On April 12, 1994, the President reported that on April 10 and 11, following shelling of Gorazde, one of the "safe areas," and a decision by U.N. and NATO leaders, U.S. planes bombed Bosnian Serbian nationalist positions around Gorazde. On August 22, 1994, President Clinton similarly reported that on August 5, U.S. planes under NATO had strafed a Bosnian Serb gun position in an exclusion zone. On September 22, 1994, two British and one U.S. aircraft bombed a Serbian tank in retaliation for Serb attacks on U.N. peacekeepers near Sarajevo; and on November 21 more than 30 planes from the United States, Britain, France, and the Netherlands bombed the runway of a Serb airfield in Croatia.

As the conflict in Bosnia continued, leaders in Congress called for greater congressional involvement in decisions. Senator Dole introduced S. 2042, calling for the United States to end unilaterally its arms embargo, conducted in accordance with a U.N. Security Council Resolution, against Bosnia and Herzegovina. On May 10, 1994, Senate Majority Leader George Mitchell introduced an amendment to authorize and approve the President's decision to carry out NATO decisions to support and protect UNPROFOR forces around designated safe areas; to use airpower in the Sarajevo region; and to authorize air strikes against Serb weapons around certain safe areas if these areas were attacked. The Mitchell amendment favored lifting the arms embargo but not unilaterally; it also stated no U.S. ground combat troops should be deployed in Bosnia unless previously authorized by Congress. The Senate adopted both the Dole proposal, as an amendment, and the Mitchell amendment on May 12, 1994, by votes of 50-49. The less stringent Mitchell amendment passed on a straight party line vote. Yet thirteen Democrats voted for the Dole amendment, indicating a sentiment in both parties to assist the Bosnians in defending themselves. The Senate then adopted S. 2042 as amended. The House did not act on the measure.

The Defense Authorization Act for FY1995 (P.L. 103-337, signed October 5, 1994) provided in Section 1404 that if the Bosnian Serbs did not accept the Contact Group proposal by October 15, 1994, the President should introduce a U.N. Security Council resolution to end the arms embargo by December 1, 1994; if the Security Council had not acted by November 15, 1994, no funds could be used to enforce the embargo other than those required of all U.N. members under Security Council Resolution 713. That sequence of events occurred and the United States stopped enforcing the embargo. In addition, Section 8100 of the Defense Appropriations Act, FY1995 (P.L. 103-335, signed September 30, 1994), stated the sense of the Congress that funds made available by this law should not be available for the purposes of deploying U.S. armed forces to participate in implementation of a peace settlement in Bosnia unless previously authorized by Congress.

On May 24, 1995, President Clinton reported "consistent with the War Powers Resolution" that U.S. combat-equipped fighter aircraft and other aircraft continued to contribute to NATO's enforcement of the no-fly zone in airspace over Bosnia-Herzegovina. U.S. aircraft, he noted, are also available for close air support of U.N. forces in Croatia. Roughly 500 U.S. soldiers were still deployed in the former Yugoslav Republic of Macedonia as part of the U.N. Preventive Deployment Force (UNPREDEP). U.S. forces continue to support U.N. refugee and embargo operations in this region.

On September 1, 1995, President Clinton reported "consistent with the War Powers Resolution," that "U.S. combat and support aircraft" had been used beginning on August 29, 1995, in a series of NATO air strikes against Bosnian Serb Army (BSA) forces in Bosnia-Herzegovina that were threatening the U.N.-declared safe areas of Sarajevo, Tuzla, and Gorazde." He noted that during the first day of operations, "some 300 sorties were flown against 23 targets in the vicinity of Sarajevo, Tuzla, Gorazde and Mostar."

On September 7, 1995 the House passed an amendment to the FY1996 Department of Defense Appropriations Bill (H.R. 2126), offered by Representative Mark Neumann (R-Wi.) that prohibited the obligation or expenditure of funds provided by the bill for any operations beyond those already undertaken. However, in conference the provision was softened to a sense-of-the-Congress provision that said that President must consult with Congress before deploying U.S. forces to Bosnia. The conference report was rejected by the House over issues unrelated to Bosnia on September 29, 1995 by a vote of 151-267. The substitute conference report on H.R. 2126, which was subsequently passed and signed into law, did not include language on Bosnia, in part due to the President's earlier objections to any provision in the bill that might impinge on his powers as Commander-in-Chief. On September 29, the Senate passed by a vote of 94-2 a sense-of-the-Senate amendment to H.R. 2076, the FY1996 State, Commerce, Justice Appropriations bill, sponsored by Senator Judd Gregg (R-N.H.) that said no funds in the bill should be used for the deployment of U.S. combat troops to Bosnia-Herzegovina unless Congress approves the deployment in advance or to evacuate endangered U.N. peacekeepers. The conference report on H.R. 2076, agreed to by the House and the Senate, included the "sense of the Senate" language of the Gregg amendment.

In response to mounting criticism of the Administration's approach to Bosnian policy, on October 17-18, 1995, Secretary of State Christopher, Secretary of Defense Perry and Joint Chiefs of Staff Chairman, Shalikashvili testified before House and Senate Committees on Bosnia policy and the prospect of President Clinton deploying approximately 20,000 American ground forces as part of a NATO peacekeeping operation. During testimony before the Senate Foreign Relations Committee on October 17, Secretary Christopher stated that the President would not be bound by a resolution of the Congress prohibiting sending of U.S. forces into Bosnia without the express prior approval of Congress. Nevertheless, on October 19, 1995, President Clinton in a letter to Senator Robert C. Byrd stated that "[w]hile maintaining the constitutional authorities of the Presidency, I would welcome, encourage and, at the appropriate time, request an expression of support by the Congress" for the commitment of U.S. troops to a NATO implementation force in Bosnia, after a peace agreement is reached.

Subsequently, on October 30, 1995, the House, by a vote of 315-103, passed H. Res. 247, expressing the sense of the House that "no United States Armed forces should be deployed on the ground in the territory of the Republic of Bosnia and Herzegovina to enforce a peace agreement until the Congress has approved such a deployment." On November 13, President Clinton's 9-page letter to Speaker Gingrich stated he would send a request "for a congressional expression of support for U.S. participation in a NATO-led Implementation Force in Bosnia ... before American forces are deployed in Bosnia." The President said there would be a "timely opportunity for Congress to consider and act upon" his request for support. He added that despite his desire for congressional support, he "must reserve" his "constitutional prerogatives in this area." On November 17, 1995, the House passed (243-171) H.R. 2606, which would "prohibit the use of funds appropriated or otherwise available" to the Defense Department from "being used for the deployment on the ground of United States Armed Forces in the Republic of Bosnia-Herzegovina as part of any peacekeeping operation or as part of any implementation force, unless funds for such deployment are specifically appropriated" by law.

On December 4, 1995, Secretary of Defense Perry announced the deployment of about 1,400 U.S. military personnel (700 to Bosnia/700 to Croatia) as part of the advance elements of the roughly 60,000 person NATO Implementation Force in Bosnia, scheduled to deploy in force once the Dayton Peace Agreement is signed in Paris on December 14, 1995. Secretary Perry noted that once the NATO I-Force was fully deployed, about 20,000 U.S. military personnel would be in Bosnia, and about 5,000 in Croatia.

On December 6, 1995, President Clinton notified the Congress, "consistent with the War Powers Resolution," that he had "ordered the deployment of approximately 1,500 U.S. military personnel to Bosnia and Herzegovina and Croatia as part of a NATO 'enabling force' to lay the groundwork for the

prompt and safe deployment of the NATO-led Implementation Force (IFOR),"
which would be used to implement the Bosnian peace agreement after its
signing. The President also noted that he had authorized deployment of roughly
3,000 other U.S. military personnel to Hungary, Italy and Croatia to establish
infrastructure for the enabling force and the IFOR.

In response to these developments, Congress addressed the question of
U.S. ground troop deployments in Bosnia. Lawmakers sought to take action
before the final Bosnian peace agreement was signed in Paris on December 14,
1995, following which the bulk of American military forces would be deployed
to Bosnia. On December 13, 1995, the House considered H.R. 2770, sponsored
by Representative Dornan, which would have prohibited the use of Federal
funds for the deployment "on the ground" of U.S. Armed Forces in Bosnia-
Hercegovina "as part of any peacekeeping operation, or as part of any
implementation force." H.R. 2770 was defeated in the House by a vote of 210-
218. On December 13, the House considered two other measures. It approved
H.Res. 302, offered by Representative Buyer, by a vote of 287-141. H.Res. 302,
a non-binding measure, reiterated "serious concerns and opposition" to the
deployment of U.S. ground troops to Bosnia, while expressing confidence, "pride
and admiration" for U.S. soldiers deployed there. It called on the President and
Defense Secretary to rely on the judgement of U.S. ground commander in Bosnia
and stated that he should be provided with sufficient resources to ensure the
safety and well-being of U.S. troops. H.Res. 302, further stated that the U.S.
government should "in all respects" be "impartial and evenhanded" with all
parties to the Bosnian conflict "as necessary to ensure the safety and protection"
of American forces in the region.

Subsequently, the House defeated H.Res 306, proposed by Representative
Hamilton, by a vote of 190-237. H.Res 306 stated that the House "unequivocally
supports the men and women of the United States Armed Forces who are
carrying out their mission in support of peace in Bosnia and Herzegovina with
professional excellence, dedicated patriotism and exemplary bravery."

On December 13, the Senate also considered three measures related to
Bosnia and U.S. troop deployments. The Senate defeated H.R. 2606 by a vote of
22-77. This bill would have prohibited funds to be obligated or expended for U.S.
participation in peacekeeping in Bosnia unless such funds were specifically
appropriated for that purpose. The Senate also defeated S. Con. Res. 35, a non-
binding resolution of Senators Hutchison and Inhofe. This resolution stated that
"Congress opposes President Clinton's decision to deploy" U.S. troops to Bosnia,
but noted that "Congress strongly supports" the U.S. troops sent by the
President to Bosnia.

The Senate did pass S.J. Res. 44, sponsored by Senators Dole and McCain,
by a vote of 69-30. This resolution stated that Congress "unequivocally supports
the men and women of our Armed Forces" who were to be deployed to Bosnia.
S.J. Res. 44 stated that "notwithstanding reservations expressed about President
Clinton's decision" to deploy U.S. forces, "the President may only fulfill his
commitment" to deploy them to Bosnia "for approximately one year" if he made

a determination to Congress that the mission of the NATO peace implementation force (IFOR) will be limited to implementing the military annex to the Bosnian peace agreement and to protecting itself. The Presidential determination must also state that the United States will "lead an immediate international effort," separate from IFOR, "to provide equipment, arms, training and related logistics assistance of the highest possible quality" to the Muslim-Croat Federation so that it may provide for its own defense. The President could use "existing military drawdown authorities and requesting such additional authority as may be necessary." S.J. Res. 44 also required President Clinton to submit to Congress a detailed report on the armament effort within 30 days, and required regular Presidential reports to Congress on the implementation of both the military and non-military aspects of the peace accords.

The House and Senate did not appoint and direct conferees to meet to reconcile the conflicting elements of the Bosnia related measures each had passed on December 13, 1995. A number of Members and Senators had wished to express their views on the troop deployment before the Dayton Accords were formally signed in Paris. That action had occurred, and the leadership of both parties apparently believed nothing further would be achieved by a conference on the measures passed. As result, no final consensus on a single specific measure was reached on the issue by the two chambers. The President meanwhile continued with the Bosnian deployment. On December 21, 1995, President Clinton notified Congress "consistent with the War Powers Resolution," that he had ordered the deployment of approximately 20,000 U.S. military personnel to participate in the NATO-led Implementation Force (IFOR) in the Republic of Bosnia-Herzegovina, and approximately 5,000 U.S. military personnel would be deployed in other former Yugoslav states, primarily in Croatia. In addition, about 7,000 U.S. support forces would be deployed to Hungary, Italy and Croatia and other regional states in support of IFOR's mission. The President ordered participation of U.S. forces "pursuant to" his "constitutional authority to conduct the foreign relations of the United States and as Commander-in-Chief and Chief Executive."[65]

HAITI: CAN THE PRESIDENT ORDER ENFORCEMENT OF A U.N. EMBARGO?

On July 3, 1993, Haitian military leader Raoul Cedras and deposed President Jean-Bertrand Aristide signed an agreement providing for the restoration of President Aristide on October 30. The United Nations and Organization of American States took responsibility for verifying compliance. In conjunction with the agreement, President Clinton offered to send 350 troops and military engineers to Haiti to help retrain the Haitian armed forces and work on construction projects. A first group of American and Canadian troops arrived on October 6. When additional U.S. forces arrived on October 11, a group of armed civilians appeared intent upon resisting their landing, and on

---

[65]For additional information see *Bosnia-Former Yugoslavia: Ongoing Conflict and U.S. Policy*, CRS Issue Brief 91089.

October 12 defense officials ordered the ship carrying them, the *U.S.S. Harlan County*, to leave Haitian waters.

Because the Haitian authorities were not complying with the agreement, on October 13 the U.N. Security Council voted to restore sanctions against Haiti. On October 20, President Clinton reported "consistent with the War Powers Resolution" that U.S. ships had begun to enforce the U.N. embargo. Some Members of Congress complained that Congress had not been consulted on or authorized the action. On October 18, Senator Dole said he would offer an amendment to the Defense Appropriations bill (H.R. 3116) which would require congressional authorization for all deployments into Haitian waters and airspace unless the President made specified certifications. Congressional leaders and Administration officials negotiated on the terms of the amendment. As enacted, section 8147 of P.L. 103-139 stated the sense of Congress that funds should not be obligated or expended for U.S. military operations in Haiti unless the operations were (1) authorized in advance by Congress, (2) necessary to protect or evacuate U.S. citizens, (3) vital to the national security of the United States and there was not sufficient time to receive congressional authorization, or (4) the President reported in advance that the intended deployment met certain criteria.

Enforcement of the embargo intensified. On April 20, 1994, President Clinton further reported "consistent with the War Powers Resolution" that U.S. naval forces had continued enforcement in the waters around Haiti and that 712 vessels had been boarded. On May 6, 1994, the U.N. Security Council adopted Resolution 917 calling for measures to tighten the embargo. On June 10, 1994, President Clinton announced steps being taken to intensify the pressure on Haiti's military leaders that included assisting the Dominican Republic to seal its border with Haiti, using U.S. naval patrol boats to detain ships suspected of violating the sanctions, a ban on commercial air traffic, and sanctions on financial transactions.

As conditions in Haiti worsened, President Clinton stated he would not rule out the use of force, and gradually this option appeared more certain. Many Members continued to contend congressional authorization was necessary for any invasion of Haiti. On May 24, 1994, the House adopted the Goss amendment to the Defense Authorization bill (H.R. 4301) by a vote of 223-201. The amendment expressed the sense of Congress that the United States should not undertake any military action against the mainland of Haiti unless the President first certified to Congress that clear and present danger to U.S. citizens or interests required such action. Subsequently, on June 9 the House voted on the Goss amendment again. This time the House reversed itself and rejected the amendment by a vote of 195-226. On June 27, a point of order was sustained against an amendment to the State Department appropriations bill that sought to prohibit use of funds for any U.N. peacekeeping operation related to Haiti. On June 29, 1994, the Senate in action on H.R. 4226 repassed a provision identical to Section 8147 of P.L. 103-139 but rejected a measure making advance congressional authorization a binding requirement. On August 5 it tabled (rejected) by a vote of 31 to 63 an amendment to H.R. 4606 by

Senator Specter prohibiting the President from using U.S. armed forces to depose the military leadership unless authorized in advance by Congress, necessary to protect U.S. citizens, or vital to U.S. interests.

President Clinton sought and obtained U.N. Security Council authorization for an invasion. On July 31, the U.N. Security Council authorized a multinational force to use "all necessary means to facilitate the departure from Haiti of the military leadership ... on the understanding that the cost of implementing this temporary operation will be borne by the participating Member States" (Resolution 940, 1994).

On August 3, the Senate adopted an amendment to the Department of Veterans appropriation, H.R. 4624, by a vote of 100-0 expressing its sense that the Security Council Resolution did not constitute authorization for the deployment of U.S. forces in Haiti under the Constitution or the War Powers Resolution. The amendment, however, was rejected in conference. President Clinton said the same day that he would welcome the support of Congress but did not agree that he was constitutionally mandated to obtain it. Some Members introduced resolutions, such as H.Con.Res. 276, calling for congressional authorization prior to the invasion.

On September 15, 1994, in an address to the Nation, President Clinton said he had called up the military reserve and ordered two aircraft carriers into the region. His message to the military dictators was to leave now or the United States would force them from power. The first phase of military action would remove the dictators from power and restore Haiti's democratically elected government. The second phase would involve a much smaller force joining with forces from other U.N. members which would leave Haiti after 1995 elections were held and a new government installed.

While the Defense Department continued to prepare for an invasion within days, on September 16 President Clinton sent to Haiti a negotiating team of former President Jimmy Carter, former Joint Chiefs of Staff Chairman Colin Powell, and Senate Armed Services Committee Chairman Sam Nunn. Again addressing the Nation on September 18, President Clinton announced that the military leaders had agreed to step down by October 15, and agreed to the immediate introduction of troops, beginning September 19, from the 15,000 member international coalition. He said the agreement was only possible because of the credible and imminent threat of multinational force. He emphasized the mission still had risks and there remained possibilities of violence directed at U.S. troops, but the agreement minimized those risks. He also said that under U.N. Security Council resolution 940, a 25-nation international coalition would soon go to Haiti to begin the task of restoring democratic government. Also on September 18, President Clinton reported to Congress on the objectives in accordance with the sense expressed in Section 8147 (c) of P.L. 103-139, the FY1994 Defense Appropriations Act.

U.S. forces entered Haiti on September 1994. On September 21, President Clinton reported "consistent with the War Powers Resolution" the deployment of 1,500 troops, to be increased by several thousand. (At the peak in September there were about 21,000 U.S. forces in Haiti.) He said the U.S. presence would not be open-ended but would be replaced after a period of months by a U.N. peacekeeping force, although some U.S. forces would participate in and be present for the duration of the U.N. mission. The forces were involved in the first hostilities on September 24 when U.S. Marines killed ten armed Haitian resisters in a fire-fight.

On September 19, the House agreed to H.Con.Res. 290 commending the President and the special delegation to Haiti, and supporting the prompt and orderly withdrawal of U.S. forces from Haiti as soon as possible; on September 19, the Senate agreed to a similar measure, S.Res. 259. On October 3, 1994, the House Foreign Affairs Committee reported H.J.Res. 416 authorizing the forces in Haiti until March 1, 1995, and providing procedures for a joint resolution to withdraw the forces. In House debate on October 6 the House voted against the original contents and for the Dellums substitute. As passed, H.J.Res. 416 stated the sense that the President should have sought congressional approval before deploying U.S. forces to Haiti, supporting a prompt and orderly withdrawal as soon as possible, and requiring a monthly report on Haiti as well as other reports. This same language was also adopted by the Senate on October 6 as S.J. Res. 229, and on October 7 the House passed S.J.Res. 229. President Clinton signed S.J.Res. 229 on October 25, 1994 (P.L. 103-423).

After U.S. forces began to disarm Haitian military and paramilitary forces and President Aristide returned on October 15, 1994, the United States began to withdraw some forces. On March 31, 1995, U.N. peacekeeping forces assumed responsibility for missions previously conducted by U.S. military forces in Haiti. By September 21, 1995, President Clinton reported the United States had 2,400 military personnel in Haiti as participants in the U.N. Mission in Haiti (UNMIH), and 260 U.S. military personnel assigned to the U.S. Support Group Haiti.[66]

PROPOSED AMENDMENTS

After 22 years of experience, controversy continues over the War Powers Resolution's effectiveness and appropriateness as a system for maintaining a congressional role in the use of armed forces in conflict.

One view is that the War Powers Resolution is basically sound and does not need amendment.[67] Those who hold this view believe it has brought about better communication between the two branches in times of crisis, and has given

---

[66]For further information on Haiti, see *Haiti After President Aristide's Return: Concerns of the 104th Congress*, CRS Issue Brief 95090.

[67] Fascell, Representative Dante B. Testimony. U.S. Congress. Senate. Committee on Foreign Relations. The War Powers after 200 years: Congress and the President at Constitutional Impasse. Hearings, July 13 - September 29, 1988. p. 11.

Congress a vehicle by which it can act when a majority of Members wish to do so. The Resolution served as a restraint on the use of armed forces by the President in some cases because of awareness that certain actions might invoke its provisions. For example, the threat of invoking the War Powers Resolution may have been helpful in getting U.S. forces out of Grenada, in keeping the number of military advisers in El Salvador limited to 55, and in prodding Congress to take a stand on authorizing the war against Iraq.

A contrary view is that the War Powers Resolution is an inappropriate instrument that restricts the President's effectiveness in foreign policy and should be repealed.[68] Those who hold this view believe that the basic premise of the War Powers Resolution is wrong because in it, Congress attempts excessive control of the deployment of U.S. military forces, encroaching on the responsibility of the President.[69]   Supporters of repeal contend that the President needs more flexibility in the conduct of foreign policy and that the time limitation in the War Powers Resolution is unconstitutional and impractical. Some holding this view contend that Congress has always had the power, through appropriations and general lawmaking, to inquire into, support, limit, or prohibit specific uses of U.S. Armed Forces if there is majority support. The War Powers Resolution does not fundamentally change this equation, it is argued, but it complicates action, misleads military opponents, and diverts attention from key policy questions.

A third view is that the War Powers Resolution has not been adequate to accomplish its objectives and needs to be strengthened or reshaped.[70] Proponents of this view assert that Presidents have continued to introduce U.S. armed forces into hostilities without consulting Congress and without congressional authorization. Presidents have cited section 4(a)(1) on only one occasion -- Mayaguez -- and by the time the action was reported, it was virtually over. The provision permitting Congress to withdraw troops by concurrent resolution is under a cloud because of the *Chadha* decision.

Holders of this third view have proposed various types of amendments to the War Powers Resolution. These include returning to the version originally passed by the Senate, establishing a congressional consultation group, adding

---

[68] Examples of bills to repeal the War Powers Resolution include S.2030 introduced by Senator Barry Goldwater on October 31, 1983, H.R. 2525, introduced by Representative Robert Dornan on May 27, 1987 and S.5, introduced by Senator Robert Dole on January 4, 1995. See also the most recent major legislative floor debate on repeal of the War Powers Resolution, held on June 7, 1995. This debate centered on an amendment to H.R. 1561, offered by Representative Henry Hyde, which would have repealed most of the key elements of the War Powers Resolution. The amendment was defeated by a vote of 217-201. *Congressional Record*, June 7, 1995, pp. H5655-H5674.

[69] *Congressional Record*, July 12, 1983, p. S9670.

[70]A recent broad-gauged proposal reflective of this view is S. 564, Use of Force Act, introduced by Senator Biden on March 15, 1995.

a cutoff of funds, and providing for judicial review, each of which is discussed below.

RETURN TO SENATE VERSION: ENUMERATING EXCEPTIONS FOR EMERGENCY USE

In 1977, Senator Thomas Eagleton proposed that the War Powers Resolution return to the original language of the version passed by the Senate, and this proposal has been made several times since. This would require prior congressional authorization for the introduction of forces into conflict abroad without a declaration of war except to respond to or forestall an armed attack against the United States or its forces or to protect U.S. citizens while evacuating them. The amendment would eliminate the construction that the President has 60 to 90 days in which he can militarily act without authorization. Opponents fear the exceptions to forestall attacks or rescue American citizens abroad would serve as a blanket authorization and might be abused, yet might not allow the needed speed of action and provide adequate flexibility in other circumstances.

SHORTEN OR ELIMINATE TIME LIMITATION

Another proposal is to shorten the time period that the President could maintain forces in hostile situations abroad without congressional authorization from 60 to 30 days, or eliminate it altogether. Some proponents of this amendment contend the current War Powers Resolution gives the President 60 to 90 days to do as he chooses and that this provides too much opportunity for mischief or irreversible action. The original Senate version provided that the use of armed forces in hostilities or imminent hostilities in any of the emergency situations could not be sustained beyond 30 days without specific congressional authorization, extendable by the President upon certification of necessity for safe disengagement. Opponents of this and related measures argue that they induce military opponents to adopt strategies to win given conflicts in Congress that they could not win in the field over time.

REPLACE AUTOMATIC WITHDRAWAL REQUIREMENT

The War Powers Resolution has an automatic requirement for withdrawal of troops 60 days after the President submits a section 4(a)(1) report. Some Members of Congress favor replacing this provision with expedited procedures for a joint resolution to authorize the action or require disengagement. One of the main executive branch objections to the War Powers Resolution has been that the withdrawal requirement could be triggered by congressional inaction, and that adversaries can simply wait out the 60 days. By providing for withdrawal by joint resolution, this amendment would also deal with the provision for withdrawal by concurrent resolution, under a cloud because of the *Chadha* decision. On the other hand, a joint resolution requiring disengagement could be vetoed by the President and thus would require a two-thirds majority vote in both Houses for enactment.

CUTOFF OF FUNDS

Some proposals call for prohibiting the obligation or expenditure of funds for any use of U.S. armed forces in violation of the War Powers Resolution or laws passed under it except for the purpose of removing troops.[71] Congress could enforce this provision by refusing to appropriate further funds to continue the military action. This has always been the case, some contend, and would not work because Congress would remain reluctant to withhold financial support for U.S. Armed Forces once they were abroad.

ELIMINATION OF ACTION BY CONCURRENT RESOLUTION

Many proposed amendments eliminate section 5(c) providing that U.S. forces engaged in hostilities abroad without congressional authorization are to be removed if Congress so directs by concurrent resolution, and section 7 providing priority procedures for a concurrent resolution. Those who hold this view contend the concurrent resolution section is invalid because of the *Chadha* decision.

EXPEDITED PROCEDURES

Several proposals call for new and more detailed priority procedures for joint resolutions introduced under the War Powers Resolution. These would apply to joint resolutions either authorizing a military action or calling for the withdrawal of forces, and to congressional action to sustain or override a Presidential veto of the joint resolution.[72]

---

[71] S.J. Res. 323, introduced by Senators Byrd, Warner, and Nunn, May 19, 1988. On September 29, 1983, Senators Cranston, Eagleton, and Stennis introduced an amendment to this effect that had been proposed in the Senate Foreign Relations in July 1977 and known as Committee Print No. 2, July 1, 1977. In U.S. Congress. Senate. Committee on Foreign Relations. War Powers. Hearings, July 13,14 and 15, 1977. Wash., GPO, 1977. p.338. For a review of the use of funding cutoffs by Congress since 1970 see: Richard F. Grimmett, *Congressional Use of Funding Cutoffs Since 1970 Involving U.S. Military Forces Withdrawals From Overseas Deployments*. CRS Report for Congress 95-1126. December 1, 1995, 6p.

[72] See Krotoski, Mark L. Essential Elements of Reform of the War Powers Resolution. *Santa Clara Law Review*. Vol. 28, Summer 1989, p. 609-750.

CONSULTATION GROUP

Several proposed amendments have focused on improving consultation under the War Powers Resolution, particularly by establishing a specific consultation group in Congress for this purpose. Senators Byrd, Nunn, Warner, and Mitchell have proposed the President regularly consult with an initial group of 6 Members--the majority and minority leaders of both Chambers plus the Speaker of the House and President pro tempore of the Senate. Upon a request from a majority of this core group, the President is to consult with a permanent consultative group of 18 Members consisting of the leadership and the ranking and minority members of the Committees on Foreign Relations, Armed Services, and Intelligence. The permanent consultative group would also be able to determine that the President should have reported an introduction of forces and to introduce a joint resolution of authorization or withdrawal that would receive expedited procedures.[73]

Other Members have favored a consultation group, but consider that amendment of the War Powers Resolution is not required for Congress to designate such a group.[74] On October 28, 1993, House Foreign Affairs Chairman Lee Hamilton introduced H.R. 3405 to establish a Standing Consultative Group. Its purpose would be to facilitate improved interaction between the executive branch and Congress on the use of U.S. military forces abroad, including under the War Powers Resolution or United Nations auspices. Members of the Consultative Group would be appointed by the Speaker of the House and the Majority Leader of the Senate, after consultation with the minority leaders. The Group would include majority and minority representatives of the leadership and the committees on foreign policy, armed services, intelligence, and appropriations.

Another proposal would attempt to improve consultation by broadening the instances in which the President is required to consult. This proposal would cover all situations in which a President is required to report, rather than only circumstances that invoke the time limitation, as is now the case.[75]

JUDICIAL REVIEW

Proposals have been made that any Member of Congress may bring an action in the United States District Court for the District of Columbia for judgment and injunctive relief on the grounds that the President or the U.S. Armed Forces have not complied with any provision of the War Powers

---

[73] S.J.Res. 323, introduced May 19, 1988.

[74] Fascell, Representative Dante. Testimony before Foreign Relations Committee, July 13, 1988.

[75] Strengthening Executive-Legislative Consultation on Foreign Policy. Foreign Affairs Committee Print, October 1983, p. 67.

Resolution. The intent of this legislation is to give standing to Members to assert the interest of the House or Senate, but whether it would impel courts to exercise jurisdiction is uncertain. Proposals have also called for the court not to decline to make a determination on the merits, on the grounds that the issue of compliance is a political question or otherwise nonjusticiable; to accord expedited consideration to the matter; and to prescribe judicial remedies including that the President submit a report or remove Armed Forces from a situation.[76]

CHANGE OF NAME

Other proposals would construct a Hostilities Act or Use of Force Act and repeal the War Powers Resolution.[77] A possible objection to invoking the War Powers Resolution is reluctance to escalate international tension by implying that a situation is war. Some would see this as a step in the wrong direction; in the Korean and Vietnam conflicts, some contend, it was self-deceptive and ultimately impractical not to recognize hostilities of that magnitude as war and bring to bear the Constitutional provision giving Congress the power to declare war.

UNITED NATIONS ACTIONS

With the increase in United Nations actions since the end of the Cold War, the question has been raised whether the War Powers Resolution should be amended to facilitate or restrain the President from supplying forces for U.N. actions without congressional approval. Alternatively, the United Nations Participation Act might be amended, or new legislation enacted, to specify how the War Powers Resolution is to be applied, and whether the approval of Congress would be required only for an initial framework agreement on providing forces to the United Nations, or whether Congress would be required to approve an agreement to supply forces in specified situations, particularly for U.N. peacekeeping operations.

---

[76] H.J. Res. 95, War Powers Amendments of 1995, introduced by Representative DeFazio, June 16, 1995.

[77] H.R. 3912, Introduced by Representative Lungren, Feb. 4, 1988. Biden, Joseph R. Jr. and John B. Ritch. The War Power at a Constitutional Impasse: a "Joint Decision" Solution. *Georgetown Law Journal*, Vol. 77:367.

APPENDIX 1. INSTANCES REPORTED UNDER THE WAR POWERS RESOLUTION

This appendix lists reports Presidents have made to Congress under the War Powers Resolution. Each entry contains the President's reference to the War Powers Resolution.[78] The reports generally cite the President's authority to conduct foreign relations and as Commander in Chief; each entry indicates any additional legislative authority a President cites for his action.

(1) <u>Danang</u>. On April 4, 1975, President Ford reported the use of naval vessels, helicopters, and Marines to transport refugees from Danang and other seaports to safer areas in Vietnam. His report mentioned section 4(a)(2) of the War Powers Resolution and authorization in the Foreign Assistance Act of 1961 for humanitarian assistance to refugees suffering from the hostilities in South Vietnam. Monroe Leigh, Legal Adviser to the Department of State, testified later that the President "advised the members of the Senate and House leadership that a severe emergency existed in the coastal communities of South Vietnam and that he was directing American naval transports and contract vessels to assist in the evacuation of refugees from coastal seaports."[79]

(2) <u>Cambodia</u>. On April 12, 1975, President Ford reported the use of ground combat Marines, helicopters, and supporting tactical air elements to assist with the evacuation of U.S. nationals from Cambodia. The report took note of both section 4 and section 4(a)(2) of the War Powers Resolution. On April 3, 1975, the day the President authorized the Ambassador to evacuate the American staff, he directed that the leaders of the Senate and House be advised of the general plan of evacuation. On April 11, the day he ordered the final evacuation, President Ford again directed that congressional leaders be notified.

(3) <u>Vietnam</u>. On April 30, 1975, President Ford reported the use of helicopters, Marines, and fighter aircraft to aid in the evacuation of U.S. citizens and others from South Vietnam. The report took note of section 4 of the War Powers Resolution. On April 10, the President had asked Congress to clarify its limitation on the use of forces in Vietnam to insure evacuation of U.S.

---

[78] Two of the reports did not mention the War Powers Resolution but met the basic requirement of reporting specified deployments or uses of forces. For the text of the reports until April 12, 1994, and other key documents and correspondence see U.S. Congress. House. Committee on Foreign Affairs. Subcommittee on International Security, International Organizations and Human Rights. The War Powers Resolution, Relevant Documents, Reports, Correspondence. Committee Print., 103rd Congress, second session, May 1994. 267 p.

[79] U.S. Congress. House. Committee on International Relations. War Powers: A test of compliance relative to the Danang sealift, the evacuation of Phnom Penh, the evacuation of Saigon, and the Mayaguez incident. Hearings, May 7 and June 4, 1975. Washington, U.S. Govt. Printing Off., 1975. p. 3.

citizens and to cover some Vietnamese nationals, but legislation to this effect was not completed. On April 28, the President directed that congressional leaders be notified that the final phase of the evacuation of Saigon would be carried out by military forces within the next few hours.[80]

(4) Mayaguez. On May 15, 1975, President Ford reported that he had ordered U.S. military forces to rescue the crew of and retake the ship Mayaguez that had been seized by Cambodian naval patrol boats on May 12, that the ship had been retaken, and that the withdrawal of the forces had been undertaken. The report took note of section 4(a)(1) of the War Powers Resolution. On May 13, Administration aides contacted ten Members from the House and 11 Senators regarding the military measures directed by the President.[81]

(5) Iran. On April 26, 1980, President Carter reported the use of six aircraft and eight helicopters in an unsuccessful attempt of April 24 to rescue the American hostages in Iran. The report was submitted "consistent with the reporting provision" of the War Powers Resolution. President Carter said the United States was acting in accordance with its right under Article 51 of the United Nations Charter to protect and rescue its citizens where the government of the territory in which they are located is unable or unwilling to protect them. The Administration did not inform congressional leaders of the plan on grounds that consultation could endanger the success of the mission.

(6) Sinai. The United States, Egypt, and Israel signed an executive agreement on August 3, 1981, outlining U.S. participation in a Multinational Force and Observers unit to function as a peacekeeping force in the Sinai after Israel withdrew its forces. In anticipation of this accord, on July 21, 1981, President Reagan requested congressional authorization for U.S. participation. Congress authorized President Reagan to deploy military personnel to the Sinai in the Multinational Force and Observers Participation Resolution, P.L. 97-132, signed December 29, 1981.

On March 19, 1982, President Reagan reported the deployment of military personnel and equipment to the Multinational Force and Observers in the Sinai. The President said the report was provided "consistent with section 4(a)(2) of the War Powers Resolution" and cited the Multinational Force and Observers Participation Resolution.

(7) Lebanon. On August 24, 1982, President Reagan reported the dispatch of 800 Marines to serve in the multinational force to assist in the withdrawal of members of the Palestine Liberation force from Lebanon. The report was provided "consistent with" but did not cite any specific provision of the War Powers Resolution. President Reagan began discussions with congressional

---

[80] Ibid., p. 6.

[81] Ibid., p. 78.

leaders on July 6 after the plan had been publicly announced, and after leaks in the Israeli press indicated that he had approved the plan on July 2.[82]

(8) Lebanon. On September 29, 1982, President Reagan reported the deployment of 1,200 Marines to serve in a temporary multinational force to facilitate the restoration of Lebanese government sovereignty. He said the report was being submitted "consistent with the War Powers Resolution." On this second Multinational Force in Lebanon there was a considerable amount of negotiation between the executive branch and Congress, but most of it occurred after the decision to participate had been made and the Marines were in Lebanon.[83]

(9) Chad. On August 8, 1983, President Reagan reported the deployment of two AWACS electronic surveillance planes and eight F-15 fighter planes and ground logistical support forces to Sudan to assist Chad and other friendly governments helping Chad against Libyan and rebel forces. He said the report was being submitted consistent with Section 4 of the War Powers Resolution. On August 23, 1983, a State Department spokesman announced that the planes were being withdrawn.

(10) Lebanon. On August 30, 1983, after the Marines participating in the Multinational Force in Lebanon were fired upon and two were killed, President Reagan submitted a report "consistent with section 4 of the War Powers Resolution." In P.L.98-119, the Multinational Force in Lebanon Resolution, signed October 12, 1983, Congress determined section 4(a) had become operative on August 29, 1983, and authorized the forces to remain for 18 months.

(11) Grenada. On October 25, 1983, President Reagan reported that U.S. Army and Marine personnel had begun landing in Grenada to join collective security forces of the Organization of Eastern Caribbean States in assisting in the restoration of law and order in Grenada and to facilitate the protection and evacuation of U.S. citizens. He submitted the report "consistent with the War Powers Resolution." President Reagan met with several congressional leaders at 8 p.m. on October 24.[84] This was after the directive ordering the landing had been signed at 6 p.m., but before the actual invasion that began at 5:30 a.m., October 25.

(12) Libya. On March 26, 1986, President Reagan reported (without any mention of the War Powers Resolution) that, on March 24 and 25, U.S. forces conducting freedom of navigation exercises in the Gulf of Sidra had been

---

[82] Oberdorfer, Don and John M. Goshko. Peace-keeping Force. *Washington Post*, July 7, 1982, p. 1.

[83] Gwetzman, Bernard. U.S. To Send Back Marines to Beirut. *New York Times*, Sept. 21, 1982, p. 1.

[84] U.S. Declares Goal in to Protect Americans and Restore Order. *Washington Post*, Oct. 26, 1983. p. A7.

attacked by Libyan missiles. In response, the United States fired missiles at Libyan vessels and at Sirte, the missile site.

(13) Libya. On April 16, 1986, President Reagan reported, "consistent with the War Powers Resolution", that on April 14 U.S. air and naval forces had conducted bombing strikes on terrorist facilities and military installations in Libya. President Reagan had invited approximately a dozen congressional leaders to the White House at about 4 p.m. on April 14 and discussed the situation until 6 p.m. He indicated that he had ordered the bombing raid and that the aircraft from the United Kingdom were on their way to Libya and would reach their targets about 7 p.m.

(14) Persian Gulf [85]. On September 23, 1987, President Reagan reported that, on September 21, two U.S. helicopters had fired on an Iranian landing craft observed laying mines in the Gulf. The President said that while mindful of legislative-executive differences on the interpretation and constitutionality of certain provisions of the War Powers Resolution, he was reporting in a spirit of mutual cooperation.

(15) Persian Gulf. On October 10, 1987, President Reagan reported "consistent with the War Powers Resolution" that, on October 8, three U.S. helicopters were fired upon by small Iranian naval vessels and the helicopters returned fire and sank one of the vessels.

(16) Persian Gulf. On October 20, 1987, President Reagan reported an attack by an Iranian Silkworm missile against the U.S.-flag tanker Sea Isle City on October 15 and U.S. destruction, on October 19, of the Iranian Rashadat armed platform used to support attacks and mine-laying operations. The report was submitted "consistent with the War Powers Resolution."

(17) Persian Gulf. On April 19, 1988, President Reagan reported "consistent with the War Powers Resolution" that in response to the U.S.S. Samuel B. Roberts striking a mine on April 14, U.S. Armed Forces attacked and "neutralized" two Iranian oil platforms on April 18 and, after further Iranian attacks, damaged or sank Iranian vessels. The President called the actions "necessary and proportionate." Prior to this action, the President met with congressional leaders.

(18) Persian Gulf. On July 4, 1988, President Reagan reported that on July 3 the USS Vincennes and USS Elmer Montgomery fired upon approaching Iranian small craft, sinking two. Firing in self-defense at what it believed to be a hostile Iranian military aircraft, the Vincennes had shot down an Iranian

---

[85] Earlier, on September 21, 1987, Secretary of State George P. Shultz submitted a report concerning the Iraqi aircraft missile attack on the U.S.S. Stark in the Persian Gulf similar to reports in this list submitted by Presidents. The report did not mention the War Powers Resolution but said the U.S. presence had been maintained in the Gulf pursuant to the authority of the President as Commander-in-Chief.

civilian airliner. The President expressed deep regret. The report was submitted "consistent with the War Powers Resolution."

(19) Persian Gulf. On July 14, 1988, President Reagan reported that, on July 12, two U.S. helicopters, responding to a distress call from a Japanese-owned Panamanian tanker, were fired at by two small Iranian boats and returned the fire. The report was submitted "consistent with the War Powers Resolution."

(20) Philippines. On December 2, 1989, President Bush submitted a report to congressional leaders "consistent with" the War Powers Resolution, describing assistance of combat air patrols to help the Aquino government in the Philippines restore order and to protect American lives.

After the planes had taken off from Clark Air Base to provide air cover, Vice President Quayle and other officials informed congressional leaders. On December 7, House Foreign Affairs Committee Chairman Dante Fascell wrote President Bush expressing his concern for the lack of advance consultation. In reply, on February 10, 1990, National Security Adviser Brent Scowcroft wrote Chairman Fascell that the President was "committed to consultations with Congress prior to deployments of U.S. Forces into actual or imminent hostilities in all instances where such consultations are possible. In this instance, the nature of the rapidly evolving situation required an extremely rapid decision very late at night and consultation was simply not an option."

(21) Panama. On December 21, 1989, President Bush reported "consistent with the War Powers Resolution" that he had ordered U.S. military forces to Panama to protect the lives of American citizens and bring General Noriega to justice. By February 13, 1990, all the invasion forces had been withdrawn. President Bush informed several congressional leaders of the approaching invasion of Panama at 6 p.m. on December 19, 1989. This was after the decision to take action was made, but before the operation actually began at 1:00 a.m., December 20.

(22) Liberia. On August 6, 1990, President Bush reported to Congress that following discussions with congressional leaders, a reinforced rifle company had been sent to provide additional security to the U.S. Embassy in Monrovia and helicopter teams had evacuated U.S. citizens from Liberia. The report did not mention the War Powers Resolution or cite any authority.

(23) Iraq. On August 9, 1990, President Bush reported to Congress "consistent with the War Powers Resolution" that he had ordered the forward deployment of substantial elements of the U.S. Armed Forces into the Persian Gulf region to help defend Saudi Arabia after the invasion of Kuwait by Iraq. The Bush Administration notified congressional leaders that it was deploying U.S. troops to Saudi Arabia on August 7, the date of the deployment. After the forces had been deployed, President Bush held several meetings with congressional leaders and members of relevant committees, and committees held hearings to discuss the situation.

(24) Iraq. On November 16, 1990, President Bush reported, without mention of the War Powers Resolution but referring to the August 9 letter, the continued buildup to ensure "an adequate offensive military option." Just prior to adjournment, Senate Majority Leader Mitchell and Speaker Foley designated Members to form a consultation group, and the President held meetings with the group on some occasions, but he did not consult the members in advance on the major buildup of forces in the Persian Gulf area announced November 8.

(25) Iraq. On January 18, 1991, President Bush reported to Congress "consistent with the War Powers Resolution" that he had directed U.S. Armed Forces to commence combat operations on January 16 against Iraqi forces and military targets in Iraq and Kuwait. On January 12, Congress had passed the Authorization for Use of Military Force against Iraq Resolution (P.L. 102-1), which stated it was the specific statutory authorization required by the War Powers Resolution. P.L. 102-1 required the President to submit a report to the Congress at least once every 60 days on the status of efforts to obtain compliance by Iraq with the U.N. Security Council resolution, and Presidents submitted subsequent reports on military actions in Iraq "consistent with" P.L. 102-1. An exception is report submitted June 28, 1993, described below.

(26) Somalia. On December 10, 1992, President Bush reported "consistent with the War Powers Resolution" that U.S. armed forces had entered Somalia on December 8 in response to a humanitarian crisis and a U.N. Security Council Resolution determining that the situation constituted a threat to international peace. He included as authority applicable treaties and laws, and said he had also taken into account views expressed in H.Con. Res. 370, S. Con. Res. 132, and the Horn of Africa Recovery and Food Security Act, P.L. 102-274. On December 4, the day the President ordered the forces deployed, he briefed a number of congressional leaders on the action.

(27) Bosnia. On April 13, 1993, President Clinton reported "consistent with Section 4 of the War Powers Resolution" that U.S. forces were participating in a NATO air action to enforce a U.N. ban on all unauthorized military flights over Bosnia-Hercegovina, pursuant to his authority as Commander in Chief. Later, on April 27, President Clinton consulted with about two dozen congressional leaders on potential further action.

(28) Somalia. On June 10, 1993, President Clinton reported that in response to attacks against U.N. forces in Somalia by a factional leader, the U.S. Quick Reaction Force in the area had participated in military action to quell the violence. He said the report was "consistent with the War Powers Resolution, in light of the passage of 6 months since President Bush's initial report...." He said the action was in accordance with applicable treaties and laws, and said the deployment was consistent with S.J.Res. 45 as adopted by the Senate and amended by the House. (The Senate did not act on the House amendment, so Congress did not take final action on S.J.Res. 45.)

(29) Iraq. On June 28, 1993, President Clinton reported "consistent with the War Powers Resolution" that on June 26 U.S. naval forces had launched

missiles against the Iraqi Intelligence Service's headquarters in Baghdad in response to an unsuccessful attempt to assassinate former President Bush in Kuwait in April 1993.

(30)   Macedonia[86].   On July 9, 1993, President Clinton reported "consistent with Section 4 of the War Powers Resolution" the deployment of approximately 350 U.S. armed forces to Macedonia to participate in the U.N. Protection Force to help maintain stability in the area of former Yugoslavia. He said the deployment was directed in accordance with Section 7 of the United Nations Participation Act.

(31) Bosnia. On October 13, 1993, President Clinton reported "consistent with the War Powers Resolution" that U.S. military forces continued to support enforcement of the U.N. no-fly zone in Bosnia, noting that more that 50 U.S. aircraft were now available for NATO efforts in this regard.

(32) Haiti.   On October 20, 1993, President Clinton submitted a report "consistent with the War Powers Resolution" that U.S. ships had begun to enforce a U.N. embargo against Haiti.

(33) Macedonia.   On January 8, 1994, President Clinton reported "consistent with the War Powers Resolution" that approximately 300 members of a reinforced company team (RCT) of the U.S. Army's 3rd Infantry Division (Mechanized) had assumed a peacekeeping role in Macedonia as part of the United Nations Protection Force (UNPROFOR) on January 6, 1994.

(34) Bosnia. On February 17, 1994, President Clinton reported "consistent with the War Powers Resolution" that the United States had expanded its participation in United Nations and NATO efforts to reach a peaceful solution in former Yugoslavia and that 60 U.S. aircraft were available for participation in the authorized NATO missions.

(35) Bosnia.   On March 1, 1994, President Clinton reported "consistent with" the War Powers Resolution that on February 28 U.S. planes patrolling the "no-fly zone" in former Yugoslavia under the North Atlantic Treaty Organization (NATO) shot down 4 Serbian Galeb planes.

(36) Bosnia. On April 12, 1994, President Clinton reported "consistent with" the War Powers Resolution that on April 10 and 11, U.S. warplanes under NATO command had fired against Bosnian Serb forces shelling the "safe" city of Gorazde.

(37) Rwanda. On April 12, 1994, President Clinton reported "consistent with" the War Powers Resolution that combat-equipped U.S. military forces had been deployed to Burundi to conduct possible non-combatant evacuation operations of U.S. citizens and other third-country nationals from Rwanda, where widespread fighting had broken out.

---

[86] See footnote 64 above.

(38) <u>Macedonia</u>. On April 19, 1994, President Clinton reported "consistent with the War Powers Resolution" that the U.S. contingent in the former Yugoslav Republic of Macedonia had been augmented by a reinforced company of 200 personnel.

(39) <u>Haiti</u>. On April 20, 1994, President Clinton reported "consistent with the War Powers Resolution" that U.S. naval forces had continued enforcement in the waters around Haiti and that 712 vessels had been boarded.

(40) <u>Bosnia</u>. On August 22, 1994, President Clinton reported the use on August 5 of U.S. aircraft under NATO to attack Bosnian Serb heavy weapons in the Sarajevo heavy weapons exclusion zone upon request of the U.N. Protection Forces. He did not cite the War Powers Resolution but referred to the April 12 report that cited the War Powers Resolution.

(41) <u>Haiti</u>. On September 21, 1994, President Clinton reported "consistent with the War Powers Resolution" the deployment of 1,500 troops to Haiti to restore democracy in Haiti. The troop level was subsequently increased to 20,000.

(42) <u>Bosnia</u>. On November 22, 1994, President Clinton reported "consistent with the War Powers Resolution" the use of U.S. combat aircraft on November 21, 1994 under NATO to attack bases used by Serbs to attack the town of Bihac in Bosnia.

(43) <u>Macedonia</u>. On December 22, 1994, President Clinton reported "consistent with the War Powers Resolution" that the U.S. Army contingent in the former Yugoslav Republic of Macedonia continued its peacekeeping mission and that the current contingent would soon be replaced by about 500 soldiers from the 3rd Battalion, 5th Cavalry Regiment, 1st Armored Division from Kirchgons, Germany.

(44) <u>Somalia</u>. On March 1, 1995, President Clinton reported "consistent with the War Powers Resolution" that on February 27, 1995, 1,800 combat-equipped U.S. armed forces personnel began deployment into Mogadishu, Somalia, to assist in the withdrawal of U.N. forces assigned there to the United Nations Operation in Somalia (UNOSOM II).

(45) <u>Haiti</u>. On March 21, 1995, President Clinton reported "consistent with the War Powers Resolution" that U.S. military forces in Haiti as part of a U.N. Multinational Force had been reduced to just under 5,300 personnel. He noted that as of March 31, 1995, approximately 2,500 U.S. personnel would remain in Haiti as part of the U.N. Mission in Haiti UNMIH).

(46) <u>Bosnia</u>. On May 24, 1995, President Clinton reported "consistent with the War Powers Resolution" that U.S. combat-equipped fighter aircraft and other aircraft continued to contribute to NATO's enforcement of the no-fly zone in airspace over Bosnia-Herzegovina. U.S. aircraft, he noted, are also available for close air support of U.N. forces in Croatia. Roughly 500 U.S. soldiers

continue to be deployed in the former Yugoslav Republic of Macedonia as part of the U.N. Preventive Deployment Force (UNPREDEP). U.S. forces continue to support U.N. refugee and embargo operations in this region.

(47) <u>Bosnia</u>. On September 1, 1995, President Clinton reported "consistent with the War Powers Resolution," that "U.S. combat and support aircraft" had been used beginning on August 29, 1995, in a series of NATO air strikes against Bosnian Serb Army (BSA) forces in Bosnia-Herzegovina that were threatening the U.N.-declared safe areas of Sarajevo, Tuzla, and Gorazde." He noted that during the first day of operations, "some 300 sorties were flown against 23 targets in the vicinity of Sarajevo, Tuzla, Goradzde and Mostar."

(48) <u>Haiti</u>. On September 21, 1995, President Clinton reported "consistent with the War Powers Resolution" that currently the United States has 2,400 military personnel in Haiti as participants in the U.N. Mission in Haiti (UNMIH). In addition, 260 U.S. military personnel are assigned to the U.S. Support Group Haiti.

(49) <u>Bosnia</u>. On December 6, 1995, President Clinton notified Congress, "consistent with the War Powers Resolution," that he had "ordered the deployment of approximately 1,500 U.S. military personnel to Bosnia and Herzegovina and Croatia as part of a NATO 'enabling force' to lay the groundwork for the prompt and safe deployment of the NATO-led Implementation Force (IFOR)," which would be used to implement the Bosnian peace agreement after its signing. The President also noted that he had authorized deployment of roughly 3,000 other U.S. military personnel to Hungary, Italy, and Croatia to establish infrastructure for the enabling force and the IFOR.

(50) <u>Bosnia</u>. On December 21, 1995, President Clinton notified Congress "consistent with the War Powers Resolution" that he had ordered the deployment of approximately 20,000 U.S. military personnel to participate in the NATO-led Implementation Force (IFOR) in the Republic of Bosnia-Herzegovina, and approximately 5,000 U.S. military personnel would be deployed in other former Yugoslav states, primarily in Croatia. In addition, about 7,000 U.S. support forces would be deployed to Hungary, Italy and Croatia and other regional states in support of IFOR's mission. The President ordered participation of U.S. forces "pursuant to" his "constitutional authority to conduct the foreign relations of the United States and as Commander-in-Chief and Chief Executive."

APPENDIX 2. INSTANCES NOT FORMALLY REPORTED TO THE CONGRESS

In some instances where armed forces have been deployed in potentially hostile situations abroad, Presidents did not submit reports to Congress and the question of whether a report was required by the War Powers Resolution might be raised. Instances such as these not reported since 1973 include:[87]

- evacuation of civilians from Cyprus in 1974
- evacuation of civilians from Lebanon in 1976
- Korean tree-cutting incident of 1976
- transport of European troops to Zaire in 1978
- dispatch of additional military advisers to El Salvador in 1981
- shooting down of two Libyan jets over the Gulf of Sidra on August 19, 1981, after one had fired a heat-seeking missile
- the use of training forces in Honduras after 1983
- dispatch of AWACS to Egypt after a Libyan plane bombed a city in Sudan March 18, 1983
- shooting down of two Iranian fighter planes over Persian Gulf on June 5, 1984, by Saudi Arabian jet fighter planes aided by intelligence from a U.S. AWACS
- interception by U.S. Navy pilots on October 10, 1985, of an Egyptian airliner carrying hijackers of the Italian cruise ship *Achille Lauro*
- use of U.S. Army personnel and aircraft in Bolivia for anti-drug assistance on July 14, 1986
- buildup of fleet in Persian Gulf area in 1987
- force augmentations in Panama in 1988 and 1989
- shooting down 2 Libyan jet fighters over the Mediterranean Sea on January 4, 1989
- dispatch of military advisers and Special Forces teams to Colombia, Bolivia, and Peru, in the Andean initiative, announced September 5, 1989, to help those nations combat illicit drug traffickers
- transport of Belgian troops and equipment into Zaire September 25-27, 1991
- evacuation of non-essential U.S. Government workers and families from Sierra Leone, May 3, 1992

---

[87] The list does not include military assistance or training operations generally considered routine, forces dispatched for humanitarian reasons such as disaster relief, or covert actions. War powers questions have not been raised about U.S. armed forces dispatched for humanitarian aid in peaceful situations, such as 8,000 marines and sailors sent to Bangladesh on May 12, 1991, to provide disaster relief after a cyclone. The War Powers Resolution applies only to the introduction of forces into situations of hostilities or imminent hostilities and forces equipped for combat.

INDEX